THE
MAJORS
2015

THE
MAJORS
2015

THE THRILLING BATTLE FOR GOLF'S GREATEST TROPHIES

IAIN CARTER

FOREWORD BY PADRAIG HARRINGTON

First published 2015 by
Elliott and Thompson Limited
27 John Street
London WC1N 2BX
www.eandtbooks.com

ISBN: 978-1-78396-187-0

Plate section picture credits:
Page 1: Robert Beck /Sports Illustrated/Getty Images; Page 2:
TIMOTHY A. CLARY/AFP/Getty Images (top); DON EMMERT/
AFP/Getty Images (bottom); Page 3: Robert Beck /Sports Illustrated/
Getty Images (top); Harry How/Getty Images (bottom); Page 4: Robert
Beck /Sports Illustrated/Getty Images; Page 5: Ross Kinnaird/R&A/
R&A via Getty Images (top); Thomas Lovelock /Sports Illustrated/Getty
Images (bottom); Page 6: BEN STANSALL/AFP/Getty Images; Page 7:
Andrew Redington/Getty Images (top); David Cannon/Getty Images
(bottom); Page 8: Andrew Redington/Getty Images

9 8 7 6 5 4 3 2 1

A catalogue record for this book is available from the British Library.

Typesetting: Marie Doherty
Printed and bound by CPI Group (UK) Ltd, Croydon, CR0 4YY

In memory of Iain Thomas, an inspirational boss who sent me to my first Masters in 1993.

Contents

Foreword

By Padraig Harrington

Majors are the tournaments that define our golfing careers. Every year they are my focal point and I set out my stall to try to make sure that these are the events where I'm ready to play my best golf.

Players have different ways of approaching them and we are all striving to find the magic formula. For me, I have always liked to play the week before a major to ensure that I am at my competitive best.

It is also important to play the right type of golf, which is the reason why in 2007 I competed in the Irish PGA on a links course the week before my Open Championship victory at Carnoustie, a formula that also worked the following year for The Open at Royal Birkdale.

My ambition was always to win multiple majors, rather than just one and when people describe me as a three-time major winner, I think to myself, 'three for now', as I hope to add to my tally before I retire.

The majors of 2015 made it an exciting year for golf. The emergence of Jordan Spieth and Jason Day is great for the future of the game while Zach Johnson proved that it's not just a young man's pursuit.

Iain Carter has been a fixture at every major since 2003 and his reporting and commentary are always insightful and accurate.

I hope you find the book's subject matter as fascinating as I do.

PH

Introduction

Rain was falling, it was chilly and, although it was July, it was not a day to be by the British seaside. Unless you were among the thousands of people gathered at one particular spot on a cold, damp Scottish east coast. This was St Andrews, the 'Home of Golf'. Of course we wanted the sun to shine, we wanted a baked golf course and shirtsleeves to be the order of the day. But what can you do about the weather? As Tiger Woods likes to say of things he would rather not discuss, it is what it is. And it did not matter that we were wrapped in waterproofs and struggling for feeling in our chilled hands. All of us among those thousands of people were witnessing the climax of the most historic and important golf tournament in the world.

That's what mattered.

They sat in grandstands, stood on the roadside, in shop fronts and hung out of windows. They wanted to see the destiny of the famous Claret Jug, the prize that goes to the winner of The Open Championship. The recipient is grandly known as the Champion Golfer of the Year — he is someone who has survived the elements and the demands of a unique golf course. Where else do they share greens between separate holes? Where else does the course start and finish in the heart of a historic town? Where else are there no bunkers on either the first or last hole? Where else would you rather be at the end of an Open Championship?

This is the tournament that set the template for a game that has become a multi-million-pound industry. It visits St Andrews every five years or so. The rest of the time it is staged at eight other courses located on various parts of the British coastline. There are four more Scottish venues: Muirfield, Carnoustie, Turnberry and Royal Troon. In England, Royal Lytham & St Annes, Royal Birkdale, Royal Liverpool and Royal St George's take turns. And, in the not too distant future, Royal Portrush in Northern Ireland will be invited to return to the roster. These are places that have links courses of the highest calibre to test the world's best players as well as the space to accommodate the vast infrastructure accompanying these events.

The Open Championship is special and, in the modern era, it features 156 of the world's leading players. It is one of four tournaments that define careers. The other three are the Masters, US Open and PGA, all staged in the USA. The evolution of the sport has dictated that these events are regarded as 'majors'. They are the tournaments players want to win more than any other. They've been playing The Open since Willie Park Senior won the inaugural tournament at Prestwick in 1860. Horace Rawlins was the first winner of the US Open at Newport Country Club in 1895 while the PGA Championship was first played as a matchplay event in 1916, with the America-based Scot Jim Barnes claiming the honours. The Masters is the youngest and most glamorous of the majors; Horton Smith was the inaugural winner in 1934.

The process of acquiring major status has evolved over time. No one can quite pinpoint the exact moment that these four tournaments separated themselves from the rest. In the early 20th century, the most prestigious tournaments were The Open, US Open, the Amateur Championship and US Amateur. When the great American Bobby Jones won all four in 1930 he was considered to have completed the 'Grand Slam' or, as it was also known then, 'The Impregnable Quadrilateral'.

Jones set a new benchmark for the game and went on to play a key role in the establishment of the Masters. He never turned professional but, with the paid ranks taking precedence, the status of the majors evolved. It was no single person's role to bequeath major status, more a consensus that built within the game and through the coverage by the reporting media.

They are the tournaments by which we measure players' careers. Who is the best male golfer of all time? Jack Nicklaus. Why? Because he has won 18 majors, four more than anyone else. 'Who in the world remembers who won the 1975 Westchester Classic or the 1978 Western Open?' Nicklaus once said. 'Basically, the majors are the only comparison over time, played on the same courses for generations. All the best players are always there.'

For many years it looked as though Nicklaus's record would be surpassed by Tiger Woods. When the American won the 2008 US Open, his 14th major title, he was only 32 years old. He had played, arguably, the best golf the sport had ever seen in a nine-year spell during which he dominated like no other player before. He won the 2000 US Open at Pebble Beach by 15 shots and that year's Open at St Andrews by eight. But he is still waiting for a 15th major after a dramatic collapse in fitness and form.

Woods came into 2015 ready to play his last set of majors before turning 40, still clinging onto the hope that he will one day surpass Nicklaus's tally. With each tournament that passes, however, the odds lengthen on his fulfilling a dream that once seemed inevitable.

A new generation of young stars emerged, largely inspired to take up the game by Woods' performances. Rory McIlroy already had four majors to his name, needing only to win the Masters to complete the full set. Jordan Spieth was a mere 21 years old but had already signalled his readiness to break through at this level. And Jason Day had featured on enough leaderboards to suggest the same.

There is always a vast array of potential winners at any major. There are so many variables to be taken into account. Tennis, like golf, has four marquee tournaments known as grand slams. However, it is much easier to predict who will be fighting for the titles at Wimbledon, the US, Australian and French Opens because the champion only has to beat seven other players. The big prizes are shared among fewer tennis players, usually the likes of Roger Federer, Rafael Nadal, Novak Djokovic and Andy Murray. In three of golf's 'big four', however, the champion has to beat 155 opponents. The Masters has a smaller field but still there are more than 90 other competitors to be conquered.

This is why a grand slam of golf majors is such a rare occurrence. Aside from Bobby Jones's heroics of 1930, Woods is the only other player to hold all four of the most important trophies simultaneously. After romping to those massive wins at Pebble Beach and St Andrews in 2000, he won the PGA and the following year's Masters. No one has achieved this feat in the same calendar year.

In 2015 we spent several months contemplating the possibility of a historic slam. The possibility remained alive as we stood in the rain at St Andrews on an astonishing Monday evening. Oh yes, we all wanted to be there!

In my role as the BBC's golf correspondent, I attended each of the majors; whispering into my microphone in April at the 79th Masters, in June at the 115th US Open, at the 144th Open in July and a month later at the 97th PGA Championship. Each tournament offered intriguing possibilities. Could McIlroy complete his set of slams at the Masters? How would a brand new US Open venue stand up to the test of hosting the world's best players? Would the 'Old Course' at St Andrews provide another classic Open at the home of golf? And would we have a fitting finale to the major season at Whistling Straits?

By the time we arrived in Wisconsin for that concluding major, I was attending my 60th major as a reporter. It had already turned into the most compelling year of golf I could remember. The PGA did not disappoint either. It produced one of the most emotional victories ever witnessed.

I had embarked on a long and magical journey that took the golfing circus from the US Pacific Northwest, to Scotland's east coast and the American Midwest. First, though, it was the annual trip to the Deep South. To Augusta, Georgia.

CHAPTER 1

The History of the Masters

There's not much to do in Augusta, the day after the Masters. Every year there's a mass exodus from a city that spent the previous week at the centre of the sporting world. Hotel rooms and rental properties are vacated as this otherwise unremarkable stop on Georgia's Interstate 20 returns to normality.

'The Masters is the only reason people know about Augusta,' Scott Michaux, chief sports columnist for the *Augusta Chronicle*, admits. 'It's the second largest city in Georgia, but by a wide margin to Atlanta. Augusta's identity is wrapped up in the golf tournament, otherwise it's a normal American city. There's nothing that particularly stands out. But there's this golf course. People in the town are fiercely proud of what this tournament is and what it's become.'

Once the Masters has been decided, and that rather desolate April Monday arrives, many of the fans, 'patrons' of the tournament for the previous few days, simply hang around. They idly fill time before heading back to Atlanta or Charlotte for their flights home. There is no chance of venturing back down Magnolia Lane to revisit the Augusta National Golf Club. Once the Masters is done, the gates to the general public are firmly closed.

Without much else to do, some will head to the city's vast

shopping mall. If, however, they go in search of Masters memorabilia they will be disappointed. The shirts, caps, umbrellas and sun cream that bear the tournament emblem can only be bought on the premises during the week of the event. Regulars know the score, buying huge quantities of golfing apparel while they can, as well as tee shirts, posters and teddy bears for friends and family. These gifts will be as close as most people get to the fabled tournament. The Augusta National fiercely protects its exclusivity, right down to its official merchandise.

The Augusta National Club wants its tournament to be special in every regard. It wants those with tickets to feel lucky that they are witnessing a unique event. No one, for instance, is allowed a mobile phone on the premises – violation of this rule leads to instant ejection. 'They're very strict, almost to the point that they are extreme,' Michaux says. 'But the nice thing is that it changes the tone and tenor of the event. You are there to pay attention to the people who are putting on the show. They don't have electronic scoreboards, they don't have video screens, they don't have hospitality tents and all those things make it feel like you've gone back in time. It is so perfectly put together. They just don't give a crap that you are going to be there without your cell phone all day. Who else does that? Not even Wimbledon.'

Anyone spotted running will be told to slow down and woe betide anyone with the temerity to walk barefoot or lie down on the immaculate turf. 'Wake up and move along please,' the offender will be told, politely yet firmly, by one of the Pinkerton Guards patrolling the course.

The message is clear. Make the most of your time at the Masters.

Wander around the Augusta Mall on the Monday after the Masters and there is very little to suggest that you are in the vicinity of golf's most glamorous tournament. It takes a keen eye to detect any link at all. You will find one, though, if you visit the restrooms. Walk down the corridor leading to the ground-floor toilets and you may spot a picture of a familiar-looking building. It shows the old farmhouse at the Fruitland Nurseries, a white two-storey building with a vertical lookout popping up from the centre of a symmetrically angled roof. An outdoor staircase leads to an upstairs balcony. Those stairs no longer exist, but this slightly faded photograph unmistakably depicts the building that became the clubhouse at the Augusta National Golf Club.

Built in 1854, it was the home of Dennis Redmond. He created an indigo plantation in the surrounding grounds which yielded berries used to make the blue dye that coloured denim jeans (who would have thought that the origins of the game's most exclusive club would be intertwined with the creation of clothing regarded as unacceptable in so many golfing establishments?).

Redmond soon sold up and the property was bought by a Belgian horticulturist called Prosper Berckmans. He turned the plantation into Fruitland Nurseries and grew a vast array of plants, including hundreds of different varieties of azaleas, dogwood, pears, apples and grapes. The drive that linked the house to the main Washington Road was bordered by an avenue of Magnolia trees. After his death in 1910, however, the business faltered, then failed.

Around this time golf was growing in popularity and it was clear the land would provide a perfect setting for a course. Miami businessman 'Commodore' J. Perry Stoltz planned to take advantage by building both a course and a $2-million hotel, aimed at winter visitors from the north keen to escape the snow and ice of New York and its surrounds. Augusta was becoming a tourist destination, with golf on its menu. 'In those days Florida was a swamp so you didn't go there,' says Michaux. 'People came as far as Augusta where they got the nice weather and they built nice hotels.'

Augusta residents were thrilled at the prospect of the flamboyant Stoltz investing in the area. He was already famous for his highly successful Fleetwood Hotel in Miami. Had Stoltz succeeded with his hotel project, though, the Augusta National and the Masters would never have come about. Nor would the traditional clubhouse still be standing. It was slated for demolition once the hotel had been built, and in 1925 work on the foundations of a new building began. Fate took a hand, however. Stoltz's showcase hotel was flattened by the great Miami hurricane of September 1926, which ripped through the city and killed 300 people. Stoltz was left bankrupt and his hotel plans collapsed.

The site went back on the market and two friends with contrasting backgrounds but a shared dream came into the picture – Clifford Roberts, a financial broker of humble origins, and Robert Tyre Jones Jr, from Atlanta, Georgia.

Jones's stage name was Bobby. To his friends, he was Bob. To fans, he was golfing royalty. He held the distinction of being the only man to simultaneously hold The Open and US Open titles along with the Amateur Championship and its American equivalent. That was in 1930 and, at the time, it constituted golf's grand slam. A lawyer by trade, Jones never turned professional, although he was certainly good enough.

Roberts hailed from Iowa, born in 1894 on a farm owned by his mother's parents. He was the second of five children and had a happy, itinerant childhood. His father, Charles, was often away pursuing small-time business opportunities. As Roberts said: 'My father always was interested in seeing what was on the other side of the next hill.' His mother, Rebecca, struggled with depression as she tried to raise the family amid haphazard finances. The young Clifford proved streetwise, entrepreneurial and hard-working. He had regular jobs from the age of 12 and left school early. He was also prone to getting in trouble, and not just the occasional fist fights. On his way to Sunday school in October 1910, the 16-year-old realised he had forgotten his gloves. He returned home, ignited a kerosene lamp and accidentally dropped the lighted match. The house burned down. Almost the only item that was saved was the family piano that his father Charles dragged from the smouldering ruins. Clifford's life as an adult began there and then.

He promised his mother he would make up for his negligence. Aside from helping on the family's failing farm, he took a variety of jobs assisting his father and working as a clerk in a dry goods firm. Within three years, though, Rebecca Roberts had committed suicide, firing a shotgun to her chest just three days after her 44th birthday. She wrote farewell letters to each member of the family. To Clifford, as David Owen quotes in his book *The Making of the Masters*, she wrote: 'Dear Clifford, I write to beg you not to grieve but be a man in time of trial. Papa will need you. Be a sober upright son & all will be well. I know Ma [Rebecca's mother] wants you to come to her. Love Mama.'

In the years that followed Roberts became a menswear salesman, travelling across the Midwest. The family moved to Kansas City and his father remarried. Roberts was earning just over a dollar a month plus commissions and was doing well enough to send funds home. Nevertheless these were hardly auspicious circumstances for someone who would eventually become the joint founder of golf's most exclusive club.

Roberts felt he could make his fortune in New York and landed a job with the Oklahoma-Wyoming Oil Company in 1918. Almost immediately, he was called up for national service and became a private in the Signal Corps at Camp Hancock, in a place called Augusta in the state of Georgia. He had never been there before.

After serving in France, he was discharged in 1919. He threw himself back into business in New York and Chicago although he found neither city paved with greenbacks. He became the principal in Roberts and Co and started to make modest returns as a financial negotiator and stock and bond broker. He made $70,000 in 1929, by far his most successful year. His timing, though, proved disastrous. Roberts invested much of his money in securities. In October came the Wall Street Crash. It always seemed to be a case of one step forward, two steps back.

Roberts' social life, however, was proving more fruitful. Keen to get in with a burgeoning and seemingly affluent golfing set, Roberts joined Knollwood Country Club in New York's Westchester County. He attended an exhibition match featuring the game's biggest luminary – Bobby Jones. 'Each time I saw Bob or read his public comments, I respected and liked him more,' Roberts wrote in his book about the Augusta National Club. 'I watched part of the final of the 1926 USGA Amateur Championship at Baltusrol, in New Jersey, in which George Von Elm defeated Jones 2 and 1. Shortly afterwards, I was one of some half-dozen who were having a drink with the loser and trying to think of something comforting to say to him.'

Here lie the roots of the relationship that yielded the Masters.

A mutual friend ran the Bon Air-Vanderbilt hotel in Augusta and after his time in the army Roberts had occasionally returned for winter golf holidays. The train link from New York was good and the weather invariably fine. Jones, meanwhile, had often spoken of his desire to build a championship course in the South, away from Atlanta where he struggled to find privacy. Roberts was a self-confessed 'hero-worshipper' and no one fitted the bill for his affections better than Bobby Jones. His air of humility and charm added to the attraction. The shared dream of creating a leading golf course, and the prospect of working with such a preeminent sporting figure, was enticing.

The pair visited the site of the Fruitland Nurseries in 1931 and Roberts was immediately struck by the lines of magnolias on the avenue that led to the farmhouse. They could see the potential for a fine golf course, while a group of local business-men recognised the opportunity presented by such a facility to draw visitors to the area. A leasehold company that included Roberts and Jones's wealthy father, was set up to acquire 365 acres of land for $15,000, taking on around $60,000 of debt in the process. The company, Fruitland Manor Corporation, then leased around half of the land to the prospective new golf club, which was now actively seeking members.

Several names for the new club were mooted, with Georgia-National the front-runner. Eventually Augusta-National (with the hyphen later dropped) prevailed.

Roberts and Jones envisaged a membership of 1,800, pay-ing an entrance fee of $350 and subscriptions of $60 a year. Those numbers were never achieved − today, the club has around 300 members. They planned two 18-hole courses, with the second layout to be added once the membership had passed 1,000. There would be tennis courts, outdoor squash courts, housing, a new clubhouse and, potentially, a hotel. The old Redmond farmhouse would be torn down because it would be too small to serve as a clubhouse.

Roberts set about attracting enough members to make the plan financially viable. But the economic depression rendered that impossible. Fewer than 100 signed up in the first couple of years. Most came from New York, attracted by the charismatic Jones. The most successful recruiter, though, was a nationally renowned sportswriter named Grantland Rice who was a mem-ber of the fledgling club's organisation committee.

Nowadays it is extraordinary to think that such an exclusive club was desperate to attract members. Roberts sent out thou-sands of unsolicited, unsuccessful invitations as he sought to tap into the enthusiasm for the game prevailing in the 1930s. Only the contributions of a small handful of wealthy men, including

Singer Sewing Machine heir Alfred Severin Bourne, kept the club alive in those early years. They provided five-year loans at a six per cent interest rate. The debts were never repaid.

Course construction began in February 1932 but the plans for a grand clubhouse and a second layout were shelved. Three years earlier, Jones had played at a brand new layout in California. It was his first look at Cypress Point and he loved it. He also played in Santa Cruz and was similarly impressed. Both courses were designed by Dr Alister MacKenzie, an English physician of Scottish heritage. Jones determined that MacKenzie was the architect he needed. The man Roberts referred to as 'Doc' came up with the design and the building work progressed at astonishing speed despite the ongoing financial difficulties.

MacKenzie would never be properly rewarded for what became one of the greatest courses in the world. His initial fee of $10,000 was halved and by late 1932, when the course had been in play for several months, he had received only $2,000. This didn't even come close to covering his expenses. David Owen quotes a letter written by MacKenzie on Boxing Day that year that revealed his dire circumstances: 'I'm at the end of my tether, no one has paid me a cent since last June, we have mortgaged everything we have and not yet been able to pay the nursing expenses of my wife's operation . . . Can you possibly let me have, at any rate, five hundred dollars to keep us out of the poor house?'

Eventually Roberts agreed to issue two short-term notes for $1,000 with a nominal rate of six per cent. He reasoned that MacKenzie could sell the notes to realise some cash but warned that he would have no chance of finding a buyer for them in Augusta. The locals would know that the notes were worthless, since the club was already defaulting on payments for items as mundane as toilet rolls. MacKenzie died a poor man in 1934 at the age of 63 and never saw his masterpiece come to fruition.

He hadn't seen the Augusta National for two years before his death. On his final visit, the grass hadn't yet been planted.

Despite all the problems, the course was clearly of the highest quality. The United States Golf Association's tournament committee chairman was Prescott S. Bush, whose second child George would become President of the United States. He played the course and raised the notion of it staging the 1934 US Open. It would have been the first time America's national championship had been played in a Southern State and the idea appealed to Jones. However, the proposal never materialised. This was a big blow. Without staging a prestigious event, Augusta National had little chance of surviving.

So Roberts came up with the idea of staging their own private tournament and it was included in the PGA's list of events for 1934, to be played on 22–25 March. For it to succeed, Roberts had to convince Jones to play, but the latter was reluctant. He was aware that he would have a vital role in attracting the biggest stars of the day, but that if he invited his friends to compete, he would be expected to play as well. He had retired from competition in 1930 and his game was rusty. Roberts was able to convince him, however, and made sure there would be no about-turn by announcing officially: 'Bobby Jones has agreed to make this tournament the one exception to his rule against further participation in tournament golf. He does this with the thought of helping to establish a new golfing event that it is hoped may assume the proportion of an important tournament.'

From the outset, Roberts wanted to call it 'the Masters' but Jones felt the title was immodest. For its first five years it was called the 'Augusta National Invitation Tournament'. It was the first 72-hole event to be scheduled over four days. Other championships were run over three, with the final two rounds played on Saturday. It was the first tournament to be played on a course with contouring specially designed to provide good lines of sight for spectators. The fairways were roped off and there were grandstands. It had an on-course scoreboard net-work, security guards to keep order and was covered live on nationwide radio. All of these were groundbreaking develop-ments for tournament golf in the US.

Horton Smith won the first event. It is unclear whether it held major status. Some historians argue that that did not come until the following year, when Gene Sarazen won after holing his four-wood second shot over the pond for an albatross at the 15th (the 'shot that was heard around the world'), while others say it took Sam Snead's epic playoff victory over Ben Hogan in 1954, a full 20 years later, for it to be regarded as a major.

By then the tournament was universally known as 'the Masters'. Roberts' desired moniker had never been a secret and had been picked up by players and press alike. In 1938 Jones finally came around to the idea.

The success of the tournament enabled the Augusta National Golf Club to attract civic and private investment. Membership numbers finally began to grow. The early years were still a struggle, though, with tournament entry numbers dipping after 72 players had competed in the first running; the club needed to be financially restructured. The Masters was vital to its future – without the tournament the club would undoubtedly have gone out of business.

The event had to provide value for money for spectators. Out of this need grew the Masters' tradition for hospitality, cheap refreshments and pristine presentation. It had to set itself apart from the rest and gain a unique reputation that would make people want to return. This played to Roberts' exceptional eye for detail, which extended to him insisting on referring to the fans as 'patrons'. The visiting press were also warmly welcomed and well treated, thus encouraging them to provide glowing reports about the course and the competition.

Initially, the two nines were reversed, so that the current ninth green was the home hole. They were switched because

Augusta is primarily a winter course, shutting its doors during Georgia's oppressive summer heat. When it is open, the lowest part of the course, and specifically the world-famous 12th green, is prone to early-morning frosts. By switching the nines there is more time for the putting surface to thaw before players arrive at 'Amen Corner' – the stretch of holes beginning with the 11th green and taking in the short par-3 12th and the drive on the dogleg par-5 13th. The holes are laid out around Rae's Creek and members originally knew the stretch as 'the water loop'. *Sports Illustrated* writer Herbert Warren Wind came up with the name Amen Corner in 1958. It was inspired by a jazz record- ing, 'Shouting at Amen Corner', that he had heard in his early years at Yale. Wind felt the 1958 Masters, won for the first time by Arnold Palmer, was decided through this stretch of holes – a place where prayers had been answered.

Palmer was the heartbeat of golf's boom-time in the 1950s and 60s and the Masters was a prime beneficiary. Before him, Gene Sarazen, Walter Hagen, Sam Snead, Byron Nelson and Ben Hogan had been the trailblazers. They had helped the Masters force its way into the sporting consciousness and the event was starting to assume considerable significance. Roberts wrote in 1939: 'While we may not have expected it originally, we have created a tournament of such importance that we are bound to see that it continues.' It was a vital ethos, because the world was about to go to war.

The Masters continued through to 1942 when Nelson earned a thrilling playoff victory over Hogan but soon after the club was shut and mothballed. A skeleton staff tended the course and the grass was kept in check by grazing cattle. Turkeys were also invited to make the most of the dormant golfing facilities and became welcome Christmas gifts for members (it turned out that the turkeys were profitable, while the cattle made a loss as well as damaging the fairways).

With the Second World War nearing its end, Augusta

reopened in late 1944. The clubhouse had been renovated shortly before the hostilities, with the attic converted into sleeping quarters (known as the Crow's Nest, it is still offered as overnight accommodation to amateurs competing in the Masters). Peacetime brought an influx of new members and a significant upturn in the financial fortunes of the club. At last it was possible to develop the facilities and, for the first time, Roberts considered capping the membership. What had set out to be a thriving cosmopolitan country club was now finding its identity as an ultra-exclusive golfing establishment.

Roberts still needed to win the argument with the club over whether to continue with the Masters; he succeeded and the tournament returned to the schedule in 1946. Jones was invited by Roberts to take charge of the event from 1950 but a progressive, incurable back condition prevented him from taking the post. He remained as a consultant to Roberts, who continued as tournament chairman.

Golf began to boom again and the tournament boomed with it, gathering international renown as first Palmer (with four victories) and then Jack Nicklaus became the game's dominant figures, watched by huge television audiences.

The club, meanwhile, became the preserve of the business, legal and political elite. President Eisenhower was a member and had his own on-site cabin. Being admitted for membership and being granted the right to wear the club's famous green jacket was accorded to the very few.

How exactly does one become a member? 'Well, firstly, you don't ask, that's a certainty,' says Michaux. 'You do very well in whatever your industry is and I guess you know the right person. The club doesn't go on membership drives. The one thing I do know is do not express interest in joining. Most of these guys are all members of the same elite clubs.'

The Masters also received vast revenues from discreet sponsors and from broadcast rights fees. All this would have been impossible to predict in the early days, when the establishment of a successful golf course, never mind one of the world's greatest sporting events, was in grave doubt.

Indeed, if it hadn't been for the Miami hurricane of 1926, Augusta National would never have existed. And if it hadn't been for the economic crash during the following decade, the club may well have been of a much more open and less exclusive character and the Masters would have none of its unique idiosyncrasies. As Michaux points out: 'Basically, the whole Masters tournament was founded on a series of failures.'

From these setbacks a grand tournament has emerged that illuminates early spring, played on a course of immense, undulating beauty and perfectly designed for thrilling stadium golf. It has produced and showcased great champions, men who dominated their eras; Sarazen, Nelson, Snead, Hogan and Palmer. From South Africa, Gary Player became the first overseas winner. Nicklaus triumphed six times between 1963 and 1986 when he added immeasurably to Masters folklore by charging home to victory, aged 46. Tom Watson was twice a victor and in 1980 Seve Ballesteros became the first European to don the famous green jacket that is presented to the champion. Bernhard Langer (twice), Sandy Lyle, Sir Nick Faldo (three times), Ian Woosnam and José María Olazábal (twice) claimed further European victories.

And then there was Tiger Woods, who stormed to a 12-shot win, smashing records to smithereens in an extraordinary professional debut at Augusta in 1997. He finished 18 under par. It was the first of four Masters wins for the man who transformed the game as it headed into the 21st century.

Woods' victory had added significance because he was the first black Masters champion. Augusta's rather dubious record in race relations reflected the elitism that pervaded much of American golf. The club was not alone in having an all-white membership policy but it was a stain on its reputation. Roberts is reported to have said: 'As long as I'm alive, all the golfers will be white and all the caddies will be black.'

It wasn't until 1975 that the Masters had a black competitor when Lee Elder took part. Virginia television executive Ron Townsend was the first African-American to be invited to join as a member, in 1990. The issue of minority members at private clubs had become a major talking point that summer. The PGA Championship was due to be held at Shoal Creek in Birmingham, Alabama. The club had no black members, but changed policy after the club's founder, Hall Thompson (an Augusta member), ignited controversy by telling his local newspaper: 'I think we've said that we don't discriminate in every other area except the blacks.'

In response, the PGA Tour announced that it would not hold tournaments at clubs discriminating on the basis of race, religion, sex or national origin. Although the Masters is not run by the PGA Tour, the Augusta National made sure they invited Townsend before the club reopened after summer that year. 'I think some credit has to go to the folks at the club,' Townsend said. 'It was something they wanted to do. They said it had been on their plate for the last several months.'

The Augusta National still discriminated on grounds of sex and it remained an all-male club until 2012 when former US Secretary of State Condoleezza Rice and businesswoman Darla Moore became members. This came nine years after a protest by women's rights activist Martha Burk, who picketed the club's gates during tournament week. The club, led by Chairman Hootie Johnson, refused to yield. If they were to change, they would do so on their own terms.

In fact, the eventual admission of women members was more a reflection of the way the game had changed. In his prime, Woods became the biggest sports star in the world. His 14 major titles and his utter domination, through an athleticism never seen before in the game, helped golf win the argument for a return to the Olympics. For the sport to be accepted in such an inclusive environment, discriminatory membership policies would be hard to tolerate. Two years later the Royal and Ancient Golf Club of St Andrews followed suit and invited female members for the first time.

Regardless of such controversies, the Masters moved steadily from strength to strength. Woods' great rival, the left-hander Phil Mickelson, won three times (2004, 2006 and 2010) as the tournament's resonance grew ever louder. The club was growing in other ways too. It invested heavily in buying up an entire housing area across the Berckmans Road that borders the Amen Corner side of the course. Parking facilities were thus improved and space freed up for a new driving range, now regarded as the best of its kind in the world. This was only made possible by the vast financial reserves that this once pauper club now commanded.

'There were some hold-outs who resented the plan,' Michaux says. 'I believe the last home was sold for $3 million – it was a house probably bought for $25–30,000. Throughout the process, the property values went up and people who didn't want to move had to go because they couldn't afford the taxes once their property values went up. So there was probably some resentment in the community but ultimately Augusta tries to do the fair thing for these people. They have the means to do that, they're not trying to be the evil landlord. Now they're starting to do that on the other side for some other projects.'

Those plans are likely to involve housing for the hundred or so competitors and their entourages during the Masters. It's akin to building golf's version of the Vatican City, but one that will only be occupied for a single week of the year. What a week, though. 'It's called the second Christmas or the 53rd fiscal week of the year,' explains Michaux. 'It means that much to the businesses, restaurants and to the hotels in particular. They charge fees that are seven, eight, nine, ten times their normal rates. A hotel downtown goes for $700 a night during Masters week. You can get it for $100 any other time.'

In the period when hotel rooms go for $100 a night you would barely be aware of the club's presence. Drive up the six-lane dual carriageway that is Washington Road from its intersection with the Interstate 20 and you will encounter the usual fast-food outlets, malls and shops, car dealerships and tyre fitters. At the top of the hill stands an obsolete water tower topped by a pristine white tank. If you could climb it, you would have a perfect vista of the course.

Beyond the traffic lights, a few hundred yards further on the right, hangs an unprepossessing sign: 'Augusta National Golf Club, Members Only'. On the other side of the gates runs a perfectly straight drive, bordered by the same magnolia trees that stood in the days of Dennis Redmond's indigo plantation. The drive, known as Magnolia Lane, leads to a turning area, 'Founders Circle', where a plaque commemorates the lives of Bobby Jones and Clifford Roberts. Jones died of his debilitating spinal condition on 18 December 1971, three months short of his 70th birthday. Six years later, after months of ill health, Roberts followed his mother's example and killed himself with a shotgun. Aged 83, he died on the golf course that defined his life.

Between the Founders Circle and the course stands the clubhouse. Supplemented by wings on either side, the heart of the building remains the farmhouse that has stood since 1854 – the one depicted in that faded picture hanging on the wall in Augusta's shopping centre.

On the day after the 2015 Masters, strolling around the shops, it would have been hard to imagine the sporting drama that had been played out just a couple of miles away over the four preceding days, but for the fact that the image of a very special young man was beaming out of every television in the mall.

CHAPTER 2

In Search of the Slam

There is a secret to good golf or, rather, a common denominator that runs like a thread through every great round. It applies to the hacker as much as to the greats. To fulfil their on-course potential, players will invariably have employed this simple maxim. It has little to do with technique but everything to do with execution. It is more about mental discipline and less to do with scoring and, although it lies at the heart of conquering this most frustrating of games, it is, in fact, somewhat dull. It is a cliché because it is undeniably true. The secret of good golf is to take it one shot at a time.

All golfers can recall countless occasions when they have got ahead of themselves only to suffer card-wrecking setbacks. On the rare days when you find that bubble of concentration, though, where all you consider is the shot at hand, you eliminate the errors and end up with a score likely to satisfy your ambitions.

Rarely would I dare to venture an opinion on the key elements to good golf. It is certainly not my area of expertise. I've played enough bad golf, however, to have some idea of where things go wrong, and I've interviewed enough top players to identify the mental state that yields the best play.

The players called in for press interviews on any given day are those who have excelled. To a man – or woman – they will tell you how hard they have been working. This is a given. No one survives on a professional tour without hours and hours of focused, dedicated practice. As the PGA Tour advert tells us: 'These guys are good'. If the best amateur in your club plays off scratch, it is worth remembering that most Tour pros would be rated around seven or eight strokes better. They make a lucrative living by forging inherent golfing talent with sheer graft. But for those who have played well there is usually this other common factor – of 'being in the moment' and 'not getting ahead of themselves'. Like a snooker player building a break, their policy on the course is easy to identify: Hit the shot that makes the next stroke as easy as possible. To do this, they retain a clear mental focus on how to perform whichever shot is required.

As an interviewer, it is difficult to tempt top players out of their bubbles by asking them what victory that week would mean to them. They may have started well, but it is only one round of golf. As reporters, we want to drag them into speculation, because it helps us inform our audiences of the personal context of a fine performance. We try our luck on Thursdays, Fridays and Saturdays but invariably we draw a blank. Pros know that the job is only a quarter, half or three-quarters done and there is no point in contemplating the consequences of victory. To do that would be to take their eye off the ball. It would be counter-productive and make it impossible to retain that all-important state of being in the moment.

One shot at a time. Golf's golden rule.

But every rule needs its exception. And in the summer of 2014 the break from conventional wisdom happened to come from the man playing the best golf in the world.

Rory McIlroy was sitting in the Royal Liverpool media tent after a third-round 68. As heavy rain pounded the canvas above, he could sit back and enjoy a six-stroke lead heading into the final round of The Open Championship. Aged 25, he had already won the US Open and PGA – a success rate similar to that of Tiger Woods when he began his brilliantly prolific career.

All who witnessed McIlroy's prowess that week saw he was firmly on course to add a third major. His play had been exemplary, starting with consecutive rounds of 66. On Saturday he had finished eagle, bogey, eagle. I walked every step of his round, commentating for BBC 5Live, and saw each of his 68 strokes. This was a man who was undoubtedly living, thinking and playing within the boundaries of the moment. We later learned that he had two buzz words; 'spot' and 'process'. He was concentrating totally on the spot that he wanted to hit his ball over, and on the process by which he would do it. Nothing else.

Yet McIlroy did allow himself to be drawn into the question of what might be the consequences of him turning his commanding lead into victory. And his answer was revealing.

It showed that he was fully aware of what was at stake at Hoylake, that week in July 2014. He not only let his mind contemplate his first Open triumph but also allowed it to race eight months ahead, to the following April. 'It would mean a lot of hype going into Augusta next year,' he laughed.

McIlroy was embracing the fact that an Open victory would leave him just a Masters green jacket short of a full set of major trophies. 'Not a lot of people have achieved the career grand slam,' he added. 'And if everything goes the right way tomorrow, to get three-quarters of the way there is some achievement by the age of 25. I'd be in pretty illustrious company.'

McIlroy added a cautionary 'let's not get ahead of ourselves' before trying to refocus on the here and now. 'It would mean an awful lot,' he said. 'I never thought that I'd be able to be in this position. I didn't think that I'd even have the chance at 25 to go for three legs of the grand slam.

'So I'm going to try to put all of that out of my head. It would be way too much to think about and way too much to ponder. First things first. Just play a good solid round of golf tomorrow.'

And McIlroy did exactly that. One shot at a time, 71 times over, to yield a finishing score of 271 – 17 under par – and two strokes better than Spain's Sergio García and the young American Rickie Fowler.

Both runners-up played spirited rounds that ensured McIlroy could not afford to lose sight of the 'spot' and the 'process' that had kept him at the top of the leaderboard for the entire week. The man from Holywood in Northern Ireland emerged beaming, clutching the precious Claret Jug.

McIlroy was at the start of an astonishing run of form. At Hoylake he carded rounds of 66-66-68-71; two weeks later he surged to victory in the WGC Bridgestone Invitational with scores of 69-64-66-66 at Firestone in Akron, Ohio, before collecting back-to-back major titles with his triumph at the PGA Championship at Valhalla where he carded rounds of 66-67-67-68. In those 12 rounds against the best players in the world, McIlroy failed to break 70 just once (on the day he clinched The Open title). He was a combined 48 under par through this blistering spell of golf in which he leapt in status from a twice to four-time major winner. McIlroy was proven correct with the comments he made on the Saturday evening of that glorious week at Hoylake. With just the Masters to be won to complete a full set of majors, there was, indeed, plenty of hype as he headed towards Augusta the following April.

But by the time the appointed week rolled around it wasn't just McIlroy who was generating huge interest. The Northern Irishman remained the prime figure and the bookmakers' favourite to make it three majors in a row, but a growing list of players vied for their share of the limelight. There was a returning Tiger Woods, a resurgent Dustin Johnson, the in-form Jimmy Walker. And there was a fresh-faced youngster from Texas.

Jordan Spieth was playing his second Masters, having finished runner-up to Bubba Watson on his debut, 12 months earlier. He was just 21 years old, but his quest for a Masters victory had been a lifelong ambition. 'The Masters is more than just a golf tournament and it appeals to more than just the standard golf fan,' Spieth said. 'And I think it's really cool. That's why I love that tournament so much, because even all my friends back in the day that didn't even like golf or care much for golf always wanted to watch the Masters and would talk to me about it.'

He had very nearly won at his first attempt. Victory in 2014 would have put him alongside Fuzzy Zoeller, who in 1979 became the only other debutant Masters winner apart from Horton Smith, who won the inaugural tournament in 1934. Spieth led by two strokes after seven holes of the final round but stumbled around the turn as Bubba Watson forged clear to claim his second green jacket.

'The only thing I'm thinking about is "when am I getting back next year?" That's what's on my mind, because it's tough. It's tough being in this position,' Spieth said immediately afterwards. 'I've worked my whole life to lead Augusta on Sunday, and although I feel like it's very early in my career, and I'll have more chances, it's a stinger. I had it in my hands and I could have gone forward with it and just didn't quite make the putts and that's what it came down to.'

Spieth was clearly on golf's fast-track to glory. He had won the John Deere Classic as a 19-year-old and was a wildcard pick for the American Presidents Cup team that took on the Internationals in 2013. The following season, he ended the year by winning the Dunlop Phoenix in Japan before triumphing in the Australian Open by six strokes after firing a course record 63 in tough, windy conditions in the final round at Sydney's Australian Golf Club.

That field boasted defending champion McIlroy as well as

leading Australians Adam Scott and Jason Day. Spieth would reflect. 'I think the Australian Open may have been the most important tournament that I've ever played. At the time, it had been maybe a year and a half since winning the John Deere in that playoff where I kind of squeaked in, luckily. I put myself in a position and just had a level of patience that I had not had when I was in contention prior to that.

'I was trying to get off to too fast a start and not realising the length of a round and how a final round in contention can almost feel like two rounds. You have to maintain the same patience the whole way. That's what we did that day. Didn't let anything get to us; the roars in front, the scoreboard changes. And I shot arguably the best round I've ever played when tied for the lead. So it was a huge, huge boost for me.'

The following week he triumphed in Tiger Woods' limited-field Hero Challenge event in Florida. Spieth had officially come of age and acquired the winning habit in impressive style.

At the start of 2015 he had three top-seven finishes early in the year before claiming the Valspar Championship in Tampa at the end of the Florida swing of tournaments in March. Then came a massive spell for the young Texan, with two stops in his home state in the weeks immediately before the Masters. At the Valero Texas Open he finished runner-up to Walker by four strokes. The following week at the Shell Houston Open, Spieth came up just short in a three-man playoff won by J. B. Holmes, with the youngster sharing the runner-up spoils with Johnson Wagner.

So Spieth headed to Augusta having finished first, second and second in his three previous tournaments. His game was in good order and he could speak with confidence in the wake of his Augusta runner-up finish 12 months earlier. He was itching to join the major winners' circle and to be regarded as one of the game's elite. 'The Masters was a humbling experience, not being able to pull that off,' he reflected. 'So many of these guys have won major championships, so I know what they felt and how they overcame it and succeeded. I only hope to do that and get myself in positions to do that.'

And he revealed that he was fully cognisant of those key factors that enable successful golf – a strong work ethic as well as the ability to stay in the moment: 'I've set goals from when I was 15 years old. I have yet to accomplish a couple of those, and those could take two years and some could take 20 years. In order for it to happen, I've got to keep my head down and keep moving forward and work as hard or harder than anybody.

'That's what it comes down to. The guys that have won major championships or have been the best in the world, that's what they have done, so that's what it takes.'

The history and glamour of the Masters held a strong resonance for Spieth. His background helped as well. One of his boyhood heroes was two-time winner Ben Crenshaw. Now one of the elder statesmen of the game, the 63-year-old from Austin, Texas, had announced that this would be his last Masters – the modern-day brute of a course that is Augusta National had become too much for him. But while he would never again contend, Crenshaw could still inform and inspire his fellow Texan.

Few figures have greater knowledge of the nuances of Augusta than Crenshaw's long-time bagman Carl Jackson, a former club caddie at the venue and the man who embraced his tearful boss back in 1995 when he claimed his second green jacket. 'We started working together in 1976, and the way that he treated me and the way that he communicated to me and his possession of knowledge is unbelievable, unparalleled around here,' Crenshaw said.

Spieth's on-course assistant was Michael Greller, a former schoolteacher who had kept his young boss in line, and often on line, throughout his early professional career. Greller was also aware that Jackson's knowledge was invaluable. 'This week, Michael has already talked with Carl a couple times, talking about how to best prepare for the greens,' Spieth revealed on the Tuesday of Masters week.

As a result, the player and his caddie put into place a detailed plan of preparation. 'Tomorrow, I'll play nine and probably go on the other nine and actually take a putter and just hit what we think is the hardest putt on each green and get a feel for that . . . a feel for the speed and the amount of break that the greens are giving this week. That's the idea. But I haven't spoken much specifically about it to Ben. Michael's picked Carl's brain.'

Crenshaw knew Spieth possessed the necessary attributes. 'I think the world of him,' the veteran said. 'He's way more mature than I was when I was 21. He has things together. I'm sure it has struck all of you that he's mature way beyond his years. He has an innate ability to score. He hits the ball definitely far enough. I think one of the really wonderful things that I really do like about him, he's got competitive fire. You can see it. I think he carries that off in a great fashion.

'He just seems to be moving forward in the game. When I first met him, I tell you, I'll never forget it. I looked right at him and he looked at me and I thought I was looking at Wyatt Earp. He just had that look about him, just wonderful.'

Equating the Masters and one of its top contenders to the key figure in the gunfight at the O.K. Corral might be a stretch, given the ultra-civilised, serene surroundings at the first major of the year, but Crenshaw had a point. For all Spieth's maturity and fine manners he possesses a competitive desire that few can match. Added to that, in the run-up to the 2015 Masters, was a deep-seated determination to atone for the near-miss 12 months earlier.

Furthermore, he could draw on experiences that stretched all the way back to his first victory as a junior golfer. 'It was a Young Guns Junior Golf Tour event in Dallas,' Spieth recalled.

'I played three of them that year. The first one I went down 18 with a couple of strokes lead and the guy made a birdie, I made double, I think, to lose. And so the next, a couple of weeks later, I was still playing really well and I ended up winning that one. They used to give out trophies that were taller than I was at the time. I think I was nine or 10.'

There was no dispute that a green jacket would fit his fully formed 21-year-old shoulders in 2015. As importantly, he felt at ease. 'This is in my mind the greatest place in golf . . . I come in maybe expecting to play well on a course I feel very comfortable on. I feel like it suits my game nicely. So as long as I'm getting enough rest and just keeping with what's been going on the last month, I should be able to make some birdies and get myself up there.

'Part of me wants to improve on last year and that's my goal. Another part of me says, you know, let's not over-think this place. Keep it simple and make it like a regular event. Because that's how I've had success in the last few tournaments. It is just trying to hit as many greens as possible, get into a rhythm with the putter. Once that happens, you know, see a couple go in, the hole gets bigger.'

The game's most exciting new talent wanted to play it one shot at a time.

But if Spieth was ready, what about the game's biggest personality? That was the burning question overshadowing the build-up to the 2015 Masters. McIlroy might have been favourite and bidding to join golf's most exclusive club of career grand-slammers, and Spieth might have looked ready to claim his first major, but Tiger Woods was still the primary headline grabber.

Woods had been on a voluntary break from the game since trudging away with an aching back from the first round of the Farmers Insurance Open at Torrey Pines in early February. He completed a mere 11 holes, miserably inaccurate from the tee and with his short game in tatters. His sore back seemed an excuse to save his embarrassment. This came a week after carding a second-round 82 at the Waste Management Phoenix Open in Scottsdale, his worst performance as a professional.

Woods seemed beset by the chipping yips, a mental condition where hitting the shortest shots from just off the green is rendered near-impossible. When leading pros chip, the question is usually: 'Will he hole it?'. In Woods' case, it was: 'Will the ball finish on the green?'. And often the answer was no. A chronic deceleration at impact would lead to his ball dribbling forward and finishing short of the putting surface. Or a jerky right hand would overcompensate and the blade of his wedge would send the ball careering uncontrollably over the back of the green. It was the form of an 18-handicapper.

It was also an unfathomably uncharacteristic malaise for a man regarded for most of his career as possessing the sharpest short game in golf. It led to many predicting that Woods was finished, gone at the age of 39. It was the end of a glorious but turbulent career during which he had dominated the game for nearly two decades.

How could he challenge for titles if the simple art of chipping was beyond his mental and physical capability? And how could he compete at the Masters, with its premium on short-game prowess?

For several weeks leading up to Augusta it remained uncertain whether Woods would take part. He had missed the 2014 Masters after undergoing back surgery while sitting atop the world rankings following five victories in 2013. He hadn't won a major since 2008 and last donned a green jacket when he won his fourth Masters in 2005. Now ranked 111 in the world, this colossus of the game seemed to have nothing but the bleakest of prospects.

Yet Woods, renowned for his dour and single-minded demeanour in the build-up to most tournaments, arrived at

Augusta full of smiles. Having taken himself away from the game, saying his golf was of an unacceptable standard after Torrey Pines, he didn't commit to the Masters until the week before the year's first major.

Never has a pre-practice round warm-up commanded more attention than the one he completed on the Monday of Masters week. Arriving on the range, complete with personal headphones blaring his favourite hip-hop tunes, he wore a broad grin. First he was greeted by 2003 champion Mike Weir and they discussed the Canadian left-hander's ongoing elbow problems. Woods' coach Chris Como was on hand, and there was a warm embrace with good friend and European Ryder Cup captain Darren Clarke.

Vast crowds lined the pristine range as Woods collected three bags of balls and took them to the chipping green stationed furthest from the galleries. Standing among the 'patrons', I craned my neck to witness the player's routine. Even though he was a good 50 yards from the nearest spectators, there was no hiding place. The American Golf Channel TV network screened his routine live. Everyone wanted a first glimpse of the state of Woods' short-game. Journalists in the media centre termed it 'yip-watch'. Normally such workouts would be nothing more than a low-stress warm-up to reignite familiar feels that are second-nature to any Tour pro. Not on this occasion, especially for a player who has always sought to build an impregnable aura of invincibility.

Woods' casual, relaxed demeanour, however, remained intact. He lazily went through a repertoire of wedge shots that had fans applauding each one that landed close to the bright yellow flags that punctuated the deeply verdant surroundings. Despite having been off the scene for nine long weeks, golf's biggest superstar meant business.

From the range he headed to the first tee with his old friend Mark O'Meara, the man to whom Woods had handed a green jacket following his victory in 1998. O'Meara was the senior pro who held a close and avuncular relationship with Woods throughout his glory years. Relations between the two had been strained in the wake of Woods' marital problems in 2009 and they hadn't seen each other for more than a year before they met on the first tee for that practice round, but there could still be no better qualified or comforting companion for Woods than the genial 58-year-old during that late afternoon workout.

Woods pulled his first drive wildly to the left but fears about the state of his game soon started to evaporate. He blasted an unlikely approach to five feet and casually holed for a birdie. Then he strolled to the edge of the green, threw down some balls and hit some chips to get more of a feel for the treacherous putting surface.

It was as though he didn't have a care in the world and Woods' golf was impressive as he strolled around the front nine. He hit approaches to the fourth and seventh holes to tap-in range and eventually called it quits after 11 holes as the light faded. He even stopped to chat with waiting reporters as he left, something that would never have happened in his glowering prime.

'I'm on the good side now,' he smiled. 'I felt like I had to get my game into a spot where I could compete to win a golf tournament and it's finally there. Chipping is fine. I wanted to test out some wedges. That is why I was chipping a little bit more.'

O'Meara was always Woods' most eloquent ambassador and he reprised that role with aplomb. 'The thing about the kid is you can never underestimate,' he said. 'He has great passion. It was good to be out there with him today. I saw some good signs.'

On Tuesday, when all the leading contenders file into the media centre for pre-tournament press conferences, it became clear that Woods didn't need a spokesman. He would do all the speaking himself. For someone who has always been so wary with the media, Woods was open and upbeat. It was a remarkable performance that went a considerable distance towards convincing a growing army of doubters that he could again contend at the biggest tournaments.

'I'm excited, excited to be back at this level,' Woods said. 'I feel like my game is finally ready to compete at the highest level. There's no other tournament in the world like this, and to come back to a place that I've had so many great memories at and so many great times in my life, it's always special. And then this week, to play with Mo [O'Meara], haven't seen him in a while, go back and relive some old times, brings back some great times.'

Woods left no one under any illusion about what had gone into making him feel so confident about his return. 'I worked my ass off,' he smiled. 'People would never understand how much work I put into it to come back and do this again. It was sunup to sundown, and whenever I had free time; if the kids were asleep, I'd still be doing it, and then when they were in school, I'd still be doing it.'

Woods rarely acknowledges a reporter by their first name during news conferences, but he departed from the norm when pressed on the apparent lightness of his mood. *New York Times* correspondent Karen Crouse suggested he seemed 'a lot looser'.

'Yeah, I'm a lot more flexible, you're right,' Woods joked. She pressed him: 'Psychologically; just socially, more at ease, more just socialising with the people around you. What's gone into that? What accounts for that?'

'I have no idea, Karen,' Woods replied, prompting more laughter. 'I'm just enjoying competing again. Whether I have blinders on or not, I don't feel any different. I feel like I'm preparing to try and win the Masters.'

It was a reminder to his immediate audience, to the watching millions at home and to his rivals that he was here to win.

But when he elaborated, that confidence was tempered by realism.

'Competing is still the same. I'm trying to beat everybody out there. That hasn't changed. I prepare to win and expect to go and do that. The only difference is that, yeah, I won the Masters when Jordan was still in diapers. That's the difference; guys are now younger, a whole other generation of kids are coming out. And the game has gotten bigger.

'When I first came out here, I think I averaged 296 (yards off the tee) and I was second to John Daly. Now the carry number is 320. When I won my first golf tournament on tour, I beat Davis Love in a playoff with a persimmon driver.

'The game has evolved so much since I've been out here and I think that's the biggest difference. I know I can pump it out there to 320, but I can't carry it out there each and every time like some of the big guys can. 7,100-yard golf courses are extremely short; before, they were long.

'Nobody worked out except for Vijay [Singh] and myself, and now everyone has their trainer here this week. You see guys are losing more weight, getting fit faster, doing explosive exercises, doing things that were unheard of. Now golf has become more of a sport.'

Aside from his 14 majors, that last observation is probably the one of which Woods is most proud. He feels that his devotion to workout regimes helped transform golf from a past-time to an athletic sport. But there was still an uncharacteristic softening to his approach to this Masters as he confirmed that he would embrace the fun side of the week. He would take part in the eve-of-tournament par-3 competition and his two children, Samantha and Charlie, would caddie for him.

'My two little ones are going to be out there with me,' he said. 'It's special. This tournament means so much to me in so many different ways. We all know what happened in 1997 with my dad's health.' He suffered a heart attack in 1996 that left him critically ill for several months. 'He was dead at one point earlier that year; came back, and then came here and I won the Masters.

'To now have come full circle and to have a chance to have my kids out there and be able to share that with them, it's special. . . . They are excited, I'm excited and can't wait to go out there.'

Woods was at pains to explain that his chipping woes from earlier in the season were not psychological. They were related to the new swing he had adopted under Como's tutelage. His new coach is a bio-mechanist, specialising in injury prevention. Employing a new swing technique meant that there was a 'new release pattern' and his short game had temporarily suffered as a consequence.

He also acknowledged that there had not been a eureka moment while he toiled on the range at his Florida base. 'There was really no moment like that. It was a slow and steady progression, each and every day. When the sun came up, by the time the sun set, I should be a better player than I was in the morning, and that was the case. That was our whole focus.'

Woods had hoped his game would be good enough to compete in Arnold Palmer's tournament at Bay Hill in March but he wasn't ready. He was desperate, though, to make it back for the Masters.

'There's no other tournament like it. Most guys will probably rate it as their most favourite tournament . . . it's basically a player's tournament. You go out there and it's just a player and a caddie and that's it. It's very quiet out there on the golf course; and inside the ropes, it's really just us.

'You come here to a golf course which we play every year, where other majors you don't. There's so much history involved. I just find it fascinating that they keep changing this place, it seems like every year, and (yet) it looks exactly the same, like it's never been touched. It's just fascinating. I didn't play last year so I didn't see when the Eisenhower Tree was gone. I didn't realise 17 was straight ahead. I always thought it was a little bit of a dogleg-left. It's eye opening to see it's just dead-straight. That was very, very shocking to me, to see it like that.'

But his central message was less surprising. It was that some things never change. His final public words before returning to major competition held a familiar and chilling ring: 'My greatest motivation? Winning. I like it.'

And if there is one tournament most professional players want to win, The Masters is probably it.

CHAPTER 3

April at Augusta

When Thursday of Masters week rolls around, Augusta undergoes a discernible change of atmosphere. It's time for the serious golf to start.

The players' practice rounds, usually punctuated by the frivolity of skimmed shots across the water at the 16th, have been completed. And the eve-of-tournament par-3 contest, a festival of smiles and laughter as players indulge their wives, girlfriends and children with caddie duties, is done and dusted.

We are able to strike one name – on this occasion the American Kevin Streelman – from the list of possible green jacket winners. No one has gone on to claim the Masters after winning this nine-hole ceremonial tournament. Streelman won on the third hole of a sudden-death playoff against Camilo Villegas to claim the crystal vase trophy. His caddie was an 11-year-old boy called Ethan Couch, who suffers from a benign but inoperable brain tumour. Streelman, who covered the nine holes in five under par, had found him through the Make a Wish Foundation.

A day later it is time for the real competition to begin. The seemingly interminable wait is over. The vacuum of eight long months without major championship golf is about to be filled.

Thursday, 9 April 2015

Day one at the Masters is the most eagerly anticipated date on the golfing calendar yet the city suddenly feels strangely quiet and normal again. Compared with the practice days, there are now fewer cars on the road and the traffic queues are shorter. The reason is simple – the crowds are smaller for the tournament itself than for the hustle and bustle that precedes it. The majority of ticket holders come from an exclusive list of people with the right to buy, year after year. The Augusta National may have made it easier for tickets to be bought on general sale in recent years, but the vast majority of patrons have their right to tickets handed down through their families.

So there is no chaos or crush as the gates are opened at first light. The words 'good morning, good morning, welcome to The Masters, please have your tickets ready for inspection' can be heard over and over again. The security guard, in his pristine white Pinkerton shirt and sharp black trousers, competes for attention with a passionate Christian preacher who sets up position on the opposite side of Berckmans Road. The crowds are passionately encouraged to adopt the ways of Jesus but they are more intent on the annual worship at golf's most beautiful temple. This is a congregation that knows the rules. No mobile phones and no running. They know where to station their deck chairs and they know the importance of crowding around the first tee just ahead of the first official tee time. Here they will catch sight of golf's 'Three Wise Men', those senior statesmen who helped turn the Masters into such an internationally significant sporting event.

With breakfast cooking in the clubhouse and an overcast morning greeting the start of the 79th Masters, Arnold Palmer, Jack Nicklaus and Gary Player were welcomed to the tee by Augusta National Chairman Billy Payne. Palmer was 85 years old and a four-time winner, Nicklaus, 75, had a record six green jackets and Player, aged 79 and the first overseas winner, had won three.

Palmer had been battling a dislocated shoulder suffered the previous December, but remained stubbornly determined to replicate his charismatic lunge at the ball. Nicklaus and Player, meanwhile, were hell bent on outdriving each other. Old competitive urges die very hard in great champions. The horseshoe of worshippers surrounding the first tee delighted in being in the presence of such golfing royalty.

Defending champion Bubba Watson, Rickie Fowler and Keegan Bradley – all competing later in the day – were there to enjoy the moment as well. 'Don't fan it,' Palmer jokingly told himself before hitting a low, hooky drive. 'I don't think he's kidding,' Nicklaus added. 'He said exactly the same thing to me.'

The mood is far more serious just to the rear of the tee, around the practice putting green. For the early starters, it provides the last opportunity to discern just how pacy the greens will be. It's a nerve-wracking time for them. Inevitably, the prospect of the season's first round of major golf concentrates the mind.

It is also a time for blocking out the pomp and ceremony. It is all about focus and feel. Strangely, though, that was not how things appeared to the man detailed with hitting the first competitive shot of the event. This particular competitor was already reflecting on a perfect start to his day. Little did he know that things were about to get even better.

Charley Hoffman is best known for loud shirts and long blond hair tumbling from beneath his golf cap. A solid but unspectacular presence on the PGA Tour, Hoffman earned his place in the Masters with victory in the final event of the calendar year in 2014. It was a relatively small tournament in Mexico, one that doesn't attract the biggest names. Not that this worried Hoffman. His victory had guaranteed him a second Augusta appearance.

Hoffman cut a less striking figure on this occasion. The long hair had been shorn, his shirt was a sober pale green and there were few signs of nerves or anxiety. Hoffman had been inadvertently distracted by those former greats and it did him no harm at all. 'It was cool, getting up this morning and warming up with Jack, Arnie and Gary Player,' he said. 'It puts the nerves at ease.

'I actually got Jack's and Arnie's autograph; they were nice enough to do that. I was sort of scared. Should I ask them? Should I not ask them? My mind wasn't really on golf. I was watching those guys.'

When the draw revealed he would be hitting the first tee shot, Hoffman guessed he might have the opportunity to snap up some legendary signatures. He wanted to use them to boost his charity work. 'I bought a couple of flags,' he admitted. 'I wasn't sure if I'd ask them when they were warming up or on the first tee, but I ended up asking. They were warming up next to me, Jack and Arnie, and I go: "Would you mind signing the flag for me? I'll auction them off for my foundation event and make some money for some kids." They were nice enough to do that for me.'

So much for the importance of being 'in the zone' when competing at the highest level. Yes, Hoffman did dispatch a pretty ropey opening tee shot that flew left towards the ninth fairway, but thereafter he played impeccably. Indeed, he positively revelled in the chance of going out first in a two-ball with fellow American Brian Harman.

With the old-timers peeling off after their ceremonial opening strikes, Hoffman quickly found his stride, picking up birdies at the par-5 second and the short par-4 third. 'I love playing "ready" golf,' Hoffman said. 'We didn't rush by any means but never had to wait on a shot. That's my dream, go play Augusta National first off in the Masters. You couldn't have set me up any better than that.'

The course was damp and relatively soft. This would surely play into Rory McIlroy's hands as he bid for the career grand slam. Certainly he had cause for optimism. As Hoffman put it: 'Any time you get this golf course a little bit damp, you can be aggressive to some of those back, hard pins.'

Hoffman used to grow his hair to stand out from the crowd. He wanted to be different from the pro-forma PGA Tour persona. But by 2013 he had tired of it. 'It had sort of a snowball effect that my daughter needed a haircut and I needed a haircut, so we went in together.' Now it was time for his golf, rather than his hairstyle, to catch the eye.

As McIlroy started shakily, Hoffman made hay. He fired an eagle at the par-5 15th and followed it up with a birdie at the next to move to four under par. At the last he sent in a brilliant approach to five feet and converted it for a round of 67. It was his lowest score in a major tournament. As he signed his card at noon on the first day of the 2015 Masters, Hoffman was the leader by two strokes. In 2011 he had made a creditable debut, finishing 27th. This start, which began with that impromptu autograph hunt, threatened a much more significant return.

McIlroy, meanwhile, was struggling in the company of three-time champion Phil Mickelson and another American, Ryan Moore. He tugged his tee shot into a little known creek down the left side of the long second. It took a penalty drop, a threaded third and accurate wedge to ensure the world number one saved par on a hole where most players are looking to pick up an early shot.

Before teeing off, McIlroy had addressed the issue of his assault on the career grand slam. 'A place in history is what's at stake,' he said. 'The sooner I get it out of the way, the better.' But so far it was an inauspicious start.

By early afternoon the leaderboard was taking shape, with Hoffman still at the top and McIlroy's name conspicuously absent. He laboured through the front nine and at the difficult par-4 11th a poor chip led to a second bogey. McIlroy swiped his club angrily. The Northern Irishman was one over par heading through Amen Corner.

Meanwhile, the champion left-handers were rising to the top. Bubba Watson was at two under, as was Mickelson. Hoffman was then joined at the top by Justin Rose, who birdied both par 5s on the back nine to push his score to five under. He parred in for a 67 to match his lowest score at Augusta.

By this time, Tiger Woods was underway. Sent out in the penultimate group with Welshman Jamie Donaldson and American Jimmy Walker, Woods was in the prime-time slot that attracts the biggest television audiences. Given his absence from the game, worries about his fitness and the fears over his chipping, he was attracting even more curiosity, and much of it morbid. How would this great champion fare with a scorecard in his pocket? How would his short game stack up on a course that puts such a premium on touch and feel? Would he even remain fit enough to complete 72 holes?

Woods pushed his first tee shot into the fairway bunker and made a bogey five, only to atone immediately with a routine birdie at the next. His gait was confident and his short game secure. Eyebrows were collectively raised. This was not at all bad for someone who hadn't been seen since February, when his game appeared to be in ruins.

There were also signs that Woods' competitive instincts remained intact. He flashed his notorious temper after two errant strokes at the severe dogleg ninth hole after yanking his tee shot into the adjacent first fairway. Woods let the club fall from his hands in disgust while he stood gazing incredulously at the flight of his ball. He then smashed his next shot into a towering pine, prompting him to lash the club around with fearful violence. It took a brilliant recovery from the pine straw, hooking the ball to the back of the green, to limit the damage to a bogey.

'Two dumb mistakes,' he would reflect. Woods covered the front half in a one-over-par 37. 'On nine I played the wrong shot. I was trying to turn it down there and I really shouldn't have. The hole was playing short. It's hot. The ball is flying. It's not that hard to hit the ball 300, 320 out here in this heat. And then, on top of that, I hit the wrong shot again. I tried to put the ball in the bunker when I probably should have put the ball short right and pitched up.'

McIlroy, meanwhile, was beginning to settle. The setback at the 11th proved his last and the 25-year-old took advantage of the par-5 13th and 15th holes with birdies that secured a one-under-par 71. It is often said that you can't win it on the first day but that you can certainly lose it. McIlroy made sure he was still in the mix. It was perhaps as much as could be expected from someone who had dominated so many headlines in the build-up to the one major he had yet to win. 'It's nice to just get on with the tournament,' he said. 'Now I can just relax and try to find my rhythm. I'm pretty satisfied.

'I haven't put too much pressure on myself. I obviously know what I can achieve this week, but I'm not letting myself think about it too much. Just trying to play it one round at a time. I feel like I can do better.'

Veteran Ernie Els surged up the leaderboard, getting to six under par with an eagle at the 15th, yet was still thoroughly overshadowed by the form man coming into the Masters – Jordan Spieth.

Spieth teed off at 1.15 p.m. With a win and two runner-up finishes in the three previous weeks, as well as his second place 12 months earlier at Augusta, the 21-year-old made an astonishing start, taking advantage of the compliant conditions even though temperatures had soared into the nineties on a sticky afternoon. So good was Spieth's unerring approach play and golden touch on the greens that he suggested he might shoot the lowest score in major championship history. A 62 or better looked a distinct possibility as he collected eight birdies in his first 14 holes. Playing partner Billy Horschel joked that he needed a tape recorder to play out the same words as they left every green: 'Nice hole, Jordan.'

Horschel was the perfect partner. 'Billy's fun to play with. We mess with each other,' Spieth said. The golfing gods seemed on his side as well. The eighth of those birdies came when his approach, from an awkward lie just off the 14th fairway, clattered into the flag before coming to rest. The ball had obeyed its master's call. (Spieth is one of those players prone to shouting instructions after striking the ball.) 'I was saying: "Carry the ridge!" Spieth recalled. 'I had a good number, good club, but the ball was above my feet out of the rough and I had to cut it, and you can't be left. If I hit it solid, it would get up there behind the hole and I'd have an uphill putt. I was just trying to make four.'

The birdie was a bonus. He was eight under par and the letters 'S P I E T H' topped the leaderboard, already assuming an air of permanence.

The Texan headed to the 15th with a simple thought – that he could shoot the lowest round of his life. The fact that it might also mean breaking the record for the lowest score at the Masters, and at any major, was lost on him. He knew the 15th was gettable and that one more birdie from the closing three holes would do the job. You can think that way when the hole appears the size of a bucket.

Commentating on BBC 5Live, we too began to speculate that we might be witnessing the first 62 at a major. This conversation crops up periodically, but something always seems to happen to deny the possibility. I remember reporting on my first Open Championship at Royal St George's in 1993 for BBC World Service. I had never done any on-course commentary and previous Open visits had been as an enthusiastic spectator. That day at Sandwich, the late Payne Stewart came down the last hole needing a birdie for 62.

I rushed out of the media centre with a tape recorder. If Stewart's putt dropped it would be golfing history and I needed to capture the moment. I pushed my way through the crowds to gain a decent view but such was the air of silent anticipation as the flamboyant American settled over his putt that I couldn't bring myself to whisper any form of commentary, for fear of ruining the moment. It was a rookie error, but my silence reflected the potential magnitude of what we were witnessing. Stewart's putt missed. It proved to be just another of the many major rounds of 63.

But why not Spieth, here at Augusta in 2015? He was holing everything. He had a reachable par 5 next and, with the receptive conditions, another birdie from the closing three holes was surely within reach.

One discounts the golfing gods at one's peril.

Yes, they had helped Spieth to his eighth birdie when that ball freakishly clattered into the pin, but they decree that no one – no one, ever – goes lower than 63 in a major tournament. It is simply not allowed.

Spieth belted a beautiful drive down the 15th. It looked a straightforward approach over the water from the middle of the fairway, but the yardage wasn't good. The gods determined that he would be caught in two minds. He powered his approach through the back of the green and almost into the water. He then left his chip short, hit an uncharacteristically tentative putt from the edge of the green and wound up taking a bogey six. Time to cancel the 62 alert. He slipped back to seven under.

Woods, meanwhile, found the water at the short par-3 12th but finished respectably to card a 73. 'The only thing I really struggled with was the pace of the greens,' Woods said. 'I couldn't believe how slow they were.' The big bonus was that his suspect chipping had held firm – indeed, it had been impressive by anyone's standards.

'That's the way it should be. That's why I hit thousands and thousands of shots, so it's my strength again,' said Woods. 'You know, I'm still in it. We have a long way to go. And we don't know what the Masters is going to do with the greens or the golf course. You know how they like to change things every now and then.'

This was a barely disguised message from the greatest player of the modern era. The course set-up is too easy. Firm up the greens. Then we can sort the champions from the also-rans.

Despite Woods' reservations, it proved a remarkable opening day to this most eagerly anticipated Masters. There was even room for 65-year-old Tom Watson to break par with a 71, on a course that for years he has contended is now too long for him. The champion from 1977 and 1981 said: 'It was there for the taking, the golf course. It's fun to be able to be in red figures at Augusta National. At my age, it's a minor miracle.'

Jason Day illustrated the course's susceptibility as he collected five straight back-nine birdies for a 67. Spieth himself bounced back from his setback at the 15th to claim a brilliant birdie at the last. He carded a 64 to claim a three-stroke lead. 'To make nine birdies out there, that's a dreamy round,' Spieth beamed.

Hoffman, Day, Rose and Els were his closest rivals. The day, though, belonged to the leader. 'Really cool, yeah,' he commented in youthful style, 'I'd take three more of them.'

Friday, 10 April 2015

One of the advantages of playing well in a late group on the first day is the immediate opportunity to capitalise. A lie-in on Thursday means an early start on Friday. There's little time to kill, and every chance of maintaining momentum. Once Spieth had finished his media duties there was just enough time for a bite to eat before turning out the light and attempting to get a refreshing sleep prior to an early alarm call the following morning.

'The hardest thing to do is put aside wanting to win so bad,' he said.

But he slept well and arrived early on Friday to prepare for a 9:57 a.m. tee time. The pre-tournament buzz had switched from McIlroy's bid for a career grand slam and now surrounded the Dallas youngster. The range was packed as he warmed up. McIlroy, meanwhile, was back at his rented home, hanging around ahead of a tee time that would have him finishing near dusk in the penultimate group of the day.

Spieth began solidly. The galleries were largely split between his group, alongside Horschel and Henrik Stenson, and the one featuring Woods with Donaldson and Walker. They teed off half an hour later, in the absence of live television coverage, which only begins in the afternoon at Augusta. Spieth improved his position with birdies at the par-5 second and the par-4 fifth. That one was a bonus, but it wasn't yet the spectacular golf of the opening day. That changed, however, on the long eighth.

A third birdie seemed improbable following a drive under the lip of a fairway bunker. Spieth could only advance a short distance, leaving 235 yards for his third shot. He hit a hybrid that found the undulating contours in perfect fashion, the ball settling two feet from the cup. Horschel walked up to the green. Turning back down the fairway, with the leader still 100 yards away, he held up his hands to indicate the distance left to complete the hole. He then smiled and started laughing. Spieth moved serenely to 11 under par.

It was only the second day but he was already applying significant scoreboard pressure, sending a relentless message to those lagging behind. While Augusta rewards patient and strategic play, the temptation would be to try to over-power the course; to make a big move to keep pace with Spieth. McIlroy was in that category, his quest for golfing history merely inten-sifying the threat of impatience. He could not afford unforced errors but his front nine was littered with them.

He dropped a shot at the first before immediately getting it back. There were further bogeys at the fifth and seventh, where he drove behind a tree on the claustrophobic par 4, and his frustration was laid bare on the ninth when he ran up a double-bogey six.

McIlroy turned in 40. Spieth had covered the same stretch in 33. McIlroy appeared destined for a round of 77 or worse for the sixth Masters in a row. A four-time major champion and undisputed world number one, yet he still had the capacity to throw in a destructive round just when he needed to avoid one.

As he stalked indignantly past the practice putting green to the tenth tee, he muttered animatedly to himself. It seemed as though his chances had evaporated. All the hype and hope had come to nought. This wasn't going to be his year.

'At that point I was just trying to get myself back to even par for the tournament,' McIlroy said. He stood on the 10th tee with the scoreboards showing him at three over and in grave danger of a second successive Masters missed cut.

It is a sign, though, of his growing maturity that he was able to summon up something special on the way back. It began with a birdie on the 10th. He came through Amen Corner unscathed and collected an eagle at the par-5 13th. A bogey followed at the next before a routine birdie to return to level par on the 15th.

McIlroy re-adjusted his sights. 'Then I was trying to get into the red numbers,' he said. There was a chip-in for birdie at the 17th and another shot picked up at the last. He came home in a commendable 31 for an uneven, but characterful 71 and a two-under-par total at halfway.

It had been another dramatic day. Spieth set a blistering pace and Hoffman tried to keep up with a 68. Woods shot 69 to match McIlroy's total. 'I'm still right there,' he insisted again.

The big-hitting Dustin Johnson, meanwhile, surged into contention with a remarkable round. A few weeks before, he had won the WGC Cadillac Championship at Doral. That victory was regarded as redemptive, coming straight after a six-month leave of absence to confront 'personal challenges'. Although it was denied by all parties, it was strongly rumoured he had been told by the PGA Tour to take time away from the game.

There was a scintillating quality to his golf as he collected a record three eagles during a single Masters round. Players who make an eagle at Augusta receive a piece of commemorative cut-glass crystal. Johnson would need to find plenty of room on his mantelpiece.

His day, though, reflected the extreme highs and lows of his personal life. His 67 had started with a double bogey at the first. He began the back nine with a bogey and his round finished with a dropped shot. Along with the trio of par-5 eagles at the 2nd, 8th and 15th, there were also three birdies.

By contrast, Spieth was the model of consistency. Having turned in a three-under 33 he brilliantly birdied the 10th, then the par-5 13th and 15th holes. With no bogeys, it all added up to a faultless 66. He was 14 under par, five strokes clear of Hoffman and a dozen ahead of McIlroy and Woods.

'This is just the halfway point,' he said as the maturity of his golf accompanied him into the interview room. 'I got standing ovations walking to multiple greens. I mean, that's something you can only dream about. It's Friday, too. I'd like to have the same thing happening on Sunday.'

While Woods was claiming he was still in the running, McIlroy sounded a more realistic tone while offering fulsome praise for the front-runner. 'It's really, really impressive,' he said. 'I think a few guys can still catch him. It will take, obviously, something extraordinary from myself to get up there, but you never know.'

McIlroy then made a passing nod to 2011, when he had squandered a four-stroke lead with a ruinous final-round 80. 'I know better than most people what can happen with the lead around here. But Jordan had the experience last year. He had a couple of shots lead and couldn't quite hold onto it. He'll have learned from that.'

The second-round leaderboard read:

−14 Spieth (64–66)

 −9 Hoffman (67–68)

 −7 Paul Casey (69–68)

 −7 Johnson (70–67)

 −7 Rose (67–70)

 −6 Mickelson (70–68)

Saturday, 11 April 2015

Spieth had broken a 39-year-old record set by Raymond Floyd for the opening 36 holes. His five-stroke advantage equalled another Augusta landmark; the three other players who held such a lead after the second round, Herman Keiser in 1946, Jack Nicklaus in 1975 and Floyd in 1976, all went on to win.

Spieth had been almost immaculate, with 15 birdies and only one dropped shot. 'I got off to a great start and had a chance to win last year on Sunday. I'd like to have that same opportunity this year,' Spieth said. 'I'm going to try and stay very patient these last two days and understand it's going to feel like a whole other tournament.'

The top 50 players and ties make it to the weekend, as well as those within 10 shots of the leader. This, though, wasn't an issue because of the size of Spieth's advantage. The guillotine fell at two over, 16 behind the Texan.

Among those jettisoned was Horschel. He had been beaten into submission. The winner of golf's most lucrative prize, the

$10 million FedEx Cup at East Lake in Atlanta the previous September, he slumped to a second-round 78 to miss out by two.

Other casualties included Jim Furyk (74-73), former world number one Luke Donald (75-72) and reigning US Open champion Martin Kaymer (76-75). Tom Watson couldn't repeat the heroics of his first round 71 and was 10 strokes worse in his second round.

Furthest behind was the man who still managed to rival Spieth for the loudest cheers. Ben Crenshaw shot 91-85 and it didn't matter in the slightest because this was his Augusta farewell. 'I feel like I've won the tournament,' said the two-time winner, playing his 44th Masters. The 63-year-old was embraced by his long-time caddie Carl Jackson, who hadn't been well enough to perform the bag duties that week, as he walked off the green for the final time. 'I just said "I love you," and he said "I love you" back. Can't be anymore succinct than that. We know how much each other has meant to the other one.'

Crenshaw and Jackson provided the abiding memories of the second day of the 79th Masters. 'Gentle Ben' had tied Sam Snead in playing the fifth largest number of Masters that week and there are few more popular figures at Augusta. The tears flowed as Crenshaw's wife Julie joined him. Spectators cheered a moment that will sit alongside the Masters farewells of Nicklaus, Palmer and Player. Amid the emotion, Crenshaw contemplated what the weekend might hold.

'I think most everybody knows Jordan is capable, entirely capable,' Crenshaw said of his fellow Texan. 'It's keeping his emotions in check. He's obviously in a real hot streak, very confident, very bold. He knows what he's doing. He's a great scorer. God, can he score.' The key was not to get ahead of himself 'and I think he's mature enough that . . . he won't get that way'.

Crenshaw judged Spieth well. A recurring theme during the 2015 majors was the youngster's intelligent outlook, which enabled his game to fulfil its potential. This was evident as he assessed what lay ahead.

'Each round on the weekend of a major in contention can feel like you're playing almost two rounds in one,' Spieth said. 'It just feels like it's a long day and you just can't get too up or down at the beginning, the first nine holes, with whatever's going on, and understand that at a place like Augusta National there's a lot of stuff that can happen, a lot of lead changes can happen. Holes can lend birdies and they can lend double-bogeys.

'You just have to really be patient, not try and force anything, and allow the angles to play themselves out . . . allow myself to hit these shots on the par 5s, like I have been the last couple of days, in the right spot to have the right angle into the green, to have a really easy pitch where the worst I'm going to make is par.'

Fifty-five players made it through to the final two rounds. Spieth would be the last to tee off on a Saturday that started cloudy and breezy but brightened later. Spieth had to wait until 2.55 p.m. before teeing off alongside the dogged Charley Hoffman, his closest rival at five strokes behind. While there was huge admiration for what Spieth had achieved, there was also a fear that he could kill the event stone dead. A tournament famed for drama and excitement could be reduced to a contest between Spieth and the record books, while the rest spent the weekend playing for nothing more than a runners-up finish.

Yet the fans were treated to a thrilling third round, one that will live long in the memory.

The pairings are determined by leaderboard order, as well as by the time a player's scorecard is submitted to the recorders on the previous day. First in is last out in the next round whenever scores are level. It is a random exercise that can serve up attractive pairings. This day was no exception, with McIlroy earning the same 12.45 p.m. tee time as Bubba Watson. Then there was the pairing of Woods and Sergio García, who have a history of bad blood, and the mutual-admiration combination of Aussies Adam Scott and Jason Day.

All of these players seemed to have too much to do to rein in the runaway leader but, among the later starters, Johnson, Rose and Mickelson knew that they could impose pressure. It would take a run of birdies to do so, but who knew how the leader would then react?

Spieth found the time between rounds difficult to fill, despite having friends and family in two rented houses in the area. 'It's just so hard,' he admitted. 'I think I finished my round 24 hours before I started my next; with a big lead, that's tough. I was just anxious to get started.'

As Spieth waited and fretted, he could see conditions remained soft and scoreable. The tournament committee resisted the temptation to turn on the sub-air system that would suck out moisture and make the course play faster and firmer. There would be more opportunities for spectacular golf, as Morgan Hoffmann demonstrated early in the day with an eagle at the short par-4 third. The less heralded Hoffmann of this Masters holed out from 123 yards to spark the first of many roars on a compelling Saturday.

By contrast, Watson began with a miserable seven as he found trees, rough and sand on the opening hole. McIlroy made a calm par before igniting more cheers on the second. His tee shot just missed the fairway down the left of the par 5. It was followed by a beautiful long iron to pin high, 40 feet to the right of the flag. It was an uphill putt and he could be aggressive. McIlroy gave the ball a firm rap and it never deviated from the cup. His eagle took him four under and catapulted him into the top 10.

Woods then muscled in on the act with consecutive birdies at the second, third and fourth holes. Indeed, he nearly holed out at the difficult par-3 fourth as he surged to five under. All that tempered his rising spirits was the fact that the tournament leader was still nine strokes better off.

Spieth began steadily, two-putting for par from 30 feet. At the same time Woods was somehow avoiding a bogey after hitting over the back of the treacherous ninth green. His miraculous up-and-down took him to the turn in 32, but he was eclipsed by McIlroy who birdied the eighth and ninth for a brilliant 31. McIlroy had covered his last 18 holes in 62 strokes, an extraordinary response to his front-nine 40 of the previous day. At six under par with 27 holes to play, he was within eight of the lead. Perhaps the career grand slam dream was still alive?

Spieth lipped out for a birdie at the third and handed back the stroke he had picked up on the second with a bogey at the fourth. McIlroy, meanwhile, two-putted the 13th for another birdie to move to within seven. Rose seemed to be fading, though, as he three putted the fifth to fall back to five under.

Television audiences often complain about what they regard as the undue attention given to Woods, especially in his years of decline since 2009. But this was a day when he was justifying every second on screen, even if it wasn't all good golf. On the 13th he snap-hooked his tee shot into the trees. It was the worst drive of the day, and by some margin. His ball, however, was leading a charmed life and ricocheted off the pines back into play. Woods then bunted a well-judged lay-up, pitched on and holed out to move to five under par for his round. At the next he found the trees and this time paid the penalty with a dropped shot. He birdied the 15th and then sloppily bogeyed the last for an otherwise excellent 68 that took him to six under. 'My goal was to get as close as I could to 10, if not to 10 (under par),' Woods said. 'Just in case Jordan went off a little bit, at least I was within range.'

Woods felt a seriously low round had eluded him. 'I really

had it going,' he said, clearly revelling in silencing the critics who had been predicting his demise. Nor would he concede his dream of a fifth green jacket was over. 'Anything can happen,' he insisted.

Spieth, though, was consolidating, and this despite the shakiest golf of his week. He coaxed in a curling 15-footer at the sixth but immediately handed back the shot. At the seventh he misjudged his approach to find the back bunker and his devilishly difficult escape left 40 feet to save par. Up ahead, McIlroy short-sided himself at the 16th for his first bogey, while Rose birdied the seventh to move back to six under. It was a pivotal moment for the Englishman. 'I was talking with my caddie and I said: "Listen, we just need to be a little bit more committed." The wind can swirl. We made a great choice of club at the 7th hole, we went with 52 degrees instead of the pitching wedge, which got me pin-high and I was able to make birdie there. That changed the momentum for me.'

Mickelson, too, was mounting a charge. He turned in 32 with a brilliant approach to four feet on the ninth. He was now 10 under par and the tournament temperature rose in tandem with the meteorological conditions. The air was warm, the greens remained receptive and some of the game's biggest names were capitalising.

McIlroy wasn't one of them, though. The dropped shot at 16 halted his progress and at the last he fired his drive into the first of the huge bunkers down the left. It cost him a bogey. A potential 65 turned into a 68, putting him alongside Woods on six under par.

Playing in the final group of a major for the first time, Charley Hoffman was steady. He went to the turn in one under par and showed little sign of being out his depth. The 11th saw him slot home a 40-footer that broke right to left to collect his second birdie and move to 11 under, four back.

There are few more evocative or exciting places in golf

than the Amen Corner stretch at Augusta. The grandstand to the right of the 11th green also overlooks the 12th tee. It is always packed as the leading groups come through. The downhill 11th is lined, sometimes four or five deep, down the right side by spectators. The opposite side has no room for patrons. It is a perilously difficult green to hit. Players can bale out right but that leaves a tricky chip, made all the more intimidating by the water that guards the front and left of the putting surface.

Once negotiated, they move to the 12th tee, where the mass of spectators in the grandstand and around the hitting area generates an atmosphere of rarefied intensity. Every movement is witnessed up close; a nervous twitch, a worried practice swing before the trickiest of tee shots on the hole they call 'Golden Bell'. It is the shortest of the par 3s, with Rae's Creek running in front of a green that is wider than it is deep. The putting surface is also guarded front and back by brilliant white bunkers. That Saturday, the crowds had already seen Johnson rack up a ruinous double bogey after his tee shot clung to the bank at the front of the green. From there he flew the putting surface with an awful pitch and took three to get down from the sand. His meltdown was played out in eerie silence because of the lack of nearby spectators. Indeed, the fans around the tee are also the closest spectators to the action on the green. There couldn't be a greater contrast in atmosphere between the teeing ground and the hole.

Spieth and Hoffman coped well with the demands of this devilish par 3 during the third round. Hoffman found sand but made a fine par save while Spieth knocked his tee shot to eight feet before slotting home a putt that took him to 16 under par. The record low score for the Masters was Tiger Woods' 18 under in 1997. Spieth was within touching distance with 24 holes to play.

It was 5.35 p.m. on a sultry spring Saturday afternoon and the leaderboard now read:

−16 Spieth (12)
−11 Hoffman (12)
−10 Mickelson (13)
 −7 Streelman (14), Casey (12), Rose (12)

The 34-year-old Rose was now playing confident, decisive golf but was still way back. As Spieth pushed his drive right into the pines off the 13th tee (an even more isolated spot than the 12th green), Rose was contemplating a difficult chip from a swale front left of the green. He executed the task with aplomb to pick up a birdie that he knew he couldn't afford to miss.

Spieth and Hoffman could only lay up after their inaccurate drives made it impossible to take on Rae's Creek. The leader pitched to 12 feet, Hoffman was less accurate and only managed a par. Spieth took the chance to move to 17 under, reading to perfection a gentle left-to-right breaker that took him six clear of his playing partner. He looked unstoppable.

Until he reached the 14th green, that is. Up ahead Mickelson's eagle chip at 15 missed but he made a birdie that took him to 11 under. Spieth's approach settled 25 feet from the hole and his birdie attempt came desperately close to toppling into the cup. But instead, it ran on four feet and he uncharacteristically missed to the left the return. Mickelson was now alongside Hoffman in second, five strokes behind. Rose, having added another birdie, was into fourth place at nine under par.

Rose followed with a delightful second to the 15th, pin high and 20 feet from the flag. He lagged the first putt and tapped in for his third birdie in a row. Ten under par. Back on the tee, Spieth responded to his third bogey of the day by splitting the fairway. One hole ahead on the last of Augusta's par 3s Mickelson was yelling 'Hook, hook!' as he tried to access the pin, tight to the right of the green. The left-hander's ball remained on the lower side left towards the water, leaving him with a 50-footer across the green.

Many of Mickelson's greatest golfing moments have come at Augusta and here was another for the 2004, 2006 and 2010 champion. To thunderous roars he rammed home his audacious birdie attempt, the ball taking a big left-to-right turn. 'Crazy. I mean, it's crazy to make that putt,' Mickelson admitted. 'I'm just trying to two-putt it. But I hit it all the time in practice, because it's a spot you want to be if you miss the small section by the hole. It's slow up to the hole, it's fast past the hole. I had perfect speed and it just kind of floated in the side door.

'I remember in 1991 watching Jack Nicklaus and Tom Watson both hit that putt, both made it, and I remember being up in the clubhouse feeling the ground reverberate from the roar. So it's makeable, but it's not an easy one.'

Spieth kept responding in perfect fashion. He struck a commanding second shot over the water and onto the green at the 15th. It set up a birdie, propelling him back to 17 under.

Rose would respond as well. Off the back of three consecutive birdies, he had dumped his tee shot into the bunker at the front of the par 3 that was still rocking to the reverberations of Mickleson's monster putt. This was the place to station your deckchair if you were one of the fortunate patrons to have tickets for this astonishing Saturday. No sooner had silence descended than Rose splashed out of the sand and watched his ball track straight into the hole for yet another birdie. It rocketed him to 11 under and a share of third place with Hoffman. 'I played patient golf and got rewarded,' said Rose. You could call it luck or magic, he said, 'but again, with our preparation, we knew that's a pin location where that bunker is not a bad place to be.

'I hit 9-iron, had 160 to the hole and knew I was sort of pushing my luck to get back to the pin. It puffed into a tiny bit of breeze and the ball came up short, but I had a great lie in the flat part of the trap; and the sand, if anything, was slightly wet in there. I knew I could be somewhat aggressive. I knew

I could get a little bit of check on the ball. Flew it probably 10 feet short of the flag, one bounce, bit of check. Again, I was on a pretty straight line to the pin. That's the key at Augusta. If you can miss the ball where you don't have a lot of slope to deal with, you're in a pretty good spot.'

Spieth's route to his birdie on that short hole was more conventional. The brilliance was in the tee shot, which finished 12 feet away and left an uphill putt. It was an opportunity not to be wasted and it took him to the mythical Masters score of 18 under par – Woods' record from 18 years earlier. Moments earlier, Mickelson had cut the arrears to four strokes, but with astonishing composure Spieth pressed the gas pedal again and, with the three-time champion three-putting the 17th, the leader swiftly moved seven clear of his closest rivals. Hoffman, wilting, missed his chance of a two from much shorter range.

−18 Spieth (16)
−11 Mickelson (17), Rose (16)
−10 Hoffman (16)

The golfing gods thwart sub-63 major rounds and they don't much care for players reaching the 18-under mark at Augusta either. Spieth chose driver for his penultimate tee shot and flew it left. All he could do was lift a wedge over the trees to the front of the green. Ahead, Mickelson made par after missing a reasonable birdie chance to sign for an otherwise brilliant 67. Rose made a superb up and down to remain at 11 under.

The focus, though, remained on the man who was dominating the week. Moments later, from a similar position to Rose, he buckled. Spieth took four more shots to get down for a double bogey that came completely out of the blue. Suddenly he was back to 16 under par and only five clear.

'We knew 17 was a par hole,' Spieth conceded. 'Driver should never have come out of my bag. Not that I'm playing any differently than if I were tied or behind, but it's a down-wind hole. I was getting a little erratic with the driver and I can hit 3-wood, 8-iron in there and have a 20-footer to two-putt. I was very frustrated with that decision.'

And then the lead was down to four, Rose's composure earning a brilliant birdie at the last and second place outright at 12 under. 'I had 6-iron in my hand,' he said, explaining his approach to the home green. 'I was about to pull the trigger and I just sort of said, well, with the amount of cut that I had to put on it, I didn't really factor that in until the last second, and so I said to my caddie, "I think we need a cut 5-iron in here." Obviously the ball then pitched up pin-high and left me a very quick putt, but one that if I picked the right line was always going to get to the hole. I picked a high line about probably three feet left of the cup and it just died in perfectly.'

For the first time, Spieth looked shaky. He fanned his second shot right of the 18th green, leaving him short-sided, on a downhill slope and with a bunker to negotiate. It could not have been more difficult, especially since he had double-bogeyed the previous hole. Half a hour before, he had been seven strokes clear but the situation was changing rapidly.

'It wasn't a great lie,' Spieth recalled. 'I didn't deserve a good lie by any means, but it wasn't a great lie, a little grass behind the ball.' His first instincts were to play a bump-and-run around the bunker and not go at the flag. Crucially, though, he fought the temptation to rush. 'I think I took enough time looking at that chip shot to really calm myself down and pick the right play and just trust it,' he said.

He jettisoned an idea that would, at best, leave him with a 15-footer for par. Better, he decided, to take the aerial route and play a flop shot. 'Because it's mowed into the grain here, it still wouldn't even go all the way down that hill,' Spieth reasoned. 'I felt like the bump (shot) was just as tricky given it would be tough to judge; plus, if it took a big hop, it could go over the green. The reason I chose a flop was because if it comes out solid, it's going to fly to pin high and going to go maybe 10, 15 feet past. And if it comes out the way I want it to, which is just a little heavy, with that grass behind it, it's going to land halfway down that hill and it could be really good.'

Anticipation and execution worked in perfect harmony. The ball finished eight feet away. It was an extraordinary shot under huge pressure, its brilliance emphasised by the composure of the putt that followed. Spieth ended with a highly unlikely par, a round of 70 and a four-stroke lead.

Majors can be won on the 18th green, but not often on the 18th in the third round. Those present on that Saturday evening witnessed a pivotal moment of an enthralling 2015 Masters.

Or, as Spieth expressed it, after being helped to see the right line by caddie Michael Greller: 'I had a putt that was a little tricky, but I had full trust in it breaking to the right. It was really big. It was huge. It was one of the bigger putts I've ever hit.'

The fact that it dropped helped reinforce a karma that Spieth thought would be vital in his quest to close out his first major title. It kept going a trend that had sustained him through an unpredictable third round. 'I was just anxious to get started,' he said. 'But when I got out there and saw a couple putts go in, I felt really comfortable. And that's good. That gives me a lot of confidence.

'The downside of it was that I had to make a lot of putts with five dropped shots. I can't rely on the putter that much to save me with two major champions right behind.'

There was still much for him to admire, however, when he looked up at the closing third-round leaderboard:

—16 Spieth
—12 Rose

−11 Mickelson
−10 Hoffman
−6 McIlroy, Woods, Streelman, Kevin Na, Johnson
−5 Hideki Matsuyama, Casey

For the third night running Jordan Spieth slept on the lead at the Masters, or at least he tried. He relaxed by watching the 2008 romantic comedy *Forgetting Sarah Marshall* and it was just the outlet he needed. 'It wasn't the Golf Channel or Masters coverage,' Spieth smiled. 'I had a few laughs, it takes your mind off anything that's happening, and that was great.'

Deep down, though, Spieth was struggling to forget something much more significant. The next time he teed up he would be embarking on the most important round of his life. 'I slept well the first night on the lead, partly because I was worn out, it was late and I was up early the next morning,' Spieth said. 'Friday night, with 24 hours between 18 and teeing off, I slept okay.' Saturday? 'I didn't sleep as well. I think I probably went to bed a little after midnight and ideally I would have liked to have slept eight, nine hours. I think I woke up before 7 a.m. and I was just wide awake. To wake up then and not tee off for nine hours is very difficult.'

Sunday, 12 April 2015

The magnitude of the day was reinforced by a conversation he had enjoyed with Crenshaw the previous evening. Crenshaw was a continuous source of inspiration. 'He was outside, right after media,' Spieth explained. The former champion reinforced positive thought processes and followed up with messages the next morning. 'I got a lot of really nice texts saying: "Stay patient, this is going to be yours, you've got this and you're playing great. Just keep your head down and stay focused,"' Spieth revealed.

Another key figure was Spieth's coach Cameron

McCormick. No one knows the player's game better than the Australian, who had been Spieth's teacher in Dallas from the age of 12. This was now the third consecutive week that Spieth would tee off in the last group on the final day and McCormick had carefully tailored his pupil's preparations to make sure he kept fine-tuning his game without over-working or falling prey to exhaustion.

'I've trusted Cameron since I was 12, so eight or nine years,' said Spieth. 'I have complete trust in anything he says. He's my swing coach, putting coach, short game coach, mental coach, everything.'

They chatted for 15 minutes on the Saturday night. 'We really don't talk very much during tournaments. Sometimes text here and there. He's the one that knows what I'm thinking out there more than anybody else and how to adapt to the situation. I owe everything on the course to him . . . he's a very special teacher.'

And Jordan Spieth is a very special golfer. He needed to be on a final day that saw him tee off at 2.50 p.m. with his closest rival, Justin Rose. Again the draw threw up some intriguing pairings, the most notable featuring Woods and McIlroy. This was supposed to have been the rivalry that would sustain the game for the next few years, but the ailing Woods had been left for dead by McIlroy's meteoric rise. The pairing of Nike's two best-paid golfers on the final day of the Masters, however, was a dream for marketeers and television producers. Behind the current and former world number ones came Mickelson and Hoffman and then it would be Rose and Spieth's turn. Storms were predicted, but thankfully they skirted clear to leave an uninterrupted final day.

Many wondered whether Spieth might fall victim to the fate of McIlroy, who blew a similar four-stroke lead in the last round in 2011. Greg Norman's 1996 capitulation felt as pertinent a possibility. Woods repeatedly referred to the Australian squandering his six-shot advantage to keep alive his own hopes of a come-from-behind victory. The demeanour of Rose also helped bolster the theory. He is a thoroughly likable chap but a ruthless competitor. Having surged into the picture with those five birdies in his closing six holes in the third round, the 2013 US Open Champion was full of confidence and capable of performing the role played by Sir Nick Faldo in his conquest of Norman. Spieth knew that Mickelson was equally dangerous. The man known as 'Lefty' liked the thought of playing one group in front. From there, he might be able to unsettle the young leader.

McIlroy appeared on the tee in a garish, fluorescent-yellow shirt that suggested he might be directing the departing traffic once his round was over. Woods arrived in his usual red-and-black combination, the one that used to be such an invincible outfit on the final day of majors. Those days now seemed long past and the opening tee shots reinforced the feeling. McIlroy dispatched a huge drive down the left side while Woods pulled his so far left that it finished on the parallel ninth fairway. It proved an undeserved break, as from there Woods was able to access the front of the first green. Both opened with pars.

Mickelson also came through the opening hole unscathed but Hoffman bogeyed following a poor tee shot into the trees down the left side. The stage was clear for the final pairing. As Spieth and Rose readied themselves with nervous-looking slow motion practice swings, a veteran former champion was generating cheers on the nearby 18th green. The 58-year-old Mark O'Meara, who had played a cameo role at the start of the week's narrative with his avuncular practice round with Woods, was putting the finishing touches to a remarkable 68. The 1998 champion closed on a highly creditable three under par for the tournament.

Spieth and Rose hit good tee shots as both sought strong starts. The Englishman then hit his approach to 20 feet but Spieth was even better, his 9-iron catching the ridge in the middle of the green and his ball rolling to within 12 feet. Rose smoothly drained his birdie putt and Spieth's shorter effort, after threatening to stay up on the right, obligingly fell in as well. Rose had hit the more convincing putt while the leader looked a little tentative, yet Spieth remained four strokes clear.

−17 Spieth (1)
−13 Rose (1)
−11 Mickelson (1)

Spieth's approach to the par-5 second trickled through the back of the green. 'I actually had a good number in and so I took a 3-wood out again,' he said. 'No part of me was going to lay up there. I hit a really good shot that just needed to be maybe two or three yards shorter.'

Rose, meanwhile, was left with a lengthy eagle putt across the treacherously undulating surface. Woods and McIlroy had each opened with three straight pars. Spieth took an age deliberating over his third shot before opting to putt from the fringe. He addressed the ball, but stepped back. Nervous laughter broke out among the crowd. He stepped up again, and prodded at a slick downhill putt that somehow stopped five feet short.

By contrast, Rose raced his 50-footer eight feet past. Apparently nerveless, he coaxed it home for a superb birdie-birdie start. Spieth, looking a little rattled, prodded his birdie attempt right of the hole.

−17 Spieth (2)
−14 Rose (2)
−12 Mickelson (3)

Spieth didn't look uncomfortable for long. At the short par-4 third he used a 5-iron from the tee and then a pitching wedge to the green, which he put to around 20 feet. 'Ideally I would have liked to have been up further,' Spieth said. 'But I got it to where it was a putt that would at least be a par, if not a birdie; it's a sucker pin.' It worked. His putter was on song. 'I just hit one of the better putts I've ever hit. I hit that putt five times in the practice round knowing that that's where I wanted to be. And I fed it out there and it broke five feet. It fed out there and went in with perfect speed in the middle.'

−18 Spieth (3)
−14 Rose (3)
−12 Mickelson (4)

Both players made excellent par saves at the downhill par-3 fourth to maintain the status quo, but a hole later Rose narrowed the gap again with a fine up and down from a greenside bunker. Spieth wasn't as efficient from just off the green after his hooked 7-iron failed to turn enough to find its target. The leader's first chip missed the green and he admitted he could have done worse than record his first dropped stroke of the round. 'I left it in a spot that you don't want to be,' he said. 'Didn't get the chip on the green and that's really all I had to do. Left it just short and it was actually a good bogey from there, a good two-putt. Made a nice six-footer for my bogey, which could have saved the round right there.'

−17 Spieth (5)
−14 Rose (5)
−11 Mickelson (6)

Further ahead, Johnson was mounting a charge with three birdies in a row to the eighth. The giant hitter moved to nine under par to tie Hoffman for fourth place, as McIlroy moved to seven under with a birdie at the seventh. Rose, meanwhile, was looking to turn the screw further on Spieth.

The flag at the sixth was in its usual tough position in the top right-hand corner of a vast green. Miss the table top where the hole is located and you have vast acreage to cover for the second shot. Rose fired a 7-iron and chewed his lip anxiously as the ball found the wrong side of the ridge and toppled back off the front of the green. 'Number six bit me a little bit. I hit a great iron shot in there that came up a yard short and did what it always does, rolls all the way down,' Rose would ruefully recall.

Spieth conservatively found the correct level of the putting surface, although it would still be a demanding two-putt for par. 'I hit a 6-iron,' he revealed. 'I tried to fade it in but hit it really straight and it ended up pin-high. Hit a really good putt in there and tapped it in. That's the kind of stuff I was looking for all day.'

Rose tried to throw a lob wedge up to the back but sent his ball through the green. His bogey restored Spieth's four-stroke advantage. Another hole had been ticked off.

−17 Spieth (6)
−13 Rose (6)
−11 Mickelson (7)

Then came the seventh: a gun-barrel-straight par 4 with a shelf green guarded by bunkers front and back. Spieth, emboldened, took his driver for the first time that day. He missed the fairway right and found the trees. That offered a glimmer of light for Rose but he followed the leader into trouble.

Away to the left, Woods collected a much needed birdie to help atone for bogeys on the fourth and seventh and move back to five under. Alongside him, McIlroy was moving more smoothly, tied for fifth place at eight under par. He wasn't going to complete the career grand slam, but he was on course to record his best Masters finish.

Spieth fired his second over the trees and found a gap between two bunkers at the front of the green. Rose was less fortunate. Snookered behind a tree trunk, he advanced his second as best he could. He had a decent lie but there was now a huge bunker between his ball and the hole, with little green to play with. His Masters hung in the balance.

Somehow he engineered a soaring wedge that pitched at the back of the green and then trundled back down the slope, missing the cup by the smallest of margins before dribbling six feet by. It was an extraordinary stroke, as brave as it was bold, and it kept the tournament alive. Rose holed out for an unlikely par after Spieth had offered a sporting thumbs-up that was acknowledged by a huge grin. The American, in contrast, failed to get up and down and amazingly his lead had been trimmed again, and from the most unpromising of positions.

'Half my feet were dangling over the bunker,' Spieth said, recalling his third shot. 'I was standing with the club almost on my toes and actually hit a really good pitch to get it to a make-able length. It's just a tough putt. It's another one you have to cast out to the side, and it's a feel-based putt. I just didn't quite hit it hard enough to hold its line. So that was two bogeys in three holes to get back to even. I was disappointed.'

−16 Spieth (7)
−13 Rose (7)
−12 Mickelson (8)

We were now into the most dramatic spell of the afternoon. Commentating for 5Live in the media centre, we scrutinised the images beamed in from the course that were providing a story full of twists and turns. It certainly didn't feel like a routine wire-to-wire victory. There was too much going on. At Augusta, a three-stroke lead can rapidly disappear.

Even that prospect was about to temporarily drop from the top of the news agenda.

Tiger Woods was out of contention but still surpassing most people's expectations bar, perhaps, his own. At the ninth, he fired his tee shot into the pine needles down the right of the dogleg par 4. He still had a clear view of the elevated green, though, and just needed to make good contact from his unpredictable lie. What he didn't know was that those ochre-coloured needles concealed a tree root. Woods lunged violently into the ball, struck the root and the shockwaves coursed back up through the shaft of his club which flew from his hands as if he had been electrocuted. He bent double, clutching his right wrist. Not another injury? Had the 39-year-old's comeback come to nothing? Spieth and Rose were greenside in two strokes on the par-5 eighth, but Woods was once again the story of the moment. And again it was a story of failing fitness, or so it seemed.

Shaking his wrist, in clear discomfort, he completed the hole and turned in a one-over-par 37, five under for the tournament. McIlroy was three strokes better having covered the front nine in 34. Woods continued to grimace. 'A bone kind of popped out and the joint kind of went out of place, but I put it back in,' Woods later said. This sounded far-fetched but there was no doubting he was in considerable pain as he embarked on his back nine and it took several holes before he again looked comfortable.

Rose, meanwhile, failed to convert a promising position at the eighth. Spieth made no such mistake. His ability to bounce back immediately from dropped strokes was becoming one of the hallmarks of his stellar 2015. For Spieth, it was almost becoming routine. 'I had a very basic up-and-down,' he said. 'Just a straight pitch up, that funnelled past the left side of the hole and made about a 3-footer.'

Rose knew he had made a crucial error by failing to match the leader's birdie and he compounded it at the next. 'The momentum really stopped for me around 8 or 9. Didn't get the ball up and down from the right edge of the green on 8 and then three-putted on 9,' he said. Spieth's 8-iron, meanwhile, clung onto the edge of the green 'by a rotation' instead of trundling down the steep hill that borders the front of the putting surface. As he marked his ball Spieth said to himself: 'This could be a difference-maker.' A year earlier, his approach had tumbled off the green. This time the breaks were going his way. 'That ball stays up, last year it came down. It was just symbolic in a way,' he would say later. 'I made par, Rosey had a three-putt and that gave me a five-shot lead going to the back nine. I was trying to play Rosey match play from there.'

−17 Spieth (9)

−12 Rose (9)

−11 Mickelson (9)

Rose may have wobbled, but Spieth's other pursuers were not backing off. Mickelson, by collecting a superb birdie at the 10th after an excellent approach, moved alongside Rose, then dispatched a magnificent drive down the 11th. Ahead, McIlroy collected the birdie that took him to nine under par. He was hitting the accelerator but in a vehicle carrying damage from earlier in the week. Spieth remained in the driver's seat, in his supercar.

At the 10th he holed for a birdie from the edge of the green, taking him back to 18 under. Again, Rose could not match him. This was a hole that Spieth would happily pack up and carry with him around the globe. 'You don't necessarily expect to birdie 10,' he said. 'I think I birdied it three times. That was the key hole, I think, for me.'

−18 Spieth (10)

−12 Mickelson (10), Rose (10)

Mickelson flirted with the water on the 11th before making par while Spieth sliced his drive into the trees. Again, fortune was on his side as he fashioned a recovery to escape unscathed. He chased up a 4-iron to leave himself a pitch of around 40 yards. 'I got a nice little hook on that second shot. I couldn't have hit a better shot. I didn't have many other options and a lot could have gone wrong there if it just caught a pine needle and went up in the air and hit a tree. It could have been a big number.' Spieth then floated the ball to two feet. Rose missed his 20-footer for birdie and the gap remained at six strokes with seven to play.

Roars shot up from around the 13th where Woods, now showing no ill effects from his wrist scare, drained a long-range effort for eagle. From a shorter distance, McIlroy two-putted for birdie to move to 10 under. The sense of what might have been was growing for the Northern Irishman.

Spieth could hear those roars as he stood on the par-3 12th. He was fully aware of this capricious hole's capacity for calamity. It had been part of his undoing 12 months earlier, with a visit to Rae's Creek, so it was vital he found the putting surface. He aimed over the bunker and fired his ball safely to 30 feet, rather than make the rookie error of chasing the pin. But what followed, in his words, was a 'dumb three putt.' He charged the birdie attempt six feet by and missed the return.

−17 Spieth (12)
−12 Mickelson (12), Rose (12)

Mickelson then jumped into second place outright with an excellent two-putt birdie at the 13th, cutting the arrears to four strokes and yet again raising thoughts of an extraordinary late turn-around. Both Spieth and Rose, though, were in good shape off the tee on the penultimate par 5. 'Go hard! Go hard!' the leader yelled as he struck his 5-iron towards the green. For a moment, it seemed it wouldn't have enough to clear the water but then it scampered up to eight feet from the hole.

'I think 13 were the two biggest shots I've ever hit in my life,' Spieth said of his 3-wood drive and his somewhat fortuitous second. 'Coming off a three-putt and Justin being in a pretty good spot off that tee, I needed to do something. I needed to birdie that hole. I missed the 5-iron a little. When it landed, from my angle, I thought it hit short in the water and all of a sudden the roar came up and the pitchmark was right on a little peninsula.

'That was another moment where I thought that this could be destiny, just like number nine. This was symbolic. Last year I missed a short birdie putt and now I had a good look at eagle.' He settled for a birdie, matched by Rose.

−18 Spieth (13)
−13 Mickelson (13), Rose (13)
−10 Matsuyama (16), McIlroy (14)

The game seemed almost up when Mickelson three-putted for bogey from 40 feet to seemingly drop out of contention with four holes to go. Spieth hit to similar range on that 14th hole, while Rose aggressively sought out the pin and carved out a fine birdie chance. The Englishman converted, to add a few inches to the leader's three-footer for par, but Spieth was equal to the task. Mickelson, though, roared once more, as did his supporters. Determined to make up for his lapse, he splashed out of a bunker and into the hole for an eagle three at the next. He was back within four strokes and still dreaming.

−18 Spieth (14)
−14 Mickelson (15), Rose (14)
−11 McIlroy (16)
−10 Matsuyama (17)

So to the last par 5 for Spieth and Rose. Both struck beautiful tee shots. 'I hit driver and I was left with the same scenario I had two other times that week,' Spieth explained. 'That was a number where if I hit a good, solid 4-iron, it's perfect. And if I go to hybrid, it's probably too much club but it's not in the water. If I miss a 4-iron, it could very easily go in the water.' He would take no chances. 'I was going to make sure I was over the green and I put a really good swing on a hybrid, picked a straight line.'

It paid off. He carried past the pin and went over the green, produced an average chip but converted an excellent six-footer that he needed to start outside the hole. Rose two-putted from off the front, after very nearly drowning his chances, to move to 15 under par. Spieth, though, was now on 19. Three pars were all he needed to break Woods' Augusta scoring record. Spieth tapped Greller on the back as he exited the green, suggesting he now knew the green jacket was destined for his shoulders.

−19 Spieth (15)
−15 Rose (15)
−14 Mickelson (16)

There was still some stress to be negotiated, though. Spieth missed the green at the short 16th and had a challenging six-footer for par. He holed it, while Rose came close but saw his audacious birdie attempt slip by. What could have been a two-shot swing, in fact, changed nothing.

'When Justin had that birdie putt, then I had that slider for par, that's when I really felt like it could get out of my hands if I'm not careful,' said Spieth. 'At that point, I was with my putter. I didn't care what it looked like, didn't care about my posture, didn't care about the mechanics. It was all feel-based. I was seeing the line. I was seeing the arc of the putt. It had been the same thing on 15, and I was just going with it.

'Given that left-to-righters downhill have been my nemesis, those are putts that I miss right 90 per cent of the time. Oftentimes, I look up and get out of them a little early. I stayed with my head down on that putt and just said, you know, this is a huge moment. Let's knock this thing in.'

−19 Spieth (16)
−15 Rose (16)

McIlroy's Masters ended in fine style as he holed from across the 18th green for a closing birdie to match Hideki Matsuyama's low round of the day. His 66 made him the new clubhouse leader at 12 under par. Not that he remained in that position for long, his ultimate finish of fourth a new personal best. 'I played well and I can take a lot of positives from it,' McIlroy stated. 'It is my best-ever finish here. I played the last 45 holes in 15 under par. I did a lot of things I wanted to do. I played the par 5s well. Just left myself too much to do after 27 holes; 40 on the front nine on Friday, that really left me with an uphill battle. It was just great to get in for the weekend and I made the most of a great finish on Friday.'

Woods completed a round of 73 to finish at an impressive five under. His short game was solid and showed no sign of the horrors that had sent him off tour earlier in the year. 'Considering where I was . . . to make the complete swing change and rectify all the faults and come here to a major championship and contend, I'm proud of that,' Woods said. 'Just wish I could have made a few more timely putts and moved up that board. I really like what I'm doing, I got my distance back, and everything is good.'

Not as good as life was about to become for Jordan Spieth.

His par save at the 16th removed almost all doubt, and any lingering thoughts that the Masters could slip from his grasp were removed by a fine 7-iron to the 17th green. He two-putted to remain 19 under, needing just a par at the last to set a new scoring low. Rose and Mickelson had battled gamely but ultimately this was now between Spieth and the record books. Golf's newest superstar could enjoy the final hole safe in the knowledge that, at the age of 21, he was about to become a major champion.

Mickelson holed a tester at the last for a 69 and a 14-under total, Hoffman closed with a 74. It yielded a top-10 finish for the man who had set in motion this captivating 79th Masters. Now, though, Augusta was all about Spieth.

The patrons rose to acclaim their new champion. He was greeted by a thundering ovation as he made his way up the hill at the 18th. It is normally an energy-sapping walk, but Spieth seemed to float on air, displaying a smile as wide as his native Texas. His performance on all four days had been nothing short of astonishing. He missed the home green and then chipped up to eight feet. Rose, to the right of the green, putted up to 10 feet, leaving an uphill putt to finish runner-up on his own. It stayed up and he signed for a 70, second alongside Mickelson.

It was time for those golfing gods to intervene. Spieth's meek par putt slid past the hole. His 270th shot of a glorious week was a tap-in to seal the Masters title. He equalled Woods' record at 18 under par, finishing with a second successive 70 after laying the bedrock of his stunning triumph with those opening rounds of 64 and 66. 'It's incredible,' Spieth said. 'It's one of the best feelings I've ever felt. This was arguably the greatest day of my life.'

−18 Spieth

−14 Mickelson, Rose

−12 McIlroy

−11 Matsuyama

 −9 Casey, Ian Poulter, Dustin Johnson

 −8 Hunter Mahan, Zach Johnson, Hoffman

−6 Fowler, Ryan Moore, Bill Haas, Streelman, Na
−5 García, Woods
−4 Stenson, Louis Oosthuizen
−3 Russell Henley
−2 O'Meara, Keegan Bradley, Patrick Reed, Bernd
   Wiesberger, Ángel Cabrera, Ernie Els
−1 Steve Stricker, Hoffmann, Webb Simpson, Day,
   Jonas Blixt

Rose and Mickelson recorded scores that would win most Masters but on this occasion they had been well beaten. 'It was a thrill to be out there and play in that arena,' Rose reflected. 'The final group on Sunday at the Masters is dream stuff and it's stuff that I tried to really soak in. It was an incredible day out there. The atmosphere was fantastic, playing with Jordan. He's going to fly the flag, I think, for golf for quite a while. People were getting excited about that out there, you could tell.'

After hugging his parents, Spieth was sent back onto the green to acknowledge the raucous cheers and applause that signaled the arrival of a new golfing hero. He high-fived his way to the scorer's hut to complete the paperwork before heading to the traditional presentation ceremony in the Butler Cabin. There he received his green jacket from Bubba Watson.

Spieth told CBS interviewer Jim Nantz: 'It was very nerve-wracking. I thought today may be easier, having played a round with the lead, but it wasn't. I didn't sleep well last night. It's the most incredible week of my life. This is as great as it gets in our sport. To be honest, it still hasn't kicked in. I'm still in shock a bit. I'm sure it will kick in soon. And I want to be like Bubba, I want to win two Masters!'

All of this was said under the watchful eye of delighted Augusta National Chairman Billy Payne. Although it had been a wire-to-wire victory, the same man in front throughout, it had still been a compelling, thrilling tournament.

They had set it up for low scoring, kept the greens soft and as a result identified the best players in the world. Who could argue with the quality of the leaderboard? The course had provided the perfect platform to enable the finest golfers to demonstrate their skills. If they erred they would be punished, as McIlroy had been on that calamitous front nine of his second round. Without that, he might have been challenging for that career grand slam. Instead, a precocious young talent from the Brookhaven Country Club in Dallas, Texas, had re-written the central theme of the 2015 golfing year with a breathtakingly brilliant performance.

He also won the hearts and minds of American golf with his thoroughly likeable, sporting and modest demeanour. At his news conference he was told by the moderator: 'Jordan, you epitomise the qualities that this club was founded on, and I think if Bobby Jones and Clifford Roberts were in the room right now, they would be smiling with pride, seeing you sitting in the green jacket.'

Spieth also demonstrated his grasp of golfing history. He knew that this would be a special year, because the oldest and grandest of the majors would be staged at St Andrews. He allowed his mind to throw itself forward. 'To go to the Home of Golf and what I consider one of the coolest places in the world is going to be really special as the Masters Champion,' he said. 'I'm sure that it will be a great time, and I look forward to enjoying the town, obviously the tournament, but to enjoy the whole experience of playing in an Open Championship at St Andrews.

'Hopefully at that point, maybe try and go for the third leg of a grand slam.'

The assembled media laughed at the prospect. Not for long, though.

CHAPTER 4

US Open Breaks New Ground

The contrast between the venues for the first two majors of 2015 could not have been greater. All they had in common were stunningly beautiful views and dramatic changes in elevation that television cameras could not fully capture. Otherwise they shared nothing.

On the one hand, you have the verdant and land-locked Augusta, ultra-exclusive with a rich and varied history; on the other, Chambers Bay, a parched coastal course open to all. It was a very unlikely major venue. There is no clubhouse beyond a small, grey shelter that houses a drinks dispensing machine. Situated in the middle of a new and popular park, this public facility is the result of a remarkable regeneration of a disused quarry. The fact that, within 20 years of the digging and extraction ending, it staged the US Open in June 2015 was nothing short of astonishing.

In the early 1990s the Washington State premises that spawned this spectacular and newest US Open venue was the largest sand and gravel pit in the United States. It was coming to the end of its useful life, having been a quarry of huge significance and dug out for the past century. These 900 acres provided the sand and gravel that created the Seattle skyline, the major highways of the Pacific Northwest and a string of military bases.

'Pierce County in Tacoma, Washington State, bought it for $30 million,' local historian Blaine Newnham told me. 'They had to figure out what to do with the property and bought it to facilitate their water treatment plant. But they had 300 acres left over and finally decided on a new golf course.'

It was a controversial move, headed by County Executive John Ladenburg who was prepared to sink millions of dollars of public funds into the project. 'It was called Ladenburg's folly,' Newnham, a former *Seattle Times* journalist, added. 'He eventually lost an election and claims it was because of that. But he was dogged and he was just going to do it. A lot of people didn't want to. He sold it on the basis that this was not another course just for golfers; this was an economic magnet and would draw attention to the area.'

The original idea was for a 27-hole facility. More than 50 design companies, including one headed by Phil Mickelson, tendered for the project. A local architect, John Harbottle, was favourite but another renowned designer, Robert Trent Jones Jr, made the decisive pitch.

'What John Ladenburg did was extraordinarily coura-geous,' Trent Jones said. The architect submitted plans for the requested 27 holes but suggested it would be better to opt for a design that allowed for '18 great holes', with no compromises. 'We said we'll give you what you want because we're profes-sionals,' Trent Jones explained. But he had a stronger message for Ladenburg: 'You have the opportunity to do something unique in our career. Would you be willing to take it to the highest level of our game?'

The designer knew the site was special, affording stunning views over Puget Sound, a dramatic expanse of water linked to the Pacific Ocean. The natural sandy base would help produce perfect golfing turf, yielding conditions similar to those that spawned the game on the British seaside.

'We had the natural wonder of sand,' Trent Jones said. 'As

anybody knows, we architects and golfers kill for sand. You can craft the many, many fine points of the game, the ground game as well as the aerial game. And it will drain and grow great turf. And that's what we saw.'

Initially, the course was going to be known as Chambers Creek. The design team was convinced it could make a huge impact on American golf and become a famous venue. In their pitch for the contract, they gambled on this ambitious view. Trent Jones's project manager, Jay Blasi, supplemented the company's bid by producing bag tags printed with the words 'Chambers Creek, US Open 2030'.

Their vision and their conviction that they could fashion a facility capable of staging a major was just what Ladenburg wanted to hear. He was a politician who wanted to leave a legacy for the people he represented. He gave little indication, however, that Trent Jones's enterprising plans coincided with his own ambitions.

'Ladenburg is a poker player, he gave no hint as to whether we had done well or not. We got no reaction,' the architect said. 'He was the leader. He pushed in all his political chips. This was not an inexpensive thing to do. It was above $20 million to build the golf course. We moved 1,500,000 cubic yards of sand.'

The notion that the US Open might be brought to the Pacific Northwest for the first time, and as soon as 2030, seemed far-fetched, but it was an ambition worth pursuing.

'These guys were relentless,' said Newnham, who wrote about the project in his book *America's St Andrews*. 'They told Robert Trent Jones: "Spend as much money and take as much land as you want, but we want to get the US Open".'

Blasi, who joined Jones's firm with a degree in Landscape Architecture, was just 25 years old when he saw the site for the first time in 2003. He said he felt like 'a kid in a candy store' as he climbed up and down the piles of sand. He looked over Puget Sound towards the Olympic Mountains and was gripped with excitement, recognising the immense potential of the property.

Someone else who saw what might be possible happened to be a man rapidly making himself one of golf's most influential figures. Mike Davis was on a fast track to becoming the executive director of the United States Golf Association, the body that sets the rules in America and runs the US Open.

When Chambers Bay was still in its embryonic stage, Davis was the USGA's man responsible for rules and tournaments. One of his roles was taking charge of course set-up for the biggest tournaments, including the US Open. This job helped satisfy a fascination with the game that had been with him since childhood. As a boy, he was golf-obsessed. He would design courses around his house, occasionally leading to broken windows and admonishment from his mother. 'I can remember early on, probably 5th grade, drawing out holes, and in the backyard making up holes,' he recalled. 'In fact, I can remember one time, one of the holes played over the house, and I hit a thin shot that went through the living room window, and my mother wasn't overly happy about that. I've always been intrigued with golf course architecture.'

Davis was a decent amateur player but the only way he was ever going to make a living from the game was by working on the administrative side. He graduated from his role as the USGA's Director of Rules and Competitions to the top job in 2011. Already he had helped steer the Chambers Bay project with astonishing speed.

'The first USGA representative to visit what was then known as the Chambers Creek property was a fellow by the name of Ron Read, who was our long-time USGA regional director,' Davis revealed. 'I remember being in my office in Far Hills (in New Jersey) one day and Ron called up and says: "Hey, there is this site in the Pacific Northwest that one day will be good enough for a US Open."

'I'm like, okay, here we go again!' Davis said, laughing. Crucially, though, he asked Read for more details.

'He says it's right on Puget Sound. Beautiful, overlooking the water. Well, that's good. It's got almost 1,000 acres. Really? Now all of a sudden I'm thinking, well, operationally, we don't need anywhere near 1,000 acres, but many golf courses simply do not have enough land to stage the US Open. And then he said it's going to be county-owned, so it's going to be a public-access golf course, which is a great thing for the daily golfer, to be able to play a US Open golf course.'

The location was attractive as well. 'Pacific Northwest — we've been conducting US Opens for over 120 years and have never been to this part of the country. So it was really appealing. And then I think the thing that really got me was when he said that it's all sand.'

So the place was on Davis's radar even before construction work had begun. 'We came out and looked at it,' he said. 'At that point they really hadn't even started anything. It was just piles of sand. But you could see the scale of this property and we said, wow, this is magical. And so we kept in touch.'

It ticked many of the boxes that have become the hallmark of Davis's ethos. He has modernised the USGA's approach to a championship that has always been regarded as the toughest test in golf. Typically, US Opens are set up at exclusive, historic country clubs. The courses have narrow tree-lined ribbons of fairway, surrounded by uncompromisingly thick, long grass, and lightning-fast greens. It was Davis who introduced a somewhat fairer approach, with graduated rough that was less penal to players who just missed a fairway. The thicker stuff still awaits more wayward shots.

More radically, he took the 2014 championship to a re-designed Pinehurst No 2 course in North Carolina where there was no rough at all. Designers Ben Crenshaw and Bill Coore restored the famous lay-out to its original form, where sandy wastes with wire grass and various other flora provide the penalty for errant shots. This was done with Davis's enthusiastic blessing and he delighted in staging both the men's and women's US Opens there.

The fact that Chambers Bay was a public course was attractive to the USGA boss. Locals can pay as little as $69 in the winter to play it. And then there was the geographical location. Not only did it provide a brand new market for the championship, but any event played on the West coast has the advantage of being three hours behind the other side of the United States. The climax of each day's play can be shown on prime-time evening television in the great cities of New York and Washington, as well as the golfing heartlands of the Deep South. It was, therefore, little wonder that he jumped at the chance of adding Chambers Bay to an Open roster that included the Californian venues of Pebble Beach, Torrey Pines and Olympic Club.

Despite Chambers Bay's many advantages and attractions, the course nevertheless gained major status with extraordinary speed. In fact, that seemingly optimistic hope of staging the 2030 US Open, as expressed by Blasi during the Trent Jones bid, proved pessimistic in the extreme. Davis simply couldn't wait to get his hands on the new course, although hindsight suggests he was probably too hasty and the course too immature to stage a major.

'It was crazy. It opened in 2007 and eight months later it gets the US Open,' Blaine Newnham told me. 'The USGA were looking at Winged Foot in New York, but they pulled out at the last minute and they had to have somewhere. They knew what they had here, because the USGA had helped build it. They wanted to establish themselves in the Pacific Northwest and Mike Davis loved the place from the beginning. He kind of pushed it.'

So the 115th US Open was destined for a site that would

be a mere eight years old when it staged the championship. Before Chambers Bay became a major venue, though, it held the 2010 US Amateur Championship.

In what proved a controversial tournament, Peter Uihlein celebrated his 21st birthday by winning the most prestigious title available to the unpaid ranks in America. The 2009 Walker Cup star defeated David Chung 4 and 2 in the final. Although Uihlein was approximately eight under par for the 34 holes of the deciding match, the course received heavy criticism for being too severe.

'They'd had an eight-week period without a drop of water,' Davis recalled during an interview for BBC 5Live. 'I've never seen a golf course bouncier than that.' Indeed, there were concerns two days before the event that Chambers Bay was playing too firm, so the USGA increased its watering. It was too little, too late.

The course's sandy soil doesn't retain moisture in dry, windy conditions. For the strokeplay section at the start of the US Amateur, greenkeepers decided to put twice as much water on the lay-out as originally planned. They had the hoses out on the eve of the first round and then watered again on the Monday morning. 'Our hope was that amount was going to get us through the day. It didn't,' Davis admitted.

The scoring average for the 156 players taking part that day was 79.87. Only three competitors broke par, with Augusta State's Patrick Reed leading with a brilliant 68. There were 79 golfers who shot 80 or higher and five recorded scores in the 90s, including two 95s.

A 17-year-old player called Jordan Spieth shot 83.

Played over seven days, the championship begins with 36 holes of strokeplay to determine the 64 players who qualify for the knock-out stages. By the time the 2010 event reached its head-to-head matches, the weather was deteriorating. There was a hard wind, temperatures were falling and rain was coming in sideways.

It was so bad that future Ryder Cup star Reed won the opening hole of his second round match with a nine. He was up against NCAA Champion Scott Langley who, earlier in the week, said of the firm conditions: 'It's like playing golf in my driveway. You get a lot of funny bounces out here, but that's the way the course is meant to be played.'

That opening hole proved comical. The players each took tortuous routes to the green before Langley asked Reed: 'What are you putting for?'

'I don't know. What are you putting for?' his opponent replied.

They needed to ask the rules official, who had the onerous task of keeping count. He informed Reed his four-footer was for a nine, while Langley would be putting for a 10 from 15 feet. Langley swiftly conceded and suggested they move on to the next hole.

In claiming the Amateur title, Uihlein demonstrated the sort of imagination that would prove vital for the players contending for the US Open five years later. At the drivable par-4 12th the young American knew he had no chance of stopping his downhill putt near the hole. Instead, he rolled his ball past the cup to a backboard slope, then watched it track back down the hill to nestle a couple of feet from the hole. 'You can't really get close to the flags by hitting them at the flag. You've got to use the slopes and be creative,' Uihlein said. 'You've got to hit every shot with a certain spin and height. You've really got to control your ball.'

Creativity is the buzzword at Chambers Bay. The players needed it in abundance, using the course's contours to access pin positions. The man responsible for the set-up also had scope for his imagination. Mike Davis loves to stamp his mark on the USGA's biggest tournament. He clung on to his course set-up role when he succeeded David Fay in 2011 as executive director. At the time USGA President Jim Hyler said:

'Obviously, Mike has done a terrific job with the US Open set-up and we'd be nuts if we pulled him out of that. We want him to continue to be involved in our signature event. When we talked with Mike about this job, we never dreamed he would not be involved in the set-up. It fits very well. We get the best of both worlds.'

There are times, though, when the US Open feels as though it is too much about the 50-year-old former Pennsylvania State junior champion. The talk before the championship is always about the course. Davis takes centre stage and the players are somewhat sidelined. Yes, tournament golf is about the contest between the competitors and the course, but there's also the competition between the players. That side of the equation often seems to be forgotten at US Opens, where all they are trying to find is the last man standing.

At Chambers Bay, Davis even involved himself in the design process by suggesting a bunker in the middle of the fairway, 120 yards short of the 18th green. Not only that, he wanted it to be deep and penal to intimidate anyone thinking of laying up. It ended up 12 feet deep, requiring a staircase for players to access the grim, grey sand that offered no realistic possibility of an escape to the green. 'Mike kept asking us to go deeper,' said Trent Jones Jr, who has designed more than 300 courses worldwide. 'I think it is a little incongruous, perhaps, but it'll give the players something to think about.' The controversial bunker became known as 'Chambers Basement.'

It was a course that provided Davis with more scope to meddle than most lay-outs. In the build-up to the US Open, he announced that he would switch the first and 18th holes to play as either par 4s or par 5s. The pars would be interchangeable throughout the week of the tournament, but total par would always remain 70.

There was more.

The ninth could either be played as a steeply downhill par 3 or a more gentle uphill hole. There was the prospect of playing off sloping tee grounds. The 16th could be turned into a drivable par 4 while the next could play as a long par 3 or a 120-yard tiddler, cutting its length in half. Davis would decree how these holes would play on a daily basis. His desire throughout was to take players out of their comfort zone, to make them think and add to the mental test.

Davis said that potentially players would need 10 practice rounds to get to grips with major championship golf's newest venue. But several leading stars scoffed at the notion, including the world number one. After winning by seven strokes at the PGA Tour stop at Quail Hollow in May, Rory McIlroy quipped: 'What's Mike Davis's handicap?' (It's five).

'With the way the Tour is, no one is going to go out there and play 10 practice rounds,' McIlroy added. 'I'm going to go up a little early. I'm going to play a couple of practice rounds the weekend before, and then I'll probably play another, you know, 18 holes.

'There's going to be someone lifting the trophy at the end of the week. It is a bit of an unknown to most people, so you have to prepare, but I think you can fall into the trap of trying to over-prepare. If you don't go out there and execute the shots that week, all that preparation doesn't mean anything. So I'd much rather have my game in good shape going in there and play practice rounds the way I usually would. I think that will do well for me.'

Some players did make an early visit, and the locker-room gossip suggested they were not overly impressed. The outspoken Ian Poulter broke cover when he tweeted: 'Several players have played Chambers Bay in prep for US Open. The reports back are it's a complete farce. I guess someone has to win.'

As with the 2010 US Amateur, there was little rain to soften the course in the weeks that preceded the US Open. 'We've had wonderful dry, warm weather,' Davis told listeners to BBC 5Live. 'So it looks aesthetically like one of the great links courses of the United Kingdom, so we're very pleased.'

He noted the weather was similar to five years earlier, when the course was so bouncy it had proved such a challenge to the world's leading amateurs. 'I don't believe we will get quite to that point and, frankly, I'm not sure we want to get to that point,' Davis said. 'But it really will be a golf course where you've got to think about what happens when your ball lands. Even though the fairways are 50, 60, 70 even 100 yards wide, they don't play that wide.

'The big difference between Chambers Bay and, say, a normal British Open links golf course would be that there's much more elevation change . . . It climbs some hills, then it comes back down, with a lot of movement in the fairways.'

The greens staff needed to work hard to keep the course playable in the dry early summer. This involved heavy watering and it caused a problem. Built on sand, the grass at Chambers Bay is fescue, a strain that can happily lie brown and dormant when rain is absent. However, non-native poa annua meadow grass, brought in off the soles of visiting golfers, infiltrated most of the putting surfaces. This darker, tougher strain flourishes when water is applied and grows at a different rate to the native fescue. As a consequence, all bar a couple of greens that had recently been relaid began to look mottled and scruffy. This 'camouflage' colouring could not disguise the uneven surfaces upon which the world's best players would be playing. Henrik Stenson later likened it to putting 'on broccoli.' This was one of the quotes of the year. McIlroy, meanwhile, disagreed with Stenson. He likened it to cauliflower.

The competitors were reluctant to be too critical in the build-up to the event, though. They largely kept their reservations to themselves, knowing that whoever was going to win would have to embrace the Chambers Bay experience. Anyone criticising the course and its set-up would be beaten before they had struck a shot in anger. 'Yeah, it's a beautiful venue,' Stenson told reporters ahead of the championship.

Defending champion Martin Kaymer embraced the challenge: 'I believe we are going to play three British Opens this year. We start here and then we play the real one at St Andrews, then Whistling Straits. I enjoy playing those golf courses.'

Mickelson, whose company had bid to design the course, agreed with Kaymer and gushed with praise. 'It's really a wonderful golf course,' he said. 'It's playing and set up much like what we're used to at a British Open. And I think this year is going to be very similar to St Andrews. So I think the guys that play well at St Andrews will play well this year. And guys that play well this week should play well in another month at St Andrews.'

Tiger Woods, who had made a reconnaissance trip in early June prior to shooting a career-worst 85 in the third round of the Memorial Tournament, observed: 'It's certainly different for a US Open, that's for sure.' Woods was down to 195 in the world rankings yet still drew the biggest audience for his pre-championship news conference. Even Trent Jones Jr was there and was responsible for an extraordinary moment when he appeared to seek validation for his project from the game's biggest name.

The first architect since his father in 1991 to witness a US Open played on one of his own designs, he took the microphone and asked Woods: 'We've known each other since you were 14. I appreciate you being forthright and honest about my golf course and all the odd bounces you're going to get. Do you think we gave you enough alternatives to play it in different ways, and is this a thinking golfer's championship as well as a shot maker's?'

It was a leading question, and one that illustrated that there are also some big egos in the golf design world.

'Well, it's a golf course in which, how you built it, we have so many options,' Woods replied, before shifting the emphasis away from the designer and onto the man who would determine how the course would play. 'The players don't know what Mike Davis is going to do and when he's going to do it. What tees he's going to move up, what tees he's going to leave back, and where he's going to put the pins. We have a general idea. But it's unlike any other major championship I've ever had to prepare for, having to hit so many different tee shots. There's three or four different tee shots on almost every hole.

'Basically, Mike has an opportunity to play 36 holes and 36 different options, somewhere around there.'

Woods added: 'I'm kind of happy that I'm playing in the afternoon the first day, get a chance to watch what some of the guys do in the morning to get a feel for it and see what's going on.'

The 14-time major champion stopped well short of the endorsement the architect seemed to be seeking.

Down on the range, there were bemused looks. Many of the pros were quick to acknowledge the beauty of the place but there were concerns over the greens. One leading European told me that there were areas that had no grass at all, just the native sand. He pointed out that, without heavy watering, the tough par-4 seventh was nigh on impossible. 'It's uphill and needs something like a four-iron approach. If you flush it, the landing area is so hard the ball will bounce all the way through the green. You can't hit that green unless they soften it.' Ironically, the seventh, along with the 13th, offered the best putting conditions, having been recently re-laid.

The other talking point was the latitude Davis was giving himself with the set-up. 'I don't know what they're doing there, whether they're just trying to show off or what, saying we can play a hole as a par 4 or a 5,' observed European Ryder Cup star Jamie Donaldson. 'I've played both holes, the 18th and the first as fours and fives and they're both good as a four or a five. So I don't think they need to mess about with it. Just pick one and stick to it.

'I think they've got so many options that they don't know what to do. Whatever they pick, or which tees they choose, it's the same for everybody so you've just got to get on with it.

'They could make it very tricky, which would be slightly farcical. If they don't go crazy, it could be just a great week on what is a really nice golf course.'

Former world number one Luke Donald, who had slipped out of the top 60 in the rankings and needed to qualify for the championship, told me that the course would be a huge test of attitude: 'This is a very bizarre golf course, very different to what we see week in, week out. It's not anything like a typical US Open.

'It's a unique golf course . . . In the morning it plays quite soft and in the afternoon it gets a lot firmer and the greens get faster, which is not typical of a links. Usually a links will retain the same firmness throughout the day and the greens will probably slow down a little bit. I think that's going to take some adjusting to.'

The Masters champion, meanwhile, was exuding a calm confidence despite that miserable 83 he shot as a teenager. 'That was a short-lived trip for me,' Spieth recalled. 'I tried to throw out the round that I shot on this course from my memories.'

Spieth's caddie, Michael Greller, is a local resident, who was even married at Chambers Bay, so he was well placed to provide vital course knowledge that Spieth had been lacking at the 2010 US Amateur.

From his first practice rounds the 21-year-old did what you're supposed to do. He embraced the test that awaited.

It was going to be nothing like Augusta. Instead of the lush, verdant feel of springtime in Georgia, this was the West Coast, baked, bare and potentially unfair. It would test technique, skill and, above all, mental fortitude. Just how they like it at the US Open. The title always goes to the last man standing.

CHAPTER 5

Figuring Out Chambers Bay

Jordan Spieth's Masters victory spoke volumes for his skill and temperament, but also his willingness to embrace local knowledge. There was no doubting the value of the information imparted by the sage Augusta combination of Ben Crenshaw and Carl Jackson. It helped shave a shot here, a stroke there, from scorecards that yielded a record-equalling low score. Although he plays an individual sport, Spieth loves the team ethos. He likes to refer to 'we' when he talks about his golf, and especially the good shots. If he makes a mistake, he is more likely to take sole responsibility, but when the outcome is positive it will be: 'We hit it where we wanted.'

There are many facets to 'Team Spieth', and the most obvious is his relationship with his caddie Michael Greller. They have been a hugely successful combination and the former schoolteacher's input was crucial during the US Open at Chambers Bay.

Greller's route to becoming the bagman for a golfer destined to become the world's top player was remarkable. He acquired the taste for big-time golf in 2012 when the then fifth-grade maths teacher won the right to buy practice-round tickets for the Masters. He treated his brother, his brother's wife and a friend to a once-in-a-lifetime trip to Augusta, where they followed Rory McIlroy and indulged in the club's famous reasonably-priced beer. 'I was dreaming about just getting a pass into the gates, let alone getting to walk inside the ropes,' admitted the man who, within two years, was carrying the bag of the Masters champion. 'I'm enjoying the walk now, too.'

Greller grew up in Michigan and played golf for Northwestern College in Iowa, before moving to the Pacific Northwest to be near his sister. He took the chance to gain some caddying experience in 2006 when the US Public Links Championship came to Gold Mountain Golf Club, near his home. He helped Florida State player Matt Savage reach the quarter-finals. Soon after, Greller moved schools so that he could live nearer Chambers Bay, where he could get more caddie work.

When the 2010 US Amateur Championship arrived there, Savage recommended Greller to the highly promising American player Justin Thomas, who happened to be good friends with an even more promising talent named Jordan Spieth. A year later, Greller asked Thomas to persuade Spieth to use him for the 2011 US Junior Championship back at Gold Mountain. They won, and with that victory a partnership was born. The combination became a fixture a year later when Spieth finished low amateur at the 2012 US Open at Olympic Club.

'I took a one-year leave of absence from teaching, thinking he had no status anywhere,' explained Greller, who was bringing home a steady $55,000 a year as a teacher. 'Yes, he was the number one amateur in the world but that means nothing out here. I was getting married, had a house. To go chase this kid, caddying, was kind of a big risk. And then he went crazy.'

Spieth could not have asked for a better-qualified right-hand man. Greller had an ability to relate to young people and to draw the best from them. Later, there would be an added bonus. Greller had an intimate knowledge of the golf course that would stage the US Open – the first major following their success at Augusta.

While Spieth likes to read his own putts and was aware that pins would be located in unfamiliar positions for Chambers Bay, he was sure that his caddie's unique insight would assist his tee shots. 'I think it's going to help driving the ball, sight lines and understanding things when it gets firm,' the Masters champion said. 'He's going to know where it will run off to a little better position.'

Such information was likely to prove invaluable on a course that would demand accurate driving. Furthermore, the rest of the field knew next to nothing about the new venue. Few of them were inclined to play the 10 practice rounds recommended by the USGA's Mike Davis, the man setting up the course. Spieth, though, was able to rely on someone who had looped around the layout in all conditions and wind directions.

Nevertheless, the young Texan prudently arrived early and played 18 holes on the Saturday and the Sunday prior to the second major of 2015. 'I really enjoyed it,' he told reporters. 'I didn't remember it much from the 2010 US Amateur. I was kind of going in with a blank slate, learning from Michael. I felt like I got two really good solid rounds in. I think it's going to be a fun challenge. It's a beautiful challenge, as well.'

Spieth described the course as 'inventive' and it was clear he was ready to embrace the test. He would not be among the constituency of players who were quietly rolling their eyes at the uneven, sandy greens and other idiosyncrasies of the venue. This already put him one up on a large proportion of the field. 'If you are going to talk negative about a place, you're almost throwing yourself out to begin with, because golf is a mental game,' he explained. 'Plus, the US Open is about as challenging mentally as any tournament in the world. So you have to go in positively. You have to go in with enough confidence to get yourself into contention.'

The young star's enthusiasm was palpable but there was someone else in the field who could claim to be even more excited. Michael Putnam is one of those professionals who operates outside the limelight, playing most of his golf on the WEB.COM Tour, a level below the PGA Tour. The 32-year-old was playing his fourth US Open, with a previous best finish of tied 45th in 2011. But this was going to be a special week for Putnam because, as a resident of University Place, Washington State, the venue for the 2015 US Open was his home course. 'For the last five years, since they announced that Chambers was going to host the US Open, I've gotten a lot of questions,' Putnam said. 'Are you going to play? Are you qualified? What's the tournament going to be like?'

He secured his place by winning the Columbus qualifier the week before the world's finest players descended on his local 'muni'.

'It's awesome for the city of University Place and for this area, the whole Pacific Northwest, to host the biggest golf tournament in the world,' Putnam said. Something of a local celebrity, he hit the first ball on the course when it opened in 2007. 'They called me and asked if I wanted to come and play the first official round of golf. I think they wanted to see how this place actually played for a good professional golfer. They charted the whole round, and it was a pretty neat experience.' Putnam shot 70 and joked: 'I definitely held the course record for a day.' He was also the natural choice to strike the opening tee shot when the championship began on Thursday, 18 June. 'It's a pretty neat and cool honour to have,' he smiled in anticipation.

'The course is what it is. It's not typical for this area to have a links golf course, and this gravel-pit area is not a typical course for the whole United States. A lot of players are here expecting a US Open course. They came here not seeing what they usually see for a US Open venue. But we're really proud of this course and this area.'

As a home star, Putnam was always going to attract plenty of support but, even with his extensive local knowledge, he was never likely to be a challenger for America's national championship. Australian Jason Day seemed a good bet, though.

Still searching for his first major title, Day had become a fixture in the world's top 10 after finishing a distant runner-up to Rory McIlroy in the 2011 US Open at Congressional. Day was becoming something of a specialist in the event. He came second again in 2013, and tied for fourth the following year. The 27-year-old also had the reputation for saving his best golf for the majors and seemed overdue to land one of them.

Day's 2015 form had been encouraging. He won early in the season at Torrey Pines and had two more top-four finishes as the schedule headed towards its most significant spell. But there were worries about his health. In late May, he had been one of the favourites for the Byron Nelson tournament, where back in 2010 he had become the youngest Australian to win on the PGA Tour. However, he experienced bouts of dizziness during the Wednesday pro-am in Texas and felt there was no alternative but to pull out of one his favourite events. It was reminiscent of the previous season, when he had withdrawn from the final round of the WGC Bridgestone Invitational at Akron in Ohio, his wife Ellie later revealing he had been suffering dizzy episodes since 2010.

Day was anxious to find out the cause of the problem. But he also knew the 2015 calendar was nearing its most important spell, a period when the remaining three majors come and go very quickly. He was in decent form and Chambers Bay, St Andrews and Whistling Straits would provide big opportunities. As a contemporary of McIlroy, six years older than Spieth and with a string of near-misses behind him, Day was desperately keen to keep pace with the generation taking over the game. To do that, he would surely need to win one of the remaining majors in 2015. And for that to happen he would need to be fit.

'I feel good,' Day insisted as US Open week dawned. 'I have had three sleep studies done. I had a lot of blood tests. I had an MRI on my head and my back, and everything came back negative. So I have no idea, other than I just may have been exhausted. I was training so hard, I was doing two-a-days [physical workouts] every day coming into tournaments and then, on top of it, I was doing practice, playing competitive golf and then trying to balance that with family.'

Day has a young son, Dash, and his wife was pregnant again. 'I think I just ran out of gas and I wasn't feeling good,' he added. 'I've got severe sleep deprivation, but I guess that's part and parcel of having a kid. So you've just got to deal with it. I feel good this week. I'm all good to go.'

This is exactly what Australian fans wanted to hear from their top talent, the man most likely to emulate the feats of Adam Scott and Greg Norman. Day's abilities were well known, but so too were his physical frailties. Not just the dizzy spells, but freak injuries that had frequently taken him off tour. 'I don't know what it is. Every time I get off to a decent start, there's something that happens,' he admitted. 'My thumb last year, and then whatever I had this year. I'm really glad it happened now, because I can understand what's wrong with me and then take action and move on. Over the last couple of years I've been fed up with being injured, fed up with sitting out and watching the guys play without me. It's been really frustrating and disappointing at the same time, because I feel I have the potential to go out there and play well and win a lot.

'I'm really trying to take control of my body. I hired a trainer last year, and we've changed a lot. We dropped a lot of body fat, increased a lot of lean muscle mass. I've cleaned up a lot of my diet. So the overall strength in my body is improving. We're still not quite where we need to be, but it's a slow improvement. You don't want to drop too much body fat too quick. You don't want to put on too much muscle too quick, because you start losing feel. That said, it's been frustrating because my whole career I've pretty much been injured.'

Day was under no illusions about the task that lay ahead. There are those who think that golf is more of a game than a sport. It doesn't involve running, you rarely breathe hard and, as former tennis great Andre Agassi once noted, you shouldn't regard any pursuit as a true sport 'if you can drink and smoke while playing it'. That might apply to the friendly fourball, where players swing around their paunches between bacon-sandwich breaks, but it is a vastly different story for those competing at the highest level. The fitness regimes undertaken by the likes of Day and McIlroy, inspired by Tiger Woods' career-long approach to conditioning, have changed the outlook at the top of the game. It is now a sport for athletes.

Seventy-two holes around the hugely undulating Chambers Bay would provide a stern physical test, made all the harder by the demands of competing for a major title. 'I think by the end of the week, you've probably lost 10 pounds just from all the stress that you have out there,' Day noted. 'It's usually physically and mentally demanding, and this is going to be more so physically, just because of the elevation changes. And once you start bringing that into play, then if you start losing focus, you start making mental errors. So it's a premium on making sure that you're eating right this week and you're keeping the fluids up. And just really trying to mentally prepare yourself, knowing that you're going to make mistakes out there. Usually, at the other events, it's totally different.'

Day is an engaging speaker who can hold an audience. He went on: 'You need to have the mental toughness to keep pushing forward, the right attitude and really the right emotions to control what you can control. And that's just how the USGA sets it up. Typically, this is the hardest major to play because of the course set-up. And it's a fun week, I think. It's more of a challenge. That's the way you've got to look at it. Instead of looking at all the negatives, you've got to look at what you can accomplish and go from there.'

Day, despite his health concerns, was on the same page as Spieth.

The two were paired together along with Justin Rose for the first two rounds. Spieth and Rose had seen plenty of each other throughout the season and putting them together made complete sense, after the way they had performed in each other's company in the final round of the Masters. 'I think it will be my 35th round with Justin in the last year,' Spieth smiled. 'We've had some success together. I played against him in a Ryder Cup match. I played with him in the final round of Augusta. We've had really everything – the first two rounds of a tour event and the back nine battling it at a major. It's good fun. I have a great time with him and Fulchy [Rose's caddie Mark Fulcher]. And to cap it off with Jason Day and Colin [Swatton, Day's bagman], who we've played a lot of golf with too, I was really excited to see the pairing.'

Spieth liked the timing as well. This marquee group would begin their quests for US Open glory on Thursday afternoon and play their second rounds on Friday morning. The luck of the draw can have a big influence if you catch the best weather conditions, but personal preference over start times is also a factor. 'I like late-early,' Spieth said. 'I was hoping I would get that wave. You can kind of get those 36 holes in quick and then, hopefully, have a little break. To tee off late Saturday would be ideal.

'I have a chance to make history in many ways. But in order to do that, I have to really focus on this week, focus on the major championships and how I'm going to prepare for them,' Spieth added. 'You can't win a grand slam unless you win the first. So I'm the only one with that opportunity this year.'

CHAPTER 6

US Open As It Happened

Rarely can a US Open have been more eagerly anticipated. As the first day dawned, there was a genuine sense that men's professional golf had embarked on a new and exciting era. The ensuing days would emphatically support this.

Jordan Spieth's Masters victory put him alongside Rory McIlroy at the vanguard of a game undergoing a generational shift. McIlroy and Spieth were the ones creating the biggest headlines. And if they weren't to win, then the trophy would be most likely to head in the direction of Jason Day or Patrick Reed who were still comfortably in their 20s, or 30-year-old Dustin Johnson.

The game was moving inexorably away from the previous two decades, when pre-major chatter was dominated by Tiger Woods and Phil Mickelson. They were the drivers of the game, after Woods burst onto the scene in the late 1990s and Mickelson started collecting majors in 2004.

This power shift was not being kind to Woods. Despite his encouraging return at the Masters, the 14-time major champion arrived at Chambers Bay just after carding a miserable 85. Worse still, this humiliation occurred at one of his favourite tournaments, Jack Nicklaus's Memorial event.

Mickelson, meanwhile, was still searching for his first

US Open, having endured six runner-up finishes. Like McIlroy at the Masters, he went to Chambers Bay knowing victory would complete a career grand slam. Despite some optimistic indicators, it still seemed a distant prospect. Mickelson had fired a 65 in his last round before the US Open, and, of course, had been a challenger at the Masters, but could 'Lefty' lift the one major still to elude him at the age of 45? The baked-out course offered some hope; it was in similar condition to Muirfield in 2013, when Mickelson won his Open title. But these factors couldn't prevent a growing feeling that the triumph in Scotland might prove his final victory in one of the game's big four tournaments.

McIlroy had shown inconsistent form since his unsuccessful attempt at completing the career grand slam. There were emphatic victories at Quail Hollow and in the WGC Cadillac Matchplay – a success that prevented him from attending an event billed as 'The Fight of the Century'. McIlroy is a huge boxing enthusiast and entered the matchplay at Harding Park in San Francisco knowing that the Floyd Mayweather–Manny Pacquiao welterweight title fight would be a mere hop away in a private jet. But he was grounded by his success and, after going through to the final, made do with a pizza-fuelled television viewing of the fight in the press tent. It wasn't how he anticipated spending his Saturday night, but it was no small consolation that he was through to a World Golf Championships decider. It did his media relations no harm either.

However, following his 4 and 2 victory over American Gary Woodland in the final, and then a share of eighth place at the Players' Championship at Sawgrass, McIlroy nosedived. He headed to his home continent to miss cuts in his BMW PGA Championship defence at Wentworth and then at the Irish Open. The latter was particularly frustrating because the tournament was promoted by his charitable foundation at Royal

County Down. But, as he put it: 'I'd rather, in a six-tournament period, have three wins and three missed cuts than six top-10s. Volatility in golf is actually a good thing. If your good weeks are really good, it far outweighs the bad weeks.'

He spent his extra days off sightseeing in the English capital.

Arriving at Chambers Bay, McIlroy was perfectly happy for the limelight to be elsewhere. He had had to deal with the cameras, microphones and notebooks trained on him all week at the Masters, but now Spieth was the main man. 'There's not as much attention or as much hype. I can get here and just do my thing without much worry,' he said. 'There's not as much on my mind about what I can achieve. It's hugely important, a chance to win a second US Open and my fifth major, but there was just so much hype and so much attention around Augusta. This one feels very different.'

Thursday, 18 June 2015
Conditions were perfect for the first morning of the 115th US Open. The forecast suggested a dry day but that the later starters, including Spieth, might be inconvenienced by a strengthening breeze. There were no such worries for the likes of McIlroy and Mickelson, who were among the morning wave.

All they needed was to come to terms with the course's baked-out undulations and uneven greens.

An indication of the scale of the task ahead, and the often surreal nature of the place, was immediately provided by the first man to tee off, local star Michael Putnam. The course has many distinctive characteristics and one of them is that the first tee appears to sit in the middle of nowhere. Perched on a hillside, spectators are held a long way back from the hitting area, the opposite scenario to most major opening shots, which are played in front of a claustrophobic, horseshoe-shaped set of grandstands. As Putnam struck his first drive at 7 a.m., there were just a couple of marshals standing behind the tee box. The crowds were held back and, because of the idiosyncrasies of the course, none were able to walk down the side of the first fairway to follow the action.

Even though he had played more rounds on the layout than any other competitor, Putnam still contrived to bogey that opening hole. The USGA's Mike Davis deemed it a long par 4 on the first day, with the 18th a par 5. Davis also decided that the par-3 ninth, which could be either dramatically downhill or uphill, would be played from the lower teeing ground. So the players' final preparations needed to take into account far more significant course and card alterations than usual.

Thereafter, Putnam performed creditably to card a level-par 70. There seemed every chance that he would be one of the leading stories from the first round, but he was overshadowed by an extraordinary youngster called Cole Hammer. The teenager from Houston was a highly promising junior in the throes of a growth spurt that had added around 30 yards to his already impressive drives. He watched his fellow Texan Spieth win the Masters and afterwards told himself that he needed to improve.

'That was a big inspiration,' Hammer said. He promptly won three junior tournaments and decided to enter a US Open qualifier in Dallas, primarily to measure his game against the professionals and leading amateurs. Hammer, now a wiry 5ft 9ins tall, by far exceeded expectations. He fired stunning rounds of 64 and 68, enough to earn him a place in the field. Aged 15, he became the third-youngest competitor in the history of the US Open, behind China's Andy Zhang in 2012 (14 years and six months) and American Tadd Fujikawa in 2006 (15 years and five months).

Some of the game's biggest names were out on the course but, just after 9 a.m., the Fox Sports television cameras focused on Hammer. It was a perfect human-interest story for the first morning of Fox's coverage, following their billion-dollar rights deal to take over the event. The lucrative contract should ensure bumper prize funds for the next dozen years, but the young man who now filled the lenses of their cameras would not see a cent of it. As an amateur, Hammer wasn't entitled to prize money. For him, though, the experience of competing was reward enough.

The enormity of the situation seemed to overwhelm the youngster. His face was creased with emotion, his eyes welled with tears and he quietly muttered to himself, seemingly seeking words to regain his composure. In the media tent, a place not renowned for compassion, there was a spontaneous and collective 'Ah!' of sympathy, although Hammer later revealed it was somewhat misplaced. 'I can't even describe what I felt on the first tee,' he said. 'It was like nervous excitement. It was so cool. I was just praying. I always pray right before my round on the first tee. That's all I was doing.'

The cameras stuck with him throughout a highly creditable opening nine holes, covered in two over par. They were there for the end of his round as well, on the ninth green, when he holed from around eight feet for a par and raised his putter to acknowledge the applause. He had shot 77, a respectable seven over par and good enough, on a brute of a course, to beat some of the biggest names in the game.

Mickelson wasn't one of them. He was generating even bigger cheers. The home crowds, most of them witnessing major championship golf for the first time, were being given plenty to shout about by the man they call 'Phil the Thrill'. He took the early lead when he struck a crisp wedge into the fifth that landed six feet away, his birdie moving him to two under par.

While he had started his round on the first, McIlroy was tackling the back nine. He swiftly moved into red figures with a birdie at the long par-4 11th. His approach used the contours to the right of the green to propel the ball six feet behind the cup.

The greens appeared softer than expected and, with little breeze, the early starters were able to play aggressively and pepper the flags. At the drivable 12th, a 317-yard par 4, Johnson made a significant statement of intent. He smashed a low draw, which skirted the right edge of the green. Bouncing off the bank, his ball scooted to the back before taking the contours to reverse to within eight feet. The putting surface on the 12th, which sits in one of the most sheltered positions on the course, was among the most uneven and Johnson left his eagle attempt out to the right. It was a disappointing birdie, if there is such a thing, but it took him into a share of the lead.

This set the tone for an opening morning where everyone became fully aware of what Chambers Bay could provide. The undulations enabled players to exercise imagination. Balls were fired into target spots and the slopes would determine how close they would finish to the hole. It made for enthralling viewing. There were no easy putts, though, because the greens were so uneven – indeed unacceptable – for major champion-ship golf.

McIlroy struggled to come to terms with them and the erratic roll of the ball. At the par-3 15th (his sixth), his tee shot from 169 yards fell into a front bunker. With little green to work with, he splashed out brilliantly, his ball gently landing just outside the hazard and rolling to three feet. However, he missed the putt, what should have been the easy part of the par save, and so suffered back-to-back bogeys. He returned to level par with a birdie at the next, the gorgeous 16th, bordered down the right by a very busy railway line and breathtaking views of Puget Sound.

Fortunes were changing quickly, a characteristic of the entire four days. Leaderboard operators were kept busy. There was a rapid-fire spell when Mickelson set the early pace. At three under after 11, he was soon joined by Reed. At the 13th a sloppy bogey dropped Mickelson out of the lead. Reed pressed the accelerator to go to the turn in four under, one clear of Johnson who was still progressing smoothly. Moments later Reed paid the penalty for missing the first green, his 10th, and his ball scuttled away from the hole. That dropped shot left him tied for the lead with fellow Americans Johnson, Kevin Chappell and Matt Kuchar, while Mickelson dropped another stroke on the 14th and found himself two behind. The leaderboard operators tried to keep up.

Spieth was perhaps the most avid television viewer that morning. Determined to acquire as much knowledge of how the course was playing, he noted that approach shots were sticking more quickly for the early starters. This would be useful information for his second round the following morning. Spieth was also fascinated by the pace of putts. 'I was able to see where some of the pins were, where guys were putting from. It's interesting, because it was a tough adjustment – the green speeds on the course are significantly slower than they are on the practice greens. And that's tough to adjust to when you've got 40 feet. And if you hit it five feet past the hole, it can go 30 yards away.'

Spieth would have been impressed by the start of one of his Ryder Cup teammates. Johnson became the new leader with a 10-footer to move to four under par after 13 and a third successive three took him further clear. In this mood, Johnson looks unbeatable. Not even the painfully slow pace of play was derailing him. The same couldn't be said of Bubba Watson. Coming up the last with Mickelson, he mishit his approach. 'Waiting for 30 minutes! This is pathetic professional golf!' he bellowed. Watson signed for a round of 70.

On the other half of the course Johnson powered on, seemingly oblivious that this was a US Open, supposedly the toughest test in golf. At the seventh he coaxed home another birdie. At six under, he was now two strokes clear of another of the game's longest hitters, Henrik Stenson of Sweden.

With the last playing as a par 5, Mickelson wedged to six feet but couldn't convert the birdie chance. The five-time major champion signed for a one-under-par 69. 'The first round was the one I was going to be most nervous,' Mickelson admitted. 'You don't want to have to fight to come back all the time.' His only complaint centred, inevitably, around the state of the putting surfaces. 'I think the biggest challenge is that the green speeds are different from green to green. That's going to wreak havoc on our touch. And that's the only thing I could possibly think of that is not really positive.'

Well, actually, there was one other thing.

The Chambers Bay layout was hopeless for spectators. The huge undulations and dunes were not safe to use as natural grandstands, and following a specific group was impossible. The par-5 eighth had no spectators because the terrain beyond the fairway was too hostile. 'Amy wants to come out and follow and she simply can't,' Mickelson said of his wife. 'And I'll tell you, the golf spectators are probably the most dedicated fans. Any other sport you buy a ticket, you sit in a seat and you watch 100 per cent of the action. In golf, you buy a ticket, you've got to walk miles in rough territory and you see a fraction of the event. So I give a lot of credit to the people who are out here.'

Usually, the compensation is that fans not only share the theatre with the players, but also the stage. This was forgotten by the USGA in choosing Chambers Bay. During one practice round, I followed Tiger Woods. I had no inside-the-ropes access and, having watched him play his approach to the sixth, I next witnessed him after driving off on the seventh.

But those spectators who based themselves at the par-3 ninth on the first morning were richly rewarded by the man dominating proceedings. Johnson dumped his tee shot into thick rough in front of a huge bunker that guarded the front of the green. He chopped out to the left onto a bank at the rear of the putting surface, which allowed his ball to break back at a right angle and trundle 60 feet down towards the hole. It stopped 10 feet away. It was a stroke of the utmost imagination and nerveless execution. 'I almost hit it backwards, up and around,' Johnson explained. 'That was probably the strangest one I had all day.'

Alas, he left the putt short, his only bogey in an otherwise brilliant 65 containing six birdies. 'I thought that it was a golf course where I could do well,' Johnson said. 'The fairways are wide.'

Johnson had worked hard with coach Butch Harmon in the build-up to the tournament. During a practice round, the Saturday before, he felt the components of his game falling into place. He was particularly pleased with his driving and approach play in the first round: 'The confidence is definitely there. I feel really good about where I'm at.'

The same could not be said of defending champion Martin Kaymer, who could only manage a two-over-par 72. Playing partner McIlroy was on the same mark and equally disgruntled. He failed to get up and down from a bunker at the ninth for a dismal finish that saw him drop two shots in the final three holes. Those bogeys sandwiched a missed birdie opportunity on the eighth.

Stenson, meanwhile, completed a brilliant 65 to share the lead and Reed's closing birdie brought him to within a stroke. As those cards were being signed, the big names in the afternoon wave, Spieth and Woods to the fore, were setting out. And as forecast, the breeze was freshening.

Woods was grouped with Rickie Fowler, fresh from a stunning victory at the Players' Championship, and 2010 Open Champion Louis Oosthuizen. The South African was free of injury at last and keen to start scaling the golfing heights again. Woods is always placed in marquee groups, guaranteed to command plenty of television coverage. This was no exception.

Sadly for the participants, there were lots of shots to show but not for the reasons they would have wished.

The tone was set on the first when Woods blocked his 6-iron approach into thick rubbish up a steep bank. Fowler then shanked his approach in the same direction before catching a lucky bounce that brought his ball back onto the green. Woods opened with a bogey before spraying his drive down the right of the second, leading to another dropped shot. Another followed at the fourth. Fowler, meanwhile missed a good birdie chance after a brilliant approach, the miss prompting the young American's round to fall apart.

Woods' body language suggested he was a beaten man just four holes into his first round. From the gallery someone yelled: 'We still believe, Tiger!'. But it seemed as though he did not share those sentiments. There was no conviction to his swing. He didn't know which direction the ball would fly next, and his putter was under constant pressure. After a wild drive on the eighth, Woods tried to hack out of the rough. As his ball squirted left, the club flew out of his hands, 20 yards backwards. It would have been a moment of comedy had it not been so sad. This once-great champion looked humbled and broken.

The malaise was infectious. The normally irrepressible Fowler looked haunted as the breeze strengthened and the usually inscrutable Oosthuizen started betraying signs of irritation as his round also unravelled. Woods went to the turn in a four-over-par 39 as did Oosthuizen while Fowler, fifth favourite in the betting, had three double bogeys in four holes for 43.

As the sunshine disappeared behind grey clouds, Woods' mood darkened further with bogeys at the 11th and 12th. At the next, he missed the widest fairway in US Open history (115 yards) by the length of a cricket pitch. This was getting very ugly. He dropped another stroke to fall to seven over. The former world number one needed to par the closing five holes to match Hammer, whose earliest golfing memory was watching Woods win the last of his majors in 2008.

The situation, though, kept deteriorating. At the next Woods found sand down the left and duffed his escape en route to a triple-bogey seven. He did manage his one birdie on the 16th only to suffer his greatest indignity at the last, topping a fairway wood like a Sunday hacker to send the ball careering into Mike Davis's controversial bunker, 'Chambers Basement'. The hazard was there to punish only the worst of shots. Members of a beer-fuelled crowd laughed. Woods was the only visitor to the bunker all week. The resulting bogey meant that he signed for a ruinous round of 80, his worst in a US Open.

Oosthuizen completed a 77, Fowler a miserable 81. The young American's card, astonishingly, included an eagle when he nearly holed in one at the par-4 12th. This illustrious trio were a combined 28 over par, and the two Americans had been comfortably beaten on the day by a 15-year-old. 'At least I kicked Rickie's butt today,' Woods joked, but otherwise he struggled to find any positives. 'Not very happy, that's for sure. I fought, I fought hard. And that was my number. I couldn't grind out any harder than that.'

While the Woods horror show played out, an amateur, Brian Campbell, flirted with the lead and the elite trio of Spieth, Justin Rose and Day battled away in the toughest of the conditions. The Masters champion three-putted the sixth to slip to one over par but atoned with a birdie two holes later after an excellent fairway wood to the par-5 green. Spieth then enjoyed a purple patch, bagging three birdies in a row from the 11th before dropping his only shot on the inward half at the short 15th. It was more stressful than he would have liked, but his 68 left him within three strokes of the top of the leaderboard.

Spieth reasoned that three more rounds of similar scoring would be enough to win. 'No complaints there,' was his verdict. He felt his ball-striking could have been better and wasn't up to the standard of his practice rounds, but there were reasons to be pleased. 'I thought I putted well,' the young Texan said. 'I missed a couple inside 10 feet, but that's going to happen out here. That's the inconsistency of the greens. I made a lot of them from inside 10 feet too. I hit the ball just so incredibly well Saturday, Sunday, Monday of this week, as good as I've ever hit it. I got a little off from there. It's close – just trying to find that same rhythm.'

Day looked in fine form, cruising to the turn in two under. His approach to the par-4 fourth nearly disappeared into the hole on the full, and at the ninth he curled in a 25-footer that fell in with its final revolution. There was a quiet confidence about the Australian that suggested his wait for a first major title was nearing its end.

By contrast Rose, the 2013 champion, struggled early on, finding himself three over par after five. His birdie at the long eighth was much needed. The Englishman's round came alive at the short par-4 12th, where he drove the green for a two-putt birdie. At the next, he holed from 15 feet, then tapped in for a third birdie in a row. He finished on 71 after a double bogey at the 16th. His birdie at the last didn't prevent Rose from bemoaning a 'weak' and 'tired' finish, during which he felt he threw away a much better score. He didn't enjoy the greens either. 'I couldn't see a putt staying on the line I hit it on and that makes it a little frustrating,' he said.

Day was altogether more upbeat. He played an inspired wedge from the top of a huge dune to the left of the 12th to make his first inward birdie, another followed at the 14th and two holes later he threatened the flag with a flicked approach before tapping in to help set the seal on a 68, matching Spieth. There were a couple of dropped shots on the way home but it was a solid performance from the straight-talking Queenslander. 'It was very, very tough,' he reflected. 'Bloody 15th hole, down the hill. Everyone was coming up short there. Our group kind of made a mess of it.

'On the front nine it was pretty warm, the balls were flying a long way. I was hitting normal distance. On the back nine it was a little tougher. It would have been great to finish four under, but I'll take anything under par. This is a marathon week. It's physically and mentally demanding, so I have to keep myself in it.'

Or, as the old adage goes, make sure you don't play yourself out of contention on the opening day. Woods and Fowler had done that and so, surely, had Oosthuizen. By contrast, Day and Spieth were firmly in the mix and Rose and McIlroy were still in touch.

The sunset over Puget Sound brought to an end a dramatic first day at Chambers Bay. The first US Open to be staged in the Pacific Northwest had delighted the fans – those who could see the action – and provided plenty for the fledgling Fox television crews to convey to their viewers.

They were left with an appetising leaderboard, heading into what proved a fascinating Friday.

-5 Stenson, Johnson

-4 Reed

-3 Kuchar, Ben Martin, Campbell (a)

-2 Cody Gribble, Francesco Molinari, Jason Dufner, Marc Warren, Joost Luiten, Spieth, Day

-1 Mickelson, Chappell, Brian Harman, Brandt Snedeker, Miguel Ángel Jiménez, Colin Montgomerie, Geoff Ogilvy, Charlie Beljan, Tony Finau, Ollie Schniederjans (a), Branden Grace, Shane Lowry

(a) denotes amateur

Friday, 19 June 2015

Spieth had said he was pleased with his late-early draw. It meant less hanging around on the second morning, and the perfect opportunity to maintain momentum. He had battled the worst of the opening day's weather and it remained breezy when he returned to Chambers Bay. Spieth, Day and Rose began their second rounds on the par-4 10th. It was their turn to play the back nine first.

Clad in all-grey (one of his favourite colour schemes), Spieth started perfectly. His opening approach skipped past the flag before climbing a slope that deflected the ball back towards the hole. He made no mistake from six feet, to move within two strokes of the lead. Rose also birdied, thanks to a fortunate pushed approach that bounced left off a slope, across the green and then took another contour that sucked it towards the hole. Day, meanwhile, paid the penalty for an errant tee shot and bogeyed.

Behind, the Tiger Woods debacle continued. After a fine drive, his approach to the 10th flew onto a massive dune. As the hapless former number one addressed his ball he lost balance and almost fell on his backside. It was symbolic of his current fortunes. He bogeyed, dropping to 11 over.

Golf seemed so much easier for Spieth. He did not take advantage of the short par-4 12th but two holes later struck a fabulous approach that shaved the left edge of the cup. Holing from 10 feet for a birdie, he was only one off the pace.

There was a sense of inevitability about Spieth's putt. His routine and rhythm told of his confidence and skill. He grips the putter left hand below right, his shoulders are square. He gives the slightest forward press before rocking his shoulders. The putter becomes the pendulum and the clubhead strikes through the ball as though it isn't there. Even on patchy greens, such as those at Chambers Bay, he imparts a roll that carries certainty. As his ball disappeared, he gave a brief, modest wave to the crowd, then moved on with a confident gait that suggested he was ready to do the same thing over and over again.

He did precisely that at the next, holing from around

30 feet, his putt hopping and popping along its route before falling in. It was the first of a couple of twos that sandwiched an inspired par save on the 16th. On the short 17th, a beautifully judged tee shot set up the chance that, once converted, took him to six under par and into the outright lead.

What would he give for that scenario, come Sunday night?

The next hole had been shortened and turned into a par 4; players either had to fly the fairway bunkers on the left or stay short of a cross-bunker on the right, 325 yards from the tee. The hole was downwind, bringing the cross-bunker well into play. But laying up would leave a par-5-sized approach to a green better shaped to receive a short iron. The players, effectively, had nowhere to go.

Meddling with the card in this way did not sit well with the players, the normally diplomatic Spieth among them. He drove into the hazard down the left, his ball tight up against the face. He should have taken his medicine and chipped out, but opted to smash it long. His ball struck the lip and squirted into the rough. His third went into the bunker front right of the green, and the good work from his brace of birdies was swiftly undone. Double bogey.

Television microphones picked up Spieth's stinging evaluation of the decision to play the 18th as a par 4. 'This is the dumbest hole I've ever seen in my life,' he told caddie Michael Greller.

Nor was he in the mood to back down later. 'I think 18 as a par 4 doesn't make much sense,' he said. 'Of course, at the moment when I didn't hit the right shots, it's going to make less sense. And if microphones are going to pick up what I say, they're going to pick it up. I'm not going to put a smile on and be happy with the way I played the hole. I just didn't know where I could hit that tee shot. And I wasn't going to hit a 3-iron off the tee and then hit 3-wood. So, all in all, I thought it was a dumb hole.'

Having briefly led, Spieth reached the turn three under for his round. The leaderboard read:

−5 Johnson, Stenson (yet to start)

−4 Grace (9 holes), Spieth (9*), Campbell (a) (5),
    Reed (yet to start)

*started at the tenth

If the 18th was a par 4 that day, then Mike Davis decreed the first, which runs in the opposite direction a little further up the hillside, should play its full length as a par 5. Spieth drove into the rough but put himself back in position. He then played a fine wedge that spun left as it landed close to the hole. It threatened to be sucked down a severe slope but put on the brakes just in time. He was left with around 15 feet for a bounce-back birdie and he rammed it home with intent. Again, Spieth showed his seemingly innate ability to recover instantly from setbacks. He was back at the top of the leaderboard, sharing the lead.

Day, meanwhile, reached halfway one over par, then picked up consecutive birdies. The first was extraordinary. He over-cooked a greenside bunker shot that ran through the green, gathered pace and scooted 40-odd yards down the slope. 'That is a joke!' Day complained, as his ball trundled out of sight. He was the one laughing soon after, though. A superbly judged pitch for his fourth shot rattled the flag and disappeared for an outrageous birdie. Day flung his wedge into the air and raised a clenched fist in triumph.

At the next, the driver of one of the monster freight trains that regularly lumbered past the course sounded his horn just as Day struck an enormous birdie putt. Again it hobbled and bobbled, but that horn took on a celebratory tone as the ball found the bottom of the cup. The Aussie was revelling in the heat of the battle, his eyes wide and bright as the sun beat down on the parched course.

Spieth slipped back to four under with a bogey at the seventh and for once his 'bouncebackability' was found wanting on the par 5 that followed. Nevertheless, the dream of becoming only the sixth man to win the Masters and the US Open in the same year was still very much alive as he moved to the ninth, which was using the upper tee and playing steeply downhill. It was his group's final hole of the second round. There was time for more drama, however – and drama of the most unexpected kind.

In the media centre the Radio 5Live team had just gone on air. I was anchoring the coverage with former Tour professional Jay Townsend. We had been discussing a charge from Ben Martin, which had taken the American into a share of the lead with overnight pacesetters Johnson and Stenson who had yet to tee off. Lee Westwood was four under for his round and into the red numbers for the first time since an opening 73.

Then our screens were filled with images that no one was anticipating and we were left trying to guess what was going on.

> IC: Now we've got a very worrying sight of Jason Day, who is down and appears to have injured himself. Now, I'm not sure exactly what has happened. He's playing with Jordan Spieth and with Justin Rose, and Jason Day at two under par, looks to be in a great deal of discomfort. Now, it is very, very slippery . . .

We couldn't ascertain at first what injury Day had sustained, but having been out on the course the day before, I knew first hand just how slippery it was; walking through the fescue grass, it was so bone dry it was like walking on a sheet of ice. Several people had already fallen, including Stenson's caddie Gareth Lord who fractured his wrist.

Day's collapse, however, had not been caused by a slip. His problem ran much deeper.

IC: Just seeing now on social media that Jason Day has collapsed on that ninth hole. The word is that he has told the medics that he is suffering from vertigo. His eyes can't focus and he is dizzy. He has had some medical issues in the build-up to this US Open [. . .] which is very, very worrying from the player's point of view. We had Gary Woodland yesterday, taken to hospital with dehydration as well, so this US Open is taking its toll.

At this point, Day was being helped by medical staff as Spieth and Rose looked on.

IC: Well, he's back on his feet, very gingerly. There are medics around him. His caddie is there, so too Michael Greller, Jordan Spieth's caddie. I think it is impossible to see him continuing, someone who was going along very well at two under par. He's trudging away. [. . .] Well, it looks like . . . no, it looked like he was going to continue; he has now gone down on one knee, he's taking a swig of water. The Australian, bearing in mind this is his final hole — so if he could just get through this and then get some treatment — but, even so he's got to play a bunker shot. He's shaking his head, wiping his nose and just trying to brace himself. He can barely stand up, he's clearly feeling a great deal of dizziness. This is very distressing to watch, but he is going to try and play this bunker shot and very gingerly walk into that sand trap and try and play.

JT: He looks unstable, like sometimes you see a runner finishing a marathon. But this is, just from a golfing standpoint – stepping outside of the health issues, right now – hitting a bunker shot, you don't hit the ball, you hit below it, I mean this is the worst shot he could possibly have right now. I mean, let's hope he can somehow finish out the hole without really messing up his score. He's in a great position in the golf tournament.

And that's what Day managed to do. He splashed out, took two putts and carded a courageous bogey, leaving him with a round of 70. He was transported by buggy to the recorders' hut, then treated by doctors. Day was one under par and still firmly in the hunt, but only if he could remain standing to play the weekend.

Rose also scored 70 while Spieth capitalised on an excellent final tee shot, retaining his composure to hole out for a birdie and a fine 67. At five under he was back into a share of the lead, with golfing history still firmly in his sights. That seemed, though, a secondary concern. Day's health was the big story.

Behind, Woods finished with a 76. His US Open ended at halfway, on a miserable 16 over par, while Fowler carded 73 to finish 14 over. Oosthuizen escaped the group's mediocrity with a superb 66 that ensured he would play the weekend.

Chambers Bay became a much tougher proposition in the afternoon. The course continued to dry out, and the greens grew ever bumpier. Scoring was difficult. Mickelson managed only a 74 after his encouraging opening 69. McIlroy added a second successive 72 and was bitterly disappointed at recklessly four-putting the 17th. Johnson's 71 was as uneven as the putting surfaces. His co-leader after the first round fared worse, Stenson carding a 74 that suggested he still wasn't ready to break his major duck. The Swede ripped into the state of the layout – it was at this point that he likened the greens to 'putting on broccoli'.

Other players raged at the course set-up, particularly the

shortening of the 18th. Westwood ruined his second round with a triple bogey seven there. In an interview with Sky Sports, the Englishman could not disguise his contempt and echoed the earlier sentiments of Spieth. 'Why bother tricking it up and switching around the pars of holes and things like that?' he said. 'Just lay out the golf course and let everybody play it and see who comes out on top.

'We played the 15th yesterday at 144 yards and it was from a tee that I didn't even know existed. It didn't even look like a tee. I don't see the reason for jiggling it all around and messing with the players' preparations. Mike Davis was right, if he's going to change it round like that, you are going to need 15 practice rounds, but some of us don't have the luxury of being able to do that.

'This is the first time I've known them change par 5s into par 4s. They say this course was designed for the US Open eight years ago and the two longest holes, the eighth and the first, you can't get any crowds around those holes. I mean, how ridiculous a design is that? I think most players are a bit too afraid to say what they think and, from what I've seen, people in the media are a little bit afraid as well. We live in a politically correct world . . . I think if you had a hidden camera and microphone in the locker room you'd hear a few things that you are not hearing in public.'

For all its faults, and there were many, Chambers Bay was still serving up compelling golf. In the afternoon, it was impossible not to watch Reed's assault on the top of the leaderboard. The 24-year-old had three birdies and two bogeys as he went to the turn in one under and on the way home he eagled the 12th and picked up two more birdies. These were offset by three dropped shots and he also fell victim to the controversial last hole, a bogey leaving him with a one-under 69 that contained only six pars. 'I actually felt it was a pretty disappointing round,' Reed said. 'To have five or six bogeys,

I was zero per cent on up-and-downs today. I hit the ball in the middle of the green on 18 and had no chance to putt a normal putt and stop it near the hole. To have to play Mickey Mouse golf to try to make par, unfortunately, is a bad way to end the day.'

Reed's round was good enough, though, to match his Ryder Cup partner Spieth.

−5 Spieth, Reed
−4 Grace, Johnson
−3 Luiten, Finau, Daniel Summerhays, Ben Martin
−2 Day, Jamie Lovemark, J. B. Holmes

Those at five over par and better made it through to the weekend. Woods, Fowler and several more significant names missed out. They included defending champion Martin Kaymer (72, 74), local hero Michael Putnam (70, 77), Bubba Watson (70, 77), Graeme McDowell (74, 74), Jamie Donaldson (74, 77) and young Cole Hammer (77, 84). But there was no disappointment from Hammer, just wide-eyed amazement. 'Oh, man, it was awesome,' he said. 'I had a blast. It was the best time of my life.'

Saturday, 20 June 2015

The prospect of Spieth teeing off last in the company of Reed was enticing. But their 2.50 p.m. tee-time would play second fiddle to the pair who began their third rounds almost an hour earlier. Given the distressing scenes from the previous day, the plight of Jason Day was top of the golfing agenda that Saturday morning. He was coupled with promising American Kevin Kisner.

One man who knew just what Day had gone through was former French Ryder Cup star Thomas Levet, who had been forced off tour for seven months through suffering similar symptoms earlier in his career. 'Basically, you are losing your balance. Your inner ear is not working,' Levet told me. 'The brain doesn't understand what's going on and when that happens you just drop to the floor . . . it feels as though you are walking on a water bed all day long and it takes a while to recover.

'It's very disturbing . . . for Jason Day at the moment, it is as though he is trying to hit a moving ball. It's really, really hard. I have a corridor in my house, it is about 10 metres long. At one stage, I could not stop hitting the left-hand wall when I walked through. I must have hit that side more than 50 times.'

It was another clear, sunny day, and certainly a demanding temperature for a player in Day's condition. He moved carefully between shots, often using his putter as a walking stick. He bogeyed the second and saw a birdie putt lip out on the short third. As his ball caught the edge, Day jerked his head in frustration. That small reaction clearly upset his precarious balance. He walked slowly forward to finish the hole but dropped another shot at the next. It seemed inevitable that his brave challenge would melt away during the afternoon.

At the fifth, Day's approach found a greenside bunker and he faced another challenge. He splashed out beautifully, almost holing for birdie. The resulting par save promised to provide momentum to a faltering round but, at the seventh, Day leaned on his caddie Colin Swatton. 'He just said he was exhausted,' Swatton revealed. 'He just didn't feel right. But, every time he said that, we just tried to focus on one more shot, one more hole.'

He went to the turn in 37 and was level for the championship, seven strokes off the lead and only just on the fringe of contention. 'I didn't feel that great coming out early, I felt pretty groggy on the front nine just from the drugs that I had in my system,' Day would later say.

Swatton is more than a caddie, he is also Day's coach and

has been a mentor to the player since childhood. He knows his boss better than anyone. So how did Day get through the inward half, that Saturday afternoon? 'He just dug deeper than he ever dug before,' Swatton said.

A perfect approach to the par-4 10th set up a tap-in birdie, but Day handed back the shot immediately. On the 12th he fired a superb driver into the heart of the green. A carefully lagged putt enabled him to tap in for birdie. Day again used his putter for support as he retrieved the ball. He was back to one under par but the effects of his pre-round drugs were wearing off. The vertigo was back, and he felt nauseous.

He battled on before arriving at the par-3 15th. The 27-year-old, moving like an old man, walked up to the tee and struck a sensational shot to six feet. It was a tricky putt to judge, with a right-to-left break that could easily have sent the ball to the low side if struck too hesitantly. Day made no mistake to move to two under par.

Two holes later, from 15 feet and against all the odds, Day rammed home another birdie. The crowds in the grandstand rose to acclaim what had become a remarkable round of golf. That was his fourth birdie on the inward half while most of the rest of the field were struggling to come to terms with a course that was becoming harder and faster.

Day's drive on the 18th, restored to a par 5, was poor. He sprayed it right but it came to rest conveniently on the top of a sand dune and he was able to hack his ball back into the centre of the fairway. From there, the Australian's challenge was to access a pin cut in a bowl on the front right of the green. His approach flew over the flag. Squinting, Day tried to track its progress, his eyes darting from the ball to the flag and back again until the rapid movement became too much and he averted his gaze abruptly. The shot flew a good 25 feet past the hole but the packed grandstands anticipated what would happen next. They began cheering even before Day's ball engaged reverse gear. Sure enough, it started to ease back towards its target. The cheers grew louder and louder as it came to rest four feet from the cup. Day tapped in to cap a momentous round. He was home in 31 and finished birdie-birdie, his 68 taking him to four under par for the championship.

His performance brought back memories of Ken Venturi's victory in the 1964 US Open. In those days, the final 36 holes were played in one day. In oppressive heat, Venturi showed signs of dehydration after a third-round 66 and a doctor recommended he stop. Venturi ignored the advice and shot a closing 70 to win his only major. Recalling the occasion, Venturi said: 'I was lying next to my locker and Dr Everett says: "I suggest that you don't go out. It could be fatal." I looked up at him and I said: "Well, it's better than the way I've been living." I got off the floor and I do not remember walking to the first tee.'

Those who witnessed Day's performance on that sunny Saturday at Chambers Bay will never forget it. It had been an arduous test and his caddie revealed that there had been several occasions on the front nine when his charge might have called it quits. 'The fourth was a really tough hole for him, up the hill,' he said. 'Seven, he really felt the pinch. Once we got to eight, I said: "It's all downhill from here." He had bits and pieces throughout the round where he felt great and then he didn't feel great. He was just exhausted.

'It's sneaky hot here, even though it says 75, 80 degrees, it plays a lot hotter than that. The hydration was really important and keeping his food up and energy levels. I said to him: "They're going to make a movie about that round." It was pretty impressive, it was up there with Tiger Woods playing with a broken leg at the US Open.'

Levet, watching for French television, went even further. 'It's a fabulous effort,' he said. 'It takes so much energy from you. There are also problems with headaches because with vertigo, your eyes are trying to get the balance back and they are moving so hard that the muscles are getting sore and you can get cramps in your eyes. If he were to win, I think it would be a greater feat than Tiger Woods winning in 2008. You can win on one leg, but trying to hit a moving ball with no balance is a different game altogether.'

For that to happen, though, Day would need to beat some equally determined players, including someone else overdue a first major. Dustin Johnson had squandered several opportunities in his chequered career but he looked primed to change that at Chambers Bay. After rounds of 65 and 71, the tall, athletic Johnson began with three birdies and two bogies in his first six holes. At the short ninth, playing uphill, Johnson's tee shot barely carried the bunkers at the front of the green and his ball skipped past the hole before taking a slope, which dragged it back towards the target. He was left with a delicate downhill, left-to-right putt that threatened to deviate from its line until it disappeared for a birdie that took him to six under par. A clumsy six at the 13th did not help, but Johnson's 70 put him alongside Day at four under par. The American's playing partner Branden Grace also shot 70 for the same total.

It was a popular number, with Spieth joining the trio at the top of the leaderboard. He had an extraordinary front nine, which contained only two pars. There were monster birdie putts at the second and third holes, which took him to seven under, and he collected another at the sixth. But the rest of his play was ragged and he bogeyed four of the six holes from the fourth. There was another dropped shot at the 11th.

Spieth was still firmly in the mix, though, unlike Reed. Buckling under the pressure after sharing the halfway lead, Reed covered the first 11 holes in a ruinous seven over par.

At the 15th, Spieth used the slope at the back of the par-3 green as a backstop and the resulting birdie brought him back into a share of the lead. His animated, repeated waist-high fist pumping demonstrated that it had been a big moment. He missed decent birdie chances on each of the closing holes and signed for a 71. It was his first round over par at a major that year.

Afterwards, Spieth bemoaned the four three-putts that had pegged him back, and what he regarded as a fine tee shot on the par-5 eighth that had not held the fairway. But he was excited to hold a share of the lead. Day and Johnson, having finished earlier, would form the last pair out for the final round. In the penultimate pairing, Spieth would play with Grace, and the man looking for back-to-back majors was perfectly happy with that. 'I think it will be somewhat advantageous,' Spieth argued. 'I think those two guys, as two stand-out stars of the game still searching for their first major, will battle with each other. I think I could sneak under the radar.'

The leading quartet were three clear of their nearest rivals, a group that, remarkably, included Oosthuizen, who had surged through the field following his opening 77 in the company of the long-departed Woods and Fowler. The South African shot a second successive 66 to move to one under par and join an impressive leaderboard that would generate one of the most memorable final days at a major in recent times.

−4 Day, Johnson, Grace, Spieth
−1 Oosthuizen, Cameron Smith, Lowry, Holmes
+1 Snedeker, Andres Romero, Stenson, Finau,
     Luiten, Reed

Three of the previous four majors had been processions. Twelve months earlier Kaymer was five strokes clear going into the final round at Pinehurst, at Hoylake for The Open McIlroy was six ahead and Spieth held a four-shot advantage at Augusta. Here, at Chambers Bay, he was in a four-way scrap for the lead with the possibility of an 18-hole playoff on Monday.

The course continued to receive heavy criticism, with Gary Player joining the fray. The legendary South African was at

Chambers Bay to mark the 50th anniversary of his career grand slam and conducted a series of interviews in which he blasted the event as 'the most unpleasant golf tournament I've seen in my life'.

Player has his own golf course design company and Robert Trent Jones is a rival. The nine-time major winner raged: 'The man who designed this course had to have had one leg shorter than the other. It's hard to believe you see a man miss the green by one yard and the ball ends up 50 yards down in the rough. Imagine, this is a public golf course. This is where we try to encourage people to come out and play and get more people to play the game . . . it's actually a tragedy. It's 7,900 yards long. The world is suffering from a shortage of water. Can you imagine the water this course will take?

'An average golfer playing this golf course, I'm telling you, if he's a 15-, 16-handicap, he's going to shoot 110 and he's not going to go home a very happy man. We've got to make golf where it's quicker, where it's more enjoyable, get back to their family. We don't want a husband and wife to argue because he's taking too long and neglecting his family life.'

Player also argued that the modern golf ball flies too far and ruins the game. 'We've got to cut the ball back for the pro golfer, leave it for the amateur golfer. We're making golf courses longer and longer. More expense, more water, more fertiliser, more labour.

'They're taking a beautiful golf course, making undulating greens, bunkers in front of the greens, and the folks are resigning from clubs . . . we don't want to see that. We've got to promote it in the right way. Professional golf has never been so healthy. But we're in trouble, amateur-wise.'

Sunday, 21 June 2015
Many of the criticisms of Chambers Bay were justified and on that final day, after completing his round, Billy Horschel

joined the tirade. 'I've been waiting for this moment all week,' he said. 'People out there think we complain a lot as players, and we don't. And when we do, I think we really need to be taken seriously.'

The source of his frustration was the state of the greens. He felt they discriminated against the most proficient putters. 'I understand Jordan is making plenty of putts. But I'm a really good putter as well, and I have not had a great week on the greens. And it's not due to the fact that my stroke is off or my speed is off; I've hit a lot of really good putts that have bounced all over the world. So it's just frustrating.'

Horschel shot a final round 67 to finish at four over par. 'I played awesome golf today. I played out my tail to shoot three-under par. And I really felt like I should have shot six, seven or eight under, but I wasn't able to, due to the fact that some of the putts hit some really bad spots on the greens and got off line.'

Horschel joined a long list of complainants. Stenson had talked about the 'broccoli' greens and McIlroy had gone for cauliflower. Rose said: 'It's like a game of outdoor bingo'; Ernie Els: 'The worst greens I've ever putted on'; Sergio García: 'This tournament deserves better'; and, of course, there was Spieth and 'the dumbest hole I've ever played in my life'.

Spieth's comments had been about the 18th being switched to a par 4. So the first big question of the final day was: Would Davis shorten it again? And, if he did, might it turn the climax of the US Open into a lottery?

The answer was no. Davis, noting the wind direction, opted for a 601-yard par 5 and the hole became a fitting stage for a stunning finish to the tournament.

The portents weren't encouraging, though, when Chris Kirk, a two-time winner on the PGA Tour, ran up a 10 on the 443-yard first hole. He was in the second pairing out on the final morning, playing with fellow American Ben Martin, who had spectacularly fallen from within a shot of the lead to the back of the field by carding a miserable 86 in the third round. Despite their travails, the course was set up superbly over the weekend. The best and most courageous players prospered – the likes of Spieth and Day – and there was also scope for challengers to charge through the field.

Adam Scott, the Masters winner in 2013, set the ball rolling on this remarkable final day. The former world number one's season had been disappointing and he had lost his way in the wake of the retirement of his caddie Steve Williams. The man who had been beside Tiger Woods for 13 of his 14 major victories had been a key figure in Scott's lone major success and was persuaded to return to the Australian's bag at Chambers Bay. There was little to suggest he had made much of an impact in the first three rounds as Scott recorded scores of 70, 71 and 72. He knew he needed something special to post a challenging total.

A birdie at the second brought Scott back to two over par and within six shots. At the seventh he drove into a fairway bunker from which he launched a brilliant approach. 'Be good, be good!' he told his ball as it flew towards the flag. It came to rest a couple of feet from the hole.

Birdie. One over par.

At the eighth he drew an accurate second into the par-5 green. Tap-in birdie. Level.

Scott was playing faultless, controlled golf. He picked up another birdie at the 11th to move under par for the first time in the championship. His card was clean, there were no dropped shots, and at the 16th, a par 4 played from a forward tee, he smashed his driver onto the green. For a moment he thought his broom-handle putter had holed for eagle. Instead, a fifth birdie.

At the last he came up just short of the par-5 green. His third shot was a monstrous putt that he charged past the hole, the slope returning his ball to the hole-side and Scott made the four-footer for a closing birdie and a brilliant round of 64. He punched the air in delight. He had set the target at three under par and proved it was possible to make a big move on the final day. 'I played really well, I took advantage of some of the holes playing a bit shorter and didn't have any disasters out there,' Scott said.

There would be no more avid viewer over the last couple of hours. 'I'd love to come back and play 18 holes and have another shot at it. I feel like I had nothing to lose and everything to gain. And I knew I was playing well and I just couldn't quite put it all together the first three days. It was a big effort for me. To be honest, it's the kind of round I needed to get things going for me this year.'

Until Scott's charge, the Australian commanding all the attention had been Jason Day. Observers were still marvelling at the way he finished his third round. As he and Johnson started out, Spieth – in the group ahead – was three-putting from inside 20 feet on the opening green.

Scott was not alone in surging through the field. McIlroy, who had begun his round almost three hours earlier, was muscling in on the action. The Northern Irishman had not been a factor in this US Open after opening rounds of 72, 72 and 70. Yet he curled in a 20-footer for birdie at the second and made an inspired par save from a greenside bunker at the fifth. At the seventh he manufactured a brilliant approach that crept back into range and his birdie putt dropped in via the right edge. At the par-5 next he completed a tough two-putt birdie by holing a five-footer with several inches of right-to-left break. Now he was back to one over par for the tournament and ready to charge on the back nine.

A brilliant approach from a fairway bunker on the 10th brought him back to level and it was the first of three birdies in four holes. At the 12th his right-to-left eagle attempt

Above: Jordan Spieth putting during the final round at the Masters, 2015.

Top: The clubhouse at Augusta National Golf Club.
Bottom: Masters defending champion Bubba Watson (left) places the green jacket on 2015 champion Jordan Spieth at the 79th Masters Golf Tournament, 12 April 2015.

Top: Dustin Johnson in action at the 115th US Open, at Chambers Bay.
Bottom: Jason Day is tended to by caddie Colin Swatton as he lays on the ninth green after falling due to dizziness during the second round of the US Open on 19 June.

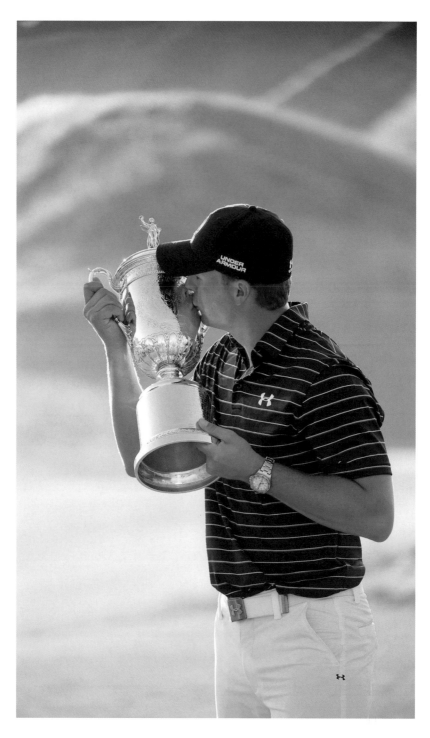

Above: Jordan Spieth victorious, with the US Open trophy during the presentation ceremony on Sunday at Chambers Bay.

Top: Chief Executive of the R&A Peter Dawson and Tiger Woods at a gathering of past Open champions for a photocall ahead of the 144th Open at the Old Course on 14 July 2015.
Bottom: Jordan Spieth and caddie Michael Greller read the 16th green during the final round of The Open on Monday at the Old Course.

Above: Zach Johnson holds up the Claret Jug in front of the clubhouse after winning the three-way playoff on day five of the 2015 Open on 20 July 2015.

Top: Rory McIlroy watches his tee shot on the fifth hole during the final round of the 2015 PGA Championship at Whistling Straits on 16 August 2015.
Bottom: Jason Day proudly holds the Wanamaker Trophy after his victory with a record major score of 20 under par during the final round of the 2015 PGA Championship.

Above: Jason Day celebrates with his caddie Colin Swatton on the 18th green after winning the 2015 PGA Championship.

broke 20 feet and left a tap-in. He then brought the crowd in the grandstands to their feet with an 80-foot birdie putt from the back of the next green. He had taken full advantage of the purest surface on the course. Now McIlroy was two under, with four to play, placing his fear-inducing name firmly on the leaderboard. 'If I could post four under par, birdie two holes coming in, then I thought I had a great chance, I really did,' McIlroy said. 'Especially with the way the greens were getting out there, they were getting baked.'

It was not to be.

McIlroy had a fine birdie chance after a terrific approach to the difficult 14th but for once his putter didn't oblige. At the next he thought he had hit a perfect tee shot to the par 3. It was a foot short. Instead of settling on the same level as the flag, his ball fell off the front of the green. When he failed to get up and down, the momentum was lost. It was the first bogey of his round and another followed on the 17th – the hole where he had four-putted on Friday evening. McIlroy had to settle for a 66 and level par for the tournament.

Although Scott soon overtook him, McIlroy had injected genuine drama to what was already developing into a remarkable final day. Day, however, was struggling. He looked off-colour and the exertions of battling his vertigo had clearly taken their toll. He moved slowly between shots, as he had done the previous day, but this time the lack of conviction spread to his golf game. At the fourth he misjudged a huge birdie attempt and his ball never came close to taking the severe left-to-right borrow for which he had aimed. It came to rest on the upper level of the green, with the pin cut on the lower back-right portion. He did well to two-putt from there, but it was a bogey. Birdies were then matched by bogeys. He went to the turn in a one-over-par 36.

Johnson covered the same ground in a blemish-free 33 and so moved to six under par – a score that looked good enough to lift the trophy. Branden Grace's birdie at the ninth kept the South African in contention at four under, while Spieth made up for his bogey at the first by conquering his demons on the eighth. This time his drive stuck in the fairway and his approach remained on the green. Two putts meant he had covered the front nine in level par.

−6 Johnson (9 holes)

−4 Spieth (10), Grace (10)

−3 Scott (64, clubhouse leader), Day (9)

Another indication of Day's discomfort came at the 10th where he needed help from his caddie to climb out of a greenside bunker. The resulting bogey dropped him further back. Oosthuizen was moving in the opposite direction. After a poor start, with three dropped shots in his first four holes, he made a birdie at the 12th to move to one over.

Individual fortunes continued to switch and turn. The leader now started to look ragged. Johnson's ability to make the game seem so effortless is apparently counter-balanced by a mental switch that transforms golf for him into something approaching an impenetrable foreign language. That switch flicked at the start of his back nine. After a bogey at the 10th, his second shot into the next found the rough just off the back-left of the green. He bumped it up to six feet but prodded uncertainly at the putt, missing out again.

Spieth and Grace were of a mood to capitalise and both made birdies on the 12th. Spieth's contention that he might be able to exert pressure on the final pair looked accurate as he and his playing partner drove the green of the short par 4 and collected stress-free birdies that now gave them a share of the lead.

−5 Spieth (12), Grace (12)

−4 Johnson (11)

−3 Scott (F)
−2 Day (11)

Johnson and Day, meanwhile, missed short birdie chances on the very patchy 12th green and knew they needed something special from the closing third of the course. Oosthuizen was back at level par and his South African compatriot Charl Schwartzel completed a superb 66 to finish at two under (not bad for someone who had been vehement in his Chambers Bay criticism ahead of the tournament, questioning whether it should even be called a golf course).

Few were doubting the layout's credentials in this final round, though. It was providing a stage for compelling sporting theatre. Grace made a stunning par save at the 13th, gutsily holing from 12 feet after Spieth completed a routine par. Scott looked on from the sidelines, wondering. The bumpy greens were becoming more and more hazardous to negotiate as the shadows lengthened.

The state of the greens was of no concern to Oosthuizen, however, as he holed his wedge shot from 120 yards on the 14th for birdie, having earlier driven into a bunker. That took him to one under. The final pair, meanwhile, hit trouble at the 13th. Day's chip from below the green failed to find the putting surface and came back to his feet. From there, he three-putted for a double bogey that finally put paid to his challenge. Johnson, who had been six under par with nine holes to play, then missed a tiddler and fell back to three under.

−5 Spieth (13), Grace (13)
−3 Scott (F), Johnson (13)

The leaders collected pars at the 14th while up ahead Oosthuizen rammed home a 30-footer on the penultimate par 3 to collect his fourth birdie in a row. He moved to within a stroke of the clubhouse lead, an incredible scenario given the way he had begun the championship with a 77, as well as the wretched start he had made on his final round.

−5 Spieth (14), Grace (14)
−3 Scott (F), Johnson (13)
−2 Schwartzel (F), Oosthuizen (15)

The level of excitement was reaching fever pitch. It was now well past two o'clock in the morning in the UK, but we were receiving messages at 5Live from listeners glued to their radios, willing to forego sleep to continue following the riveting action that was unfolding.

Spieth, still scrapping for a second successive major to keep alive the hope of a grand slam, remained the centre of attention. Playing with Grace, he watched the South African find the middle of the 15th green with his 158-yard tee shot. Spieth then sent his wedge to 10 feet, but watched in disbelief as his ball followed McIlroy's earlier example in toppling back down the bank at the front.

New names were also edging into the spotlight. Ireland's Shane Lowry birdied the drivable 337-yard 16th after nearly holing a long eagle putt. He moved back into the exclusive club of players under par. Behind him, Oosthuizen drove onto the green to set up his own eagle chance.

At the 14th, though, Johnson looked like he was falling apart. His approach sailed off to the left portion of the green, then he pushed his 30-foot birdie putt six feet past. It was hard to watch. Another major was ignominiously slipping away for perhaps the most naturally talented golfer in the world. This would surely be another ruinous three-putt. But he summoned an inner steel and slotted home the five-footer for par to staunch the bleeding.

Spieth displayed a surer touch. Left with a putt up and over a massive bank on the 15th green, he superbly negotiated the contours to make the par that had earlier eluded McIlroy. It was gutsy, determined golf from the man who had so contrastingly cruised to his Augusta victory. The co-leaders remained two clear at five under with three holes to play.

Intriguingly, Spieth had no idea of how well he was doing until he caught sight of the leaderboard as he left the fifteenth green. 'I didn't mean to. In turning back and watching Branden finish it was up there and I saw that he and I were two clear,' he explained. 'That's when it hit me . . . at the time I thought DJ was six or seven under. I didn't scoreboard-watch the whole day.'

Oosthuizen couldn't complete an eagle at the 16th but sealed a remarkable fifth birdie in a row. Now he was tieing for third place.

−5 Spieth (15), Grace (15)

−3 Scott (F), Oosthuizen (16), Johnson (14)

Playing the par-4 16th off the forward tee was classic Mike Davis. There are occasions when the USGA's executive director is too meddlesome. Chambers Bay encouraged this weakness, in offering him so many options. Directors of television sports coverage often fall into the same trap – dazzled by the variety of choice provided by modern technology, they mess up the narrative by using shots that people don't want to see at key moments. Keep it simple. Show the action. Let the sport do the talking. Save the clever stuff and the close-ups for the action replays. That was all the Fox Sports directors needed to do on the final day at Chambers Bay and, despite some funky camera angles, they largely succeeded.

Davis succeeded at the 16th as well. This was an occasion when imaginative interference was well worthwhile. He had recognised how pivotal it could be to the championship on the final day. He engaged the forward tee to tempt players to drive the green, to try to set up eagle and birdie chances. As with all classic golf course design, reward must be balanced by risk. Here, the risk was losing your drive out to the right, towards the railroad.

Grace decided to try and emulate his fellow countryman Oosthuizen, and land his 3-wood drive on the putting surface. A regular winner on the European Tour and someone with the reputation for converting winning opportunities, Grace had never before been in a leading position coming down the stretch in a major. To his great anguish he unleashed his drive and watched it sail to the right and out of bounds. His second attempt found its target, but his chance had surely gone. 'I was hitting my 3-wood great the whole day,' Grace recalled. 'It was a straightforward shot, I just spun out of it.'

Spieth, meanwhile, missed the green and chipped tentatively. He left his ball 25 feet short of the hole. 'You've gotta be kidding me!' Spieth cried out. Anything worse than a birdie would feel as though he was conceding ground.

Behind, Johnson, having found the front bunker at the short 15th, splashed out and knocked in an eight-footer for par. Oosthuizen's run of birdies ended with par at the 17th.

Fox Sports had buried microphones in several of the holes on the closing run at Chambers Bay. The idea was to catch the sound of a ball disappearing. The roars of the crowd, though, threatened to drown out any other noise. The golfing public of the Pacific Northwest were boisterous and raucous, and they were being given plenty to cheer. Rarely were they louder, though, than when Spieth dispatched his birdie attempt at the 16th. With Grace en route to a double bogey, the tournament was heading in the direction of the 21-year-old history-maker. Grace had made a crucial mistake, Johnson had wobbled throughout his back nine, Scott's target was diminishing in difficulty and Oosthuizen's charge might not be enough.

As Spieth stepped up to his putt, BBC 5Live summariser Jay Townsend described what the youngster was facing.

JT: This is a difficult birdie putt. He has to go down a slope and a big swing from left to right. It's actually difficult to stop it pin-high. It's gonna most likely run past the hole if it misses. But effectively, right now, he has a two-shot lead.

IC: Yep, because Branden Grace has paid the penalty for driving out of bounds. This for birdie for Jordan Spieth, 27 feet, it's on its way, borrowing from left to right, this looks good, really, really good . . . and in! And in for Jordan Spieth! And is that the putt that gives him back-to-back major titles? It is a massive blow to strike and Jordan Spieth, with that birdie, moves to six under par and moves into clear water with two holes to play!

JT: Well essentially he now has a three-shot lead, Grace is going to make a double bogey, it looks like. I mean, that is an unbelievable putt! We've seen numerous players not only not make that putt, but struggle to get it anywhere near to the hole. This is just the magic that this guy possesses. Absolutely incredible. Is this guy really just 21 years old?

'I thought I had won it on 16,' Spieth later stated. Yet, dramatic as that moment was, it seemed inappropriate for this US Open to effectively end two holes from home. This had to go the distance.

And it did.

−6 Spieth (16)
−3 Scott (F), Oosthuizen (17), Grace (16), Johnson (15)

For the leader, there was one par 3 and par 5 to go. Complete those holes in regulation figures and the job would surely be done. He would be halfway to the grand slam. Spieth had shown immense composure since his uncharacteristic three-putt on the first green. There had been three birdies and no further dropped shots. He had played archetypal US Open golf, exactly what the course required.

So it was a huge surprise when Spieth wildly pushed his 6-iron tee shot on the 219-yard 17th, sending it 40 yards right of the green. 'That's as far off line as I've hit a 6-iron in a long time,' Spieth admitted. 'That was a really bad shot. In mid-air I thought it might go out of bounds. I just didn't square up the club face.' His ball was nearer the railway line than his intended target.

Grace, meanwhile, found the heart of the green. As Spieth escaped the long rough where his ball had nestled, Johnson set up a birdie chance on the hole behind. Eight feet away, he was ready for one last assault. The drama was unrelenting. Up ahead, another Aussie was getting involved. Cameron Smith, who had been on the fringes of the leaderboard all week, fired in his 3-wood second and nearly holed it. He tapped in for an eagle to finish with a 68, alongside compatriot Scott at three under par.

Oosthuizen, Smith's playing partner, then completed a closing birdie to set the new target. He capped an incredible inward half of 29 for a 64, and a four-under-par total.

At six under, Spieth was 25 feet away in two on the par-3 17th and he missed his putt by a couple of feet. Grace, from similar distance, almost made a bounce-back birdie, his par leaving him at three under.

Astonishingly, Spieth then made an extraordinary and out of character error. Renowned for his putting, he managed to push his short putt for bogey and ended up dropping two shots. There was a huge intake of breath. Spieth had somehow slipped back to four under par. This championship wasn't over – not by any stretch of the imagination.

−4 Oosthuizen (F), Spieth (17)
−3 Scott (F), Smith (F), Grace (17), Johnson (15)

Transfixed, Jay Townsend and 5Live commentator Chris Jones watched as Johnson settled over his birdie chance on the 16th.

JT: Johnson might actually now be in the driver's seat. This is a tough left-to-right breaking putt.

CJ: What a putt this is for Dustin Johnson for his birdie. Left to right, he sets it on its way and . . . he misses to the right! . . . And Johnson had a chance to go to four under par, level with Oosthuizen and level with Spieth and he spurns it. What a miss!

−4 Oosthuizen (F), Spieth (17)
−3 Scott (F), Smith (F), Grace (17), Johnson (16)

So it all came down to the final two holes, and the final two groups on the course. Spieth fired a beauty of a drive down the middle of the par-5 18th, a fine response to his aberration on the previous hole. Grace drove into a fairway bunker. Meanwhile, back on the 17th, Johnson gave himself another chance, curling his tee shot in from the left, his ball stopping within six feet of the hole.

Spieth was back in the zone and powered a 3-wood from 282 yards to the top-right corner of the green. 'Hit it wind, hit it wind! Any wind up there, please hit it, just a little bit!' Spieth implored. The ball funnelled round to the left and then back down to the hole, stopping 15 feet below it. 'Awesome shot, awesome,' Greller said as he handed Spieth his putter.

'I hit it right out of the middle,' Spieth said. 'I looked up and it was bleeding right, I just asked for the wind to hold it up just a little bit. And it looked like it did . . . at the last second it stayed out of going in that bunker and instead found the rebound and stayed up on the top ledge. I was going to be pleased with anywhere on the green. And then, with the roar, I knew it had stayed on the top ledge.'

A putt for eagle, two for birdie – in yet another twist, the US Open was back within his grasp. As the young superstar of American golf received a tumultuous reception from the vast grandstand stretching down the right of the closing hole, Johnson calmly slotted home his chance to secure a rare birdie at 17. The big-hitting American had intensified the pressure cooker-atmosphere by making it a three-way share of the lead.

What is more, the home green, 600 yards away, would certainly be within two blows for him.

–4 Oosthuizen (F), Spieth (17), Johnson (17)
–3 Scott (F), Smith (F), Grace (17)

Grace could only find the green in three strokes and his 20-footer for birdie never threatened. Having paid a huge price for his error on the 16th, he signed for a 71 that left him three under par for the championship. Oosthuizen was now the only South African with a glimmer of a chance of winning, and his hopes had significantly dimmed with Spieth's brilliant fairway wood. They disappeared completely when he putted up to the hole-side, borrowing just a fraction too much from the left. Spieth tapped in for a birdie and a superb 69. He led in the clubhouse at five under par. There was little sense of triumph, though. 'My goal was to get to six under,' Spieth said. 'Walking off the 18th green, I was a little down and frustrated.'

-5 Spieth (F)
-4 Oosthuizen (F), Johnson (17)
-3 Scott (F), Smith (F), Grace (F)

It was now all down to Johnson. An eagle to win. A birdie to force an 18-hole playoff.

Johnson crashed an immense drive down the fairway. He would need only a 5-iron to make the green. 'Beauty, great swing,' said Austin Johnson, his brother and caddie, as the ball flew towards the putting surface, directly at the flag, bouncing to the back of the green and coming to rest just 12 feet from the hole. It was a stunning shot. But it left the slickest of putts.

Johnson had to wait as Day finished off his brave effort. The Australian had run out of energy as he struggled to a 74, leaving him at level par and in a share for ninth place – a brilliant effort from one of the stars of an extraordinary week. His time would come.

Now, though, the stage was set for Johnson and his eagle putt for victory. In the recorders' area, Spieth watched on television. 'I was probably more nervous then than I was on the course at any point,' he admitted.

It's difficult to know what the inscrutable Johnson was feeling. What we do know is that he borrowed a fraction too much to the left and the ball drifted by the hole and rolled on another four feet. Outright victory was gone. Four feet left, for a playoff with the Masters champion.

The tall Johnson wasted no time. Indeed, it looked as though he rushed the birdie attempt. It started left and stayed left. It shaved the hole, but never threatened to fall.

Johnson had squandered another major. His loss was Spieth's gain. He had won the US Open, and his grand slam dream was still alive. Spieth, the winner at Augusta, was the last man standing at Chambers Bay.

He had become only the sixth player to win the Masters

and the US Open in the same year. His moment of triumph came in the recorders' hut as he joined Woods, Jack Nicklaus, Ben Hogan and Arnold Palmer in accomplishing the feat.

−5 Spieth
−4 Oosthuizen, Johnson
−3 Scott, Smith, Grace
−2 Schwartzel
−1 Snedeker
E: McIlroy, Lowry, Day

'When DJ hit his second shot I thought: "Shoot, I may have lost this tournament,"' Spieth said. The moment of realisation that he'd won was an 'utter shock'.

'I was able to share the moment with Michael [Greller], which is really cool,' Spieth added. 'This is a special place for him, and we're just able to add to his history here at Chambers Bay. You only get a few moments in your life like this and I recognise that. To have two in one year and still be early in the year, that's hard to wrap my head around. The goals were the majors. They weren't about winning a certain number of times or getting in contention in a major. It was: "Let's find a winning formula in a major."'

He'd done that in style, forcing a rewriting of the record books and putting his name alongside some of the greats of the game. 'As a golf historian, that's very special and it gives me goosebumps,' he said with a smile.

He was the first to win the US Open with a birdie at the last since Bobby Jones in 1926. He was the first since Gene Sarazen in 1922 to win two majors before the age of 22, and he was the youngest winner of America's national championship in the modern era. In that regard, he overtook McIlroy, who won the US Open at Congressional at the age of 22 in 2011.

It was a staggering list of achievements, to cap an extra-ordinary championship. Could Spieth possibly make it three majors in a row at St Andrews the following month? McIlroy would be defending champion on the Old Course, his favourite venue. An equally intriguing question hung in the air: how would the man from Northern Ireland and still world number one react to this astonishing raid on his position at the top of the game?

CHAPTER 7

Golf's Oldest Championship

Not since 1960 had a golfer headed to a St Andrews Open having won the first two majors of the year. Back then, Arnold Palmer was breathing new life into the world's oldest major. It had been suffering from the indifference shown by many of the top American players in the previous decade. Palmer's attitude was different and so was his personality. Charismatic and fearless, he was the pre-eminent force in the game. And force is the correct term; he made golf attractive through the weight of a disposition that naturally connected with people. He was an astute businessman as well; it was his handshake with an American lawyer called Mark McCormack that spawned the International Management Group, which for decades has played a hugely influential role in the business of professional sport.

Nowadays, IMG manage many of the biggest stars in golf, tennis and several other sports. The company looked after the interests of Tiger Woods through the most successful period of his career. Its tentacles spread into the realms of television rights negotiations, sponsorship deals and staging events across the sporting spectrum.

Palmer was the catalyst and he recognised the value of spreading his brand globally. This is why he so willingly travelled overseas to events like The Open Championship. By talking up the notion of the 'grand slam' of majors, this golfing great re-valued The Open's currency. He helped turn it back into a 'must-play' event for all of the world's leading players.

Like Jordan Spieth in 2015, Palmer had won the Masters and US Open and continued his odyssey to the place universally known as the 'Home of Golf'. St Andrews is a historic town and, from the 11th century, was the seat of Christianity to which pilgrims flocked from all over Europe. The great cathedral, built in 1160, was for seven centuries the largest building in Scotland. The university was founded in 1413 and it remains one of the United Kingdom's great places of learning. The town's current 17,000 population is swelled in term time by around 7,000 undergraduates.

Numbers are boosted further by the thousands of tourists who make a modern-day pilgrimage to worship at the altar of golf. They come in their droves to sample the delights of a place that boasts seven layouts, including the world-famous Old Course, which was staging The Open in 2015 for a record 29th time.

The first detailing of golf in St Andrews dates from 1552 in a charter bearing the seal of the Archbishop of St Andrews, Archbishop Hamilton. It conferred on the locals the right to play the game on the Links, the area separating the North Sea from arable land. This space, which linked farmland with the beach known as the West Sands, was also used for activities such as football, livestock grazing and rabbit breeding.

But there is evidence to suggest that golf had been played on St Andrews Links long before. Indeed, the sport had been banned in Scotland by King James II nearly 100 years earlier in 1457 (in order to make people focus on archery).

The key moment in the making of St Andrews' golfing reputation came in the middle of the 18th century. Despite the spell when the game was forbidden, golf grew into an ever more attractive pursuit, with more and more people taking up the game. In 1754, 22 'noblemen and gentlemen of the Kingdom of Fife' formed the Society of St Andrews Golfers. It would later evolve into the Royal and Ancient Golf Club of St Andrews. Before then, though, the society had already established key precedents for the game. Most significantly, they ruled that a round of golf should be 18 holes in length, even though the Old Course was originally made up of 22.

The Royal and Ancient Golf Club of St Andrews built its clubhouse in 1854 and this iconic building remains synonymous with the game. Overlooking the first tee, it is arguably the most photographed structure in golf. Gradually, the R&A became regarded as the premier club in the world and published the first 'Rules of Golf' in 1897. Since then, it has been recognised as the sport's global ruling body outside the USA and Mexico.

In 1919 it took over the management of The Open Championship and it wasn't until 2004 that the club officially relinquished responsibility. Secretary Peter Dawson pushed through an organisational change that separated the club from a formal company known as R&A Limited. The new firm took over the role of administering The Open but the Royal and Ancient Golf Club, despite not owning any of the town's courses, remained inextricably linked with the championship. Dawson became Chief Executive of the R&A but remained Secretary of the golf club and his office is found upstairs in the clubhouse.

The 2015 Open was the last to be run by Dawson, who was then 65 and had taken over as R&A Secretary from Sir Michael Bonallack 16 years earlier. There are few workplaces that enjoy a better view than his office. It overlooks the first tee of the Old Course, with a vista stretching the length of the hallowed layout. From here, Dawson masterminded the running of every Open Championship since 2000, as well as dealing with issues key to the running of the global game.

It was a period in which golf went through huge changes. Dawson was at the heart of the campaign that has brought the sport back to the Olympics in 2016. He was also involved in the ongoing battle to deal with the effects of club and ball technology, as well as the long-overdue admission of women members to the R&A for the first time.

In wrestling with the many and varied issues that crossed his expansive desk, Dawson admitted his office's unique location helped soothe some of the headaches that come with his role.

'I pace a lot and if there's something really troublesome I open the door, go out on the balcony, have a look around and think golf will go on despite this problem,' he told me. 'I think to myself: "You know, there's plenty of momentum here." It's an experience that secretaries of the R&A are fortunate to have and you can see that the game is here for the long run, it's a long term thing.'

Dawson never guessed that he would become such an influential figure in golf when he emerged from Cambridge University and began his career in the manufacturing industry. 'I'd grown up playing golf as a kid, starting in the early 60s and went on to be a fairly decent player, not a great player.' His love of the game grew during the boom period that followed Tony Jacklin's 1969 Open victory at Royal Lytham & St Annes.

'We were always getting beaten by the Americans or the Australians and then suddenly in 1969 Jacklin finally did it. It had been 18 years since Max Faulkner's win at Portrush – and there was not a dry eye in the house that day,' he commented to the 2015 *Open* magazine.

'It is my most memorable Open moment, even though I've subsequently been working in golf. Jacklin began to make us think it was possible that British golf could be strong again.'

Dawson attended his first Open at Royal St George's in

1985 when Sandy Lyle was the victor. But in those days he didn't envisage ever running The Open Championship.

'No, absolutely unthinkable,' he laughed. 'Never would have crossed my mind and, in fact, it didn't even cross my mind when Sir Michael Bonallack was coming up to retirement and the job was being advertised. I never thought of applying for it but one or two people said "you should have a go at this" and, blow me, I got my application in by fax on the deadline.

'We were living in Northumberland and my wife didn't particularly want to move and my son said "Let him apply, he'll never get it". And then I got down to the shortlist and there was no one more surprised than I when it actually happened. But it's been a wonderful job and there've been many, many highlights to it. Of course, The Open Championship is the showcase of everything we do.'

In 2000, Dawson's inaugural Championship in charge, Woods claimed his first Open title and took home a £500,000 first prize. Fifteen years later the champion was paid more than £1,000,000 for the first time. The figures illustrate the way the event grew during Dawson's tenure. 'The average number of spectators has been growing, the amount of corporate support we've had has been growing, TV income has been growing and so commercially it's got a lot bigger, which has allowed us to reinvest in the Championship,' he said. 'The technology that's in there today is very different to what it was 15 or 16 years ago, particularly in scoring terms. In digital media, all of those aids for spectators and for viewers, that's got a lot bigger.

'The commercial success has allowed us to help the game a lot more. And we're in a competitive world. There are other majors, there are other sporting events in Britain . . . so we absolutely have to make sure the event stays in its prominent position and you need commercial success to do that.'

No one could argue with Dawson's business acumen and his ability to steer the R&A through the challenging economic period that followed the economic crash of 2008. But the Chief Executive attracted plenty of criticism for changes to the Old Course that he initiated in the build-up to 2015. Dawson's skills lay in the world of business and sports administration, not necessarily golf course design, it was argued. Meddling with the world's most famous layout was tantamount to putting a moustache on the Mona Lisa. When news broke of the planned alterations, five-time champion Peter Thomson said: 'It's like a bad dream.' The outspoken Ian Poulter branded them 'insane', while golf design aficionados wailed with outrage at the temerity of meddling with this precious piece of architecture.

The Old Course, after all, is unique. Apart from the first, ninth, 17th and 18th holes, the putting surfaces are vast double greens. You play to the right side (apart from on the eighth and tenth holes, which, uniquely, are on the left side) of each of these undulating target areas that stretch as big as football pitches. The second green shares with the 16th, the third with the 15th and so on. If you add together the numbers of the holes, the total is always 18.

Starting in a south-westerly direction, the first shares a wide fairway with the 18th and they are bordered by white racecourse-style fencing. Neither hole is protected by any bunkering, although the Swilcan Burn snakes immediately in front of the first green and a deep depression known as the 'Valley of Sin' lies at the front of the home putting green. A round starts and finishes in the town, and once the opening hole has been negotiated the routing runs parallel to the West Sands.

Once the seventh green has been reached, players double back on themselves by playing the short eighth and par-4 ninth before switching in the opposite direction for the next two holes. This portion of the course is known as 'the loop'. Then, from the 12th, it is a largely direct route back towards the town, which grows ever larger on the horizon. It is iconic golfing ground that has been trodden by the greats of the game throughout its history.

Hence the outrage at plans to alter the course.

Yes, it had been lengthened over the years, even to the extent that championship tees for holes like the second and 17th are situated on neighbouring courses, but there had been little formal change otherwise. The necessity of stretching the course reflects how far the modern golf ball travels when propelled by fitter, stronger modern professionals using the most up-to-date equipment.

Nevertheless, the central tenet of how to play the Old Course remained intact. The theory is that you should hit tee shots towards the left to avoid trouble. This, though, results in a more challenging approach. Taking on the right side with your drive is a risky strategy but can yield the reward of an easier route to most pins.

Ahead of the 2015 Open, the R&A and the St Andrews Links Trust announced the changes. They had been initiated by the Royal and Ancient's Championship Committee and the alterations on nine holes were overseen by renowned architect Martin Hawtree. 'We obviously know the course very well and how it plays at all levels of the game,' Dawson told me. 'No one knows it like we do or the Links Trust do. We did feel that there were a small number of things that would make it just that bit more demanding. A need for greater precision – this is nothing to do with length. It's just the ability of the modern player.'

Dawson insisted that local support for the changes was strong. He also stated that there was plenty of precedent for alterations to be made to a layout that has the reputation of being fashioned by Mother Nature and the golfing gods rather than by human hands. 'I was looking at aerial photographs of the course from 50 to 60 years ago and compared them with now. Anyone who thinks they are identical needs to come and have a look at them, they are actually quite different,' Dawson said.

So two new bunkers were added short right of the second hole, and undulations were built on a flat area to the right of the green. At the next, new bunkers were constructed down the right side to increase the risk factor of hitting on the potentially more rewarding side of the fairway. Undulations were added to the right side of the fourth green to encourage players to hit from that side with their approach shots and similar alterations were made on the sixth hole. At the next, a depression in the fairway was filled in, turning it from a concave shape to a convex one that repels balls. 'It was a mess before, a mass of divot holes,' Dawson said.

On the short par-4 ninth, which is drivable in favourable conditions, a bunker 300 yards from the tee was introduced on the left to make the tee shot more challenging. The contours of the famous 11th green were softened to provide a greater range of pin positions and make the putting surface more stable in high winds. Subtle changes were made at the back of the 15th to make recovery shots from approaches going through the green more difficult, while at the 16th Dawson sought to grow rough down the left side to encourage players to flirt with the out-of-bounds to the right.

By far the most controversial move was widening by 22 inches the famous Road Hole Bunker on the 17th. This is one of golf's greatest holes, where players drive over the corner of the Old Course Hotel and then face a challenging second shot to a narrow green protected by the bunker and the road at the back. This is where Tom Watson blew his chances of victory in 1984 when his final-round approach ended up against the wall on the other side of the road.

'Let me tell you about the Road Bunker,' Dawson said, eager to mount a stern defence of the change. 'In the past, when the bunker has been rebuilt – which needs to be done every year or two because of the amount of wear it gets – the greenkeepers have gone and rebuilt it pretty much to their own eye. As a result, it is never the same twice in a row. If you look at the film of when Doug Sanders missed the famous putt that year when he was in the Road Bunker, you could see the top half of his body over the top.' This was in 1970. Three decades later, David Duval couldn't cope with the hazard because the face was so much steeper and deeper. He couldn't see over the top and took four strokes to escape.

'And if you go back to the 1890s it was as deep as it is now. All we are doing now is trying to find a design that we think is optimal. And mapping it very closely so that every future rebuild is replicated.'

Dawson added that the moves were neither that radical nor extensive. 'It was men with shovels and wheelbarrows rather than bulldozers,' he said. 'Don't worry, it's still the Old Course.'

These sentiments were echoed by Watson, five times a champion, who was given special dispensation to play his final Open at St Andrews, 40 years on from his debut victory at Carnoustie. 'The course starts and ends in the town and the beauty is that any changes haven't changed the golf course,' the 65-year-old said. 'It still plays as it was, so many years ago. Bunkers are in the same place, greens are the same, maybe a little faster but not much. You see pictures and the greens were a little shaggier. Kinda like my eyebrows. You always see people out here playing and being so excited. More than you see at any other golf courses. They are truly excited to be here at the Old Course – and it gets me excited.'

Back in 1960, when Palmer was generating all the excitement and the greens were that little bit 'shaggier', the dream of continuing his grand slam charge came up a fraction short. The charismatic American was beaten by a single stroke by Australia's Kel Nagle.

Fast forward 55 years and the focus was on another telegenic star from the States; the 21-year-old Spieth. On the tweaked but still iconic Old Course, could he move three-quarters of the way towards a slam, a feat never before accomplished in a calendar year?

Furthermore, how would defending champion and world number one Rory McIlroy respond to the American upstart's astonishing performances in the first two majors? How would Dustin Johnson cope in the wake of his bitter Chambers Bay disappointment? And could Tiger Woods rediscover the form that had brought him the St Andrews Open titles of 2000 and 2005?

These were the big questions as the golfing juggernaut, towing a burgeoning industry nurtured from Palmer's vision, magnetism and presence, thundered towards the Home of Golf.

CHAPTER 8

Open Contenders

These were changing times for men's professional golf. Not long before, the majors had produced a revolving carousel of winners. From Padraig Harrington's 2008 victory in the PGA Championship at Oakland Hills, there were different champions in the next 16 majors. There was an unpredictable churn following Tiger Woods' years of domination. No one was ready or able to assume his mantle; it was simply a case of who would be most on top of his game during any given week.

This spell generated many fine stories, but golf struggled for consistent champions to drive its narrative. This sequence ended when Rory McIlroy claimed his second major with his PGA triumph at Kiawah Island. The Northern Irishman initiated a generational shift, with Jordan Spieth fast on his heels. Players like Jason Day, Justin Rose, Dustin Johnson and Bubba Watson had also established elite credentials.

This change at the top of the game was brought into sharper focus as the golfing world readied itself for the St Andrews Open. All four major titles rested in the hands of two young players with a combined age of 47. On the morning after Spieth's Chambers Bay victory, I used my 5Live report to urge the R&A's Peter Dawson to pair them together for the first couple of rounds on the Old Course. It would be box-office golf, and a perfect opportunity for the game to showcase talent capable of transcending the sport.

McIlroy was certainly up for the fight. Having closed with a final-round 66, he left Chambers Bay in bullish mood. 'Of course I take a lot of positives out of this,' he told reporters. 'I've never hit the ball as good in a major championship for four rounds. I was really dialled in all week and confident with that. And if I can just get the putting a little bit better, and roll a few more in and get a little bit of confidence going, I see nothing but positive signs for the next few months.'

But McIlroy didn't see what was coming. None of us did.

A fortnight later, I was sitting in a commentary box at Wimbledon, as part of the 5live radio commentary team. That particular day, Monday 6 July, was my last at Wimbledon. I was heading back on the golf beat and flying to Edinburgh to cover the Scottish Open. I had taken myself away to a quiet outside court to prepare for the women's fourth-round match between Serena and Venus Williams.

As I was making notes my phone buzzed, the first of several rapid-fire texts. The messages concerned a big item of breaking news that would strongly influence how the golfing year would be remembered. The first text was from a friend, James, a former international canoeist. 'I suppose you've seen what McIlroy has done??' it read, adding: 'Bloody ridiculous, so irresponsible, why on earth would he be playing football with The Open so close??'

'No, what's happened,' I replied.

'Check his timeline.'

Having been immersed in tennis statistics, I hadn't seen the McIlroy Instagram and Twitter accounts. Moments earlier, he had posted a picture and message revealing that he had badly injured his ankle while playing football with friends at home in Belfast. He had been there for a week's holiday and was due to fly to Scotland that Monday for practice rounds at the Old Course and Gullane, where he was scheduled to play the Aberdeen Asset Management Scottish Open.

He was pictured on crutches, a forlorn figure, with his left ankle in a protective boot. The accompanying message read: 'Total rupture of left ATFL (ankle ligament) and associated joint capsule damage in a soccer kickabout.'

His chances of playing The Open were gone, along with his anterior talofibular ligament. He later revealed: 'Any time I go back home, one of the things that I regularly do with my friends is play football. That was like the fourth or fifth time in a 10-day period where I had played. I enjoy it. We all enjoy it. And it's unfortunate that it happened. It can happen walking off a tee box. It can happen falling off a kerb on the side of the street. It can happen doing anything. Unfortunately, my foot just got stuck on the turf and I went over on it.

'I thought I had broken it. As soon as I went over on it I heard, like, a snap. Obviously that was the ligament. As well as that, I tore the joint capsule, so that's why when I looked down 30 seconds later it got the size of a tennis ball, because all the fluid came out of the joint capsule.'

It took a couple of days for official confirmation that McIlroy would be the first player since Ben Hogan in 1954 not to defend his Open title. Spieth, meanwhile, had his sights set on Hogan for far more positive reasons. He was looking to emulate his fellow Texan's feat and become only the second man to win the first three majors of the year.

As soon as he had won at Chambers Bay, Spieth's attention turned towards the Old Course. 'I can get more positive. I can improve on all aspects of my game, I believe that,' he said. 'It's just about now looking to St Andrews and how are we going to best prepare for it and how we are going to fine-tune.'

The very thought of St Andrews was evocative enough to set his juices flowing. 'The Home of Golf,' Spieth smiled. 'I've played one round at St Andrews, when we were playing in the

Walker Cup at Royal Aberdeen. We went as a team to visit St Andrews first, we played there and at Kingsbarns, before going to Aberdeen. It's one of my favourite places in the world. I remember walking around the R&A clubhouse and seeing paintings of royalty playing golf, and it was dated 14-whatever, 1460 something. I'm thinking, our country was discovered in 1492 and they were playing golf here before anyone knew that the Americas existed! And that really amazed me and helped me realise how special that place is.'

Despite having played there only once, Spieth decided against making an early visit to the Old Course. His meticulous preparations, using the local knowledge of Ben Crenshaw and Carl Jackson at Augusta and his caddie Michael Greller at Chambers Bay, reaped astonishing results in the first two majors. For the third, he would have to cram, like an under-prepared student ahead of an exam, but for the best of reasons. Spieth possesses a deep sense of loyalty to the John Deere Classic, a PGA Tour event that helped him gain experience of professional golf when he was still in the amateur ranks. The event in Silvis, Illinois, also yielded his first Tour victory when he beat Zach Johnson in a playoff in 2013. 'It never really crossed my mind to drop out,' Spieth said.

'If I thought that I wasn't going to play well next week because I played here, it would be a different story. I probably wouldn't be here. I think that this is a good preparation for me, to get good feels, to get in contention and to find out what's on and what's off when I'm in contention. The only downside here, versus playing anywhere else, is the adjustment to the time zone, but as long as I get over there and I have my schedule ahead of time, I'm going to have enough sleep by the time I tee it up on Thursday. So it's not really much of an issue, to have three full days to get over a six-hour time change. It's not like you're going 13 hours to Asia.'

Not only did Spieth commit to the John Deere Classic, he

also agreed to appear at an event immediately before, which was supporting Zach Johnson's charitable foundation.

'His game on the golf course, we know, is very mature, but off it I would say he's even better,' Johnson said of Spieth. 'I think it's a product of great parenting and the fact that he's just so level-headed. But my point in saying all that is he's stuck with his commitment, which is very honourable.'

Johnson is also on the organising board of the John Deere Classic and always seems to contend for the title. He won in 2012 and hadn't finished outside the top three in the four years leading up to the 2015 tournament. Furthermore, he backed up those successes in Illinois with top tens in two of his last three Opens.

The 2007 Masters champion struggled to find fault with Spieth's St Andrews strategy. 'The beauty of it is he's won the first two majors, but it seems like every other tournament he's played and he hasn't won, he's been right in contention,' Johnson said. 'He's just got it going, and it's fun to watch.'

There was plenty of fun to be had playing as well for the 39-year-old Johnson. Not just at the John Deere event, but at St Andrews as well. 'I love what that tournament demands,' he said. 'I love the fact that it's a major. I love the fact that it's on links-style golf courses, and courses that we just don't have over here. Some of the best courses I think I've ever played are in that tournament, and that's comforting. When I leave there, I also know what I need to work on.

'I just thoroughly enjoy it. I don't know if that's why I've had some minor success there or not. I can't answer that. But I just embrace the fact that this is what I'm going to do and this is how I'm going to do it, and there's no telling what can happen.'

Johnson, unlike his namesake Dustin, is one of the game's shorter hitters but possesses a ruthlessly efficient game around the greens. It was again evident as he posted his usual top-three finish in the event immediately before The Open. He missed out on the John Deere playoff by a single shot after rounds of 66, 68, 66 and 65. The two men to beat him were Tom Gillis and Spieth, who shot a blistering third-round 61 en route to a 20-under-par total. Spieth, who had been four strokes behind with six holes to play, then won at the second extra hole to claim his fourth title of an astonishing year. It had, indeed, been the perfect tune-up for The Open.

'I came here for a reason, and we accomplished that reason and certainly have some momentum going into next week,' Spieth said. 'I've got plenty in the tank.'

Certainly, memories of his Masters and US Open successes would be a source of confidence heading to golf's most iconic major venue. Playing at St Andrews was an enticing prospect. 'I think it's just mind-boggling that it can hold the test of time and still host a major championship, I mean, centuries and centuries after it was built,' Spieth enthused. 'And with just minor tweaks here and there. So I'm excited to get there. It's yielded very low scores. That's why I think this is advantageous, to feel like you're making a lot of birdies. I feel like you will need to make a lot of birdies.'

In claiming third place in Illinois, Johnson had made his share of birdies as well. 'I feel great about my game. I've been feeling good about my game for months,' he said. 'I would have probably felt good about next week regardless, because I know the state of my game. I know I'm controlling my trajectory, I'm controlling my spin. I feel good about things.'

That Sunday night, both Johnson and Spieth boarded a charter plane laid on by the tournament organisers to ferry Open participants to Scotland. The pair did so in the best of spirits. For one of them in particular, the return journey would prove even more pleasurable.

In the absence of McIlroy, Spieth was inevitably the main focus as Open week began. Indeed, he would have been even if the Northern Irishman had been there to defend his trophy. But other players were also commanding a degree of attention. Rickie Fowler had recovered brilliantly from his US Open disappointment to snatch the Scottish Open title at Gullane. His game looked well-suited for a rain-softened St Andrews. The same could be said of Jason Day. The Australian looked rejuvenated after the health scares of Chambers Bay. 'I feel good,' he insisted. 'I'm not thinking about falling over on my face again. I'm not worrying about it and I feel healthy – I'm good to go.'

Louis Oosthuizen was another name being mentioned. The South African's stirring run at the US Open proved that he had put years of injury misery behind him. He was back in the kind of form that had brought him his only major title, the 2010 Open, which had been staged at the Old Course. Oosthuizen, referring to his preparations and his new-found fitness, said: 'I could actually do a bit more work on the putting green and out on the range, which you need to, to be on top of your game.

'I'll feel very confident going into the week, and I just need to hit the shots I want to off the tee so I put myself in good positions. But there are a lot of great guys out there who I know are going to play well around this golf course.'

Oosthuizen was once again drawn with Woods and wanted to avoid a repeat of the US Open, when they had played together in the first round and performed horribly. 'I hope we have a better first round,' the South African laughed. 'Hopefully, we can pull each other in the right direction this time. Yeah, I always enjoy playing with him, so it should be fun. He's won twice around here. I want to see the way he plays this golf course. It's going to be good. Hopefully we make a few more birdies in the first round than we did at Chambers!'

Woods, too, was hoping the magic of St Andrews might inspire a return to his best golf. After missing the cut so badly in the previous major, he played the Greenbrier Classic and there were signs of a significant improvement. He opened with rounds of 66 and 69, although he faded to a 71 on the Saturday. His closing 67 left Woods at seven under par, sharing 32nd place. In days gone by, that would have been considered a sub-standard return but, given the state of his game, it was treated as cause for great optimism.

'I ended up playing well at Greenbrier and hit the ball the best I've hit it in probably two years on the Sunday,' Woods said. 'I've hit the ball just as well in my practice rounds.

'I'm hitting much, much more solid. I'm controlling my flights. Coming in here, being able to shape the golf ball not only both ways but also change my trajectories as well, and being very comfortable changing my trajectories. That's something that I feel you have to do here on this golf course. You have to be able to manoeuvre the golf ball, because there's a big difference between hitting the ball low with a draw and hitting the ball low with a cut. Sometimes it can be 30 to 50 yards' difference in how the ball reacts on the ground, and to be able to understand that and to be able to control that, I think that's very important.'

These days, the spin Woods imparts in his press conferences is more effective than the spin he puts on his golf ball. Often in recent years his pre-tournament briefings have convinced his audience that he could contend, even when all logic suggested otherwise. Woods is a persuasive advocate of his own golfing prowess. The act, though, was wearing a little thin by the summer of 2015. Brandel Chamblee, one of the US Golf Channel's leading analysts, was not convinced by his optimism. 'He is by far the worst on tour at scrambling this year,' the former PGA Tour pro told me. 'He's still got a bit of a two-way miss going. His irons are a bit better but the Greenbrier was a pretty easy golf course and, compared with The Open Championship, it was a field of far lesser strength. So, Tiger Woods? No. He does not have a chance of winning at the Old Course, by a long shot.'

When Woods had won there, in 2000 and 2005, he was among the longest hitters in the game. Oosthuizen was no slouch off the tee when he won in 2010, and the 1995 Open was claimed by John Daly who, at the time, hit the ball further than anyone else. Since the advent of the modern golf ball, St Andrews Opens were the domain of the big hitters. McIlroy's game is perfect for the Old Course, especially one softened by early summer downpours. He would have been a justified short-odds favourite, but he was at home with his injured ankle, wondering whether he would be able to return to the game in time to defend his PGA title the following month.

A pressing question for those playing at St Andrews concerned the likely impact of changes made to the course. Might the new bunkers and reshaped greens lessen the impact of length from the tee, and open up the championship to the medium and shorter players? This might play into the hands of someone like Johnson or, of course, his great friend Spieth. Certainly the Masters and US Open winner possessed the confidence and composure to challenge.

But in truth, there was no shortage of contenders. It looked like a wide-open Open. Even though one man had dominated the year's biggest tournaments, the destiny of the Claret Jug, that most prized of trophies, was far from certain.

And neither was the weather.

CHAPTER 9

The Five-Day Major

Eight days of major championship golf had been completed in 2015 without interruption. The weather was so kind at Augusta and Chambers Bay that there was no great advantage for either side of the draw. At St Andrews, though – as at all Open venues – there was a real fear that one half of the field might be blown out of the championship before it had even reached halfway.

According to the forecast, it seemed that those starting on Thursday afternoon would have the worst of the weather, with freshening winds predicted. Conditions were then expected to worsen the following morning, coinciding with their second rounds.

This was bad news for the likes of Adam Scott, Phil Mickelson and Zach Johnson. By contrast, Jordan Spieth and Dustin Johnson appeared to have been blessed with a kinder draw. Forecasting the weather on the British coastline, though, is a hazardous business.

Thursday, 16 July 2015
Conditions early on Thursday could hardly have been better. Ivor Robson, the silver-haired starter, was on duty at an Open for the final time. His high-pitched Scottish accent had been a fixture at the event for 41 years. By the end of the 144th

Open, it was calculated that he had announced no fewer than 18,995 players onto the first tee. Famously, Robson never left his position beneath the umbrella shielding his start sheet. On this occasion, the day would run from 6.32 a.m. until 4.13 p.m. when Rikard Karlberg was due to strike the final tee shot. The starter was as famous for his bladder control as his announcing skills.

The first name Robson called on Thursday, 16 July 2015, was Rod Pampling. The experienced Australian, who had led after the first round of the 1999 championship at Carnoustie, split the fairway as a gentle breeze swept across the famous old links. In truth, the first at St Andrews is the least intimidating drive in competitive golf. The fairway is over 100 yards wide and there are no bunkers. The only concern is hitting it too far and into the Swilcan Burn, which runs immediately in front of the green, more than 350 yards away. But with the course so verdant and soft, there was little run so that wasn't an issue.

The wind direction helped players on the outward half and several of the early starters were quickly into their stride. Irish amateur Paul Dunne was in the second group out. He was lucky to be there at all. He had nearly missed his tee time in qualifying at Woburn, where a pair of 67s earned him a place in the 156-man field. Dunne birdied the first two holes to place his name on the famous yellow scoreboards overlooking the first and 18th fairways. Few, least of all Dunne, expected it to remain there for long.

Dunne's start, however, was overshadowed by the blistering form of David Lingmerth. The diminutive Swede, who beat Justin Rose in a playoff for the Memorial title earlier in the summer, birdied six of the first seven holes. His only par came at the par-5 fifth, which statistically offered the best chance of gaining a shot. At six under he was two clear of Dunne, who went to the turn in an impressive 32, and the promising American Robert Streb, who birdied four of his first six holes.

'I got two really long ones to go in on number two and four. They were kind of bonuses, but I kept on giving myself opportunities,' Lingmerth recalled. 'I tried not to think too much. If you put your ball in play off the tee, you get short irons and you can get yourself some really good opportunities.'

That was exactly the mindset Spieth was trying to adopt for his tee off at 9.33 a.m. He was paired with Japan's Hideki Matsuyama and the man he edged out at Chambers Bay, Dustin Johnson. The 30-year-old from South Carolina was playing his first competitive round following his US Open disappointment.

The arrival of Spieth on the first tee brought to mind the legendary figure of Ben Hogan. Spieth is an altogether more approachable and engaging character than his fellow Texan who triumphed in 1953, but there were strong parallels.

Hogan went to Carnoustie that year in search of the victory that would give him a clean sweep of available majors. Those who entered The Open could not play the PGA because they overlapped. So Hogan was seeking to complete a unique hat-trick after winning the Masters and US Open in his one and only tilt at the British-based major. Legendary journalist Pat Ward Thomas wrote in the *Guardian*: 'He dresses as modestly as he talks and only the piercing, deep-set eyes reveal the force of character behind them. Imagine him as he scrutinises a long, difficult stroke, with arms quietly folded, an inscrutable quarter-smile on his lips, for all the world like a gambler watching the wheel spin. And then the cigarette is tossed away, the club taken with abrupt decision, the glorious swing flashes and a long iron pierces the wind like an arrow. That was Hogan. We shall never see his like again.'

Ward Thomas also noted the pressure that Hogan must have been feeling ahead of his victory at Carnoustie. 'From the moment he arrived in Britain, Hogan was under considerable strain. Not since [Bobby] Jones had one man been made such an overwhelming favourite, and although Hogan's confidence, which incidentally was never expressed, in his ability must be immense, he was facing a tremendous test of his powers. The knowledge that the whole golfing world was expecting him to win must have been disturbing even to his cool brain.'

Ward Thomas could have been writing about Spieth in 2015. But the 21-year-old had already charmed the British media in a way that was beyond the more taciturn Hogan. On the eve of the event, Spieth said: 'I don't think there's anything more special than playing an Open Championship at the Home of Golf. I have fond memories from playing here a few years back, vivid memories, one of those courses you play where you don't really forget much. There's only a couple of those maybe in the world. I think here and Augusta National are my two favourite places in the world.'

Just as Spieth was arriving on the first tee, Lingmerth was rolling in a birdie from 15 feet to go to the turn in a remarkable seven-under-par 29, so the man who had dominated the first two majors knew a fast start was required.

I was standing down the right of that opening hole, in front of the vast grandstand and on 'Grannie Clark's Wynd', the road that crosses the fairway. Commentating for BBC 5Live, I was peering back at the tee alongside former PGA Tour professional Andrew Magee, who vividly remembered Spieth as a junior at Brookhaven Country Club in Dallas.

> IC: Wearing a white cap, white trousers and a grey sweater, this young man in this most historic of towns, who come Sunday night might just have golfing history in his hands, comes and addresses his first shot of the 144th Open Championship beneath grey skies here on the Old Course at St Andrews. He's got one of those rescue clubs in his hands, half iron, half wood, and

he fires down this broad, green, verdant fairway, his opening tee shot and Jordan Spieth is underway with the minimum of fuss.

After the tee shots of Matsuyama and Johnson, we set off in pursuit. His second shot came to rest five or six feet from the hole, giving him a birdie chance at the very first opportunity. Matsuyama and Johnson followed in kind. After the short walk to the green, Spieth settled over his first putt of the championship.

IC: And it would be in keeping with the kind of guy that he is, were he to start his Open quest, having won the Masters and the US Open, with a birdie. He's just seen Dustin Johnson miss from around eight feet, just shaving the left edge of the hole, the big American has tapped in for his par. But this for a birdie to start for Jordan Spieth from six or seven feet. A couple of glances at the hole, just slightly widens his stance, putter head behind the ball, it comes back, sends the ball in motion . . . and in! Straight in! Don't you just know it, Jordan Spieth off and running at the very first opportunity, a birdie at the first.

Spieth was already the centre of attention – and there he remained. He went to the turn in a superb five-under-par 31, with further birdies at the second, fifth, sixth and seventh holes. Conditions were favourable but this was, nonetheless, a stunning start given all the hype that had accompanied him from the moment he had stepped off his charter flight from Illinois on the Monday morning.

Even more impressive was the start of playing partner Johnson, who had insisted there would be no hangover from Chambers Bay. 'You know, I played really well that week,'

Johnson reasoned. 'I was happy with the way I played and the way I handled myself coming down the last few holes. I thought I hit the shots that I was supposed to hit. You know, I did everything I was supposed to. It wasn't too difficult to get over it. Obviously I was a little disappointed I didn't get the job done . . . '

Johnson had warmed up for The Open with practice rounds on the Irish links of Portmarnock and Royal Dublin. He was swiftly in the groove, matching Spieth's outward nine of 31 thanks to an eagle at the fifth – where he hit a 195-yard 7-iron approach to 10 feet – along with birdies at the second, third and ninth holes. His birdie at the 10th took him to six under. As Spieth observed: 'It's hard to argue with somebody who's splitting bunkers at about 380 yards and just two-putting for birdie on five or six of the holes when there's only two par 5s. I don't have that in the bag.' Johnson's prodigious hitting enabled him to counter the effects of a strengthening breeze, which began to hamper the players on the inward nine. He picked up another birdie at the par-5 14th and kept a clean card for a brilliant 65. It was some response to Chambers Bay, and earned him yet another first-round lead at a major.

'On the way back in, it played pretty difficult,' Johnson said in his modest, somewhat ponderous drawl. 'I thought the only time I was really out of position was on 16 and 17. I made probably a 10-footer on 16 for par, and then a 15-footer on 17 for par. It's kind of hard to beat St Andrews for an Open Championship. I really like the golf course. I think it sets up well for me. You've got to drive it well. You've got to miss the bunkers.

'But then, coming into the greens, you've really got to be precise with where you're landing the ball and what side of the hole you want to land it on. And then especially when it gets windy, your short game has got to be very good, or your lag putting, because you're going to have a lot of long putts up and over hills. I think it challenges everything.'

Although he birdied the difficult par-3 11th, Spieth

struggled in comparison. He bogeyed the 13th and dropped another shot at the notorious Road Hole 17th. He failed to get up and down from Peter Dawson's remodelled bunker that so maliciously guards the green by sucking in errant approach shots. However, at the last, in golf's most historic setting, he responded in typical fashion and showed his qualities. Spieth's drive wasn't the best, pulled way left. He would have been in trouble on any other hole – indeed, it was so far left that he could not be sure of the yardage because he was bereft of reference points. So Spieth paced out the entire length of the shot; 92 yards. He pitched to 15 feet and made no mistake in completing a round of 67. 'It was certainly nice to finish that way,' he said. 'I'm very pleased with the start. I saw a 65 in our group, and if D.J. keeps driving it the way he is, then I'm going to have to play my best golf to have a chance.'

Nevertheless it was a fine start, laying to rest the fears that he would be under-prepared for the links test. To put his round into context, the first time Jack Nicklaus played an Open at St Andrews he shot 76; Tom Watson, perhaps the greatest links golfer of all time, 73; and Tiger Woods made his Old Course debut with a 74.

Woods also enjoyed the best of the conditions, but his form was of the same wretched brand that blighted his game at Chambers Bay. From the moment he limply deposited his second shot into the burn on the first, he looked a forlorn figure. While the rest of the field were taking advantage of the favourable breeze on the outward half, he laboured to the turn in a miserable 40 strokes. Four over par, 11 shots worse than Lingmerth. Woods dropped another stroke on the 10th and his lone birdie came at the 14th. He finished with a 76 and was halfway to a second successive missed cut in a major. For much of his round he looked resigned, but insisted he was determined to fight his way back. 'Motivation is never a problem with me,' he said.

But Woods was more than aware how far his game had slipped. He only needed to look across at his playing partners, Jason Day (66) and Louis Oosthuizen (67). With Johnson and Spieth also to the fore, they gave the leaderboard a similar look to those that had overlooked the greens of Chambers Bay. Day was a much healthier-looking figure this time, though, as he went bogey-free, picking up three birdies on the way out and three more heading back towards the old, grey town. 'I was playing with Tiger and Louis, the last two winners here of The Open Championship,' the Australian noted. 'I knew there were going to be a lot of eyes on me. I just wanted to make sure I played solid.'

Day found the state of Woods' game distressing. 'He was my idol growing up,' he said. 'He's why I'm a professional and why I chased the dream of becoming a professional. It's tough. The good thing about it is I saw him struggle a little bit before and he came back, so I know that he can get back out of this. It's just depending on how much he wants it. It's unfortunate to see him struggle like this . . . it's just tough to see your idol struggle.'

Oosthuizen dropped only one shot, at the difficult 13th, and finished with a rousing birdie to move to five under. It placed the 2010 champion firmly in the pack chasing Johnson.

The leader's namesake, Zach, was the pick of the afternoon starters. Establishing his credentials to land a first Open title, he rode the freshening winds after starting just after 1 p.m. He flew through the front nine in 31 and moved to six under par with a birdie at the 10th. Johnson putted superbly and manoeuvred his ball beautifully on an ever-tougher back nine. His only dropped shot came at the 17th, where he hit a poor drive and needed a 3-wood for his second. During practice, with the wind in a different direction, he had been hitting 7-iron approaches. Although he found the green, Johnson's only option was to chip his third. It got to 12 feet, from where he missed his putt. The man from Iowa City immediately atoned with a birdie for a brilliant 66. It was arguably the round of the day and it came from someone that few had considered as a genuine challenger.

'I've embraced the fact that you don't have to be perfect,' he explained. 'You've just got to try to hit that ball solid. Solid shots usually pan out. They may not be phenomenal, but hit solid shots. I'm just getting more and more experienced.'

It came as a surprise to hear Johnson enthusing so readily about the Championship. He is regarded as an archetypal PGA Tour pro, only seen in Europe at The Open or on Ryder Cup duty. Others, like Dustin Johnson, pitch up at events like the Alfred Dunhill Links, but Zach is regarded as a home-bird. Nevertheless, it was clear he was revelling in the challenges presented by golf at the British seaside.

'This is my favourite tournament consistently, year in, year out,' he stated. 'If I'm going to rank the venues, I'm not going to put this one number one. It's not that I don't like it, it's just the ones ahead of it I phenomenally love. Like Muirfield, Turnberry, Birkdale and Lytham; those stand out to me. I guess you could even say Carnoustie, to a degree. Gosh, they're all so good. I just love this kind of golf.'

Johnson's 66 put him alongside Streb, Day, the 1999 champion Paul Lawrie, South Africa's Retief Goosen and the Englishman Danny Willett. Like Johnson, Willett played in the afternoon, when the wind strengthened and temperatures plummeted. It was brilliant golf. The leading group, with Dustin Johnson ahead by a single stroke, reflected the range of the game. Day and Dustin Johnson were at the sport's vanguard; Streb and Willett were straining to break into the upper echelons; Lawrie, Goosen and Zach Johnson were experienced campaigners, major winners keen to reinforce the adage that class is permanent.

Just behind them on five under par was Spieth, along with Oosthuizen and the young American amateur Jordan

Niebrugge, who had benefitted from a painstaking preparation: 'I arrived last Friday and played four or five times so I'm used to the track. And my caddie works here.'

At the opposite end of the age scale, veteran Tom Watson was unable to cheer his huge army of fans other than by offering trademark smiles and waves. Playing his final Open, the 65-year-old's golf was poor in a 76. 'I knew I had to hit some quality shots, and I didn't,' he admitted. 'That was the disappointment. I didn't follow up some of the good shots I hit in the middle of the round and finish the deal. I failed.'

Watson did, though, beat another veteran and former St Andrews champion, Sir Nick Faldo. The 1990 winner wasn't sure whether this would be his last Open, but it would be his final appearance on the Old Course. He put together a miserable 83 that ensured he wouldn't be making the cut. It was also an unlikely prospect for Watson, who admitted he would need 'an extraordinary round' the following day to make it a weekend farewell. He also knew the round would have to be played in very hostile weather.

−7 Dustin Johnson

−6 Streb, Goosen, Lawrie, Day, Zach Johnson, Willett

−5 Niebrugge (a), Kevin Na, Charl Schwartzel,
   Spieth, Oosthuizen

−4 Greg Owen, Matt Jones, Luke Donald, David
   Howell, Marc Warren

Friday, 17 July 2015

When I peered out of my hotel window at 6 a.m. on Friday, it was dark and raining. The 5Live team were staying around seven miles inland from St Andrews. Twenty minutes later I made my way to the car and was utterly drenched during a 20-metre scamper. It was some of the heaviest rain I have ever encountered, reminiscent of the downpours that nearly put paid to the Ryder Cups at Valderrama (1997) and Celtic Manor (2010). Driving into town, I had my headlights on full beam and the windscreen wipers on maximum speed. They were still struggling to cope.

Yet, just down the road, the second round was starting on time. Jaco Van Zyl, Marcel Siem and former champion Mark Calcavecchia were the poor souls who teed off at 6.32 a.m. They lasted a mere 14 minutes. The sounding of the horn was inevitable as the rain pounded down and vast puddles accumulated on the first and 18th fairways. The road running to the rear of the famous R&A clubhouse flooded, and sandbags were hastily put in place to protect the media tent, which sat on the museum car park across the road.

More than 20mm of rain fell that morning, more than half of it in a 30-minute spell. As the rain finally eased, R&A Chief Executive Peter Dawson told the BBC: 'It's a very sandy golf course and, once it starts to drain, you'll find it'll dry out very quickly . . . if any course can take this, it's the Old Course at St Andrews.'

Then came the announcement that play would resume at 10 a.m., with winds forecast to freshen up to 35 miles per hour. The players braced themselves. 'It's definitely going to be a brutal day,' Jordan Spieth observed. 'I think it will be a true Scottish day.'

Ironically, the severity of the weather played into the hands of those who feared having the worst of things. The morning starters, who had toiled away in Thursday's afternoon winds, were left with an even softer golf course to counter-balance the breezy conditions.

Zach Johnson and Willett were best-placed to capitalise. So was home hope Marc Warren. The Scot surged to seven under par with three birdies in his first seven holes. Even he had been surprised by the morning weather. 'I looked at an app on my phone, I think it was between 7 and 9 a.m., and it was 95 per cent-plus chance of rain,' he said. 'So I thought we were going to get wet but, to be honest, I didn't really think it was going to stop play. Just shows you how much rain must have been here already. The water table is obviously very high. It is unusual for St Andrews to be stopped because of rain.'

Willett was immaculate in covering the first 10 holes in four under and topped the leaderboard. There were slip-ups at the 15th and the brutish 17th but a birdie at the last gave the Yorkshireman a highly creditable 69 to go with his opening 66. He was nine under par, two ahead of Warren. 'I just had a text message off my mum, saying "really well done, you've made the cut",' Willett laughed. He had not just made it to the weekend, he was leading a major for the first time.

'It's a childhood dream and, looking up there, it's still a little bit surreal but something I'm going to have to get used to, otherwise no point in being up there . . . hopefully we can still be up there in two days' time.'

That trust in the tournament schedule would prove to be rather optimistic.

Zach Johnson was relatively quiet on Friday. It was a plodding round that included a couple of outward birdies and a struggle on the way home. There were three bogeys sandwiching a birdie on the 13th and another at the last ensured a second under-par circuit of the Old Course. The American's 71 left him at seven under par, still handily placed. He felt that he played just as well as in the opening round. 'I just didn't score,' he said, bemoaning two three-putts. He backed the organisers, though. 'Clearly they made the right decision,' Johnson said. 'The course was unplayable, especially talking to some of the guys that had teed off or even hit a few shots. The R&A did what they needed to do and what they were supposed to do, which was tremendous. A tip of the cap to the maintenance crew because, essentially, it was a lake on one and 18.'

Johnson liked his chances and did not see any reason why he couldn't end up lifting the Claret Jug.

'No, I don't,' he said. 'It's going to be a lot of great golf to get to that point, but if you'd have asked me that question on Wednesday I'd have said the same thing. You just never know what's going to come about with the conditions and the factors presented, but I feel mentally I'm in a place that I can combat essentially whatever comes my way.'

By mid-afternoon, the winds had freshened. Their growing influence was reflected in an incident on the 17th where Australian Steven Bowditch called a penalty on himself. He addressed a short par putt and stepped away, throwing his putter to the ground in despair. Slow motion television pictures showed no movement but the player was sure his ball had changed position. The resulting penalty cost him a bogey – or so he thought, until a rules official reminded him that a recent change in the laws of the game meant that, since he was deemed not to have touched the ball and therefore not been responsible, there was no penalty. Bowditch duly celebrated with a birdie at the last.

My commentating brief that Friday was to follow British golf's biggest hope, Justin Rose. The Englishman shot a one-under-par 71 in the first round and was then hampered in his efforts to play catch-up by a severe dose of hay-fever. Rose sneezed his way through a round that threatened to take off with three early birdies. He went to the turn in 33 but at the 11th he miscued and pushed his tee shot to the par 3. It finished nearer the seventh flag on the double green and he three-putted. Another bogey followed at the next but he responded with great character to record a hat-trick of birdies, taking him to five under.

Rose was playing with Faldo, who stole the show after almost withdrawing from the championship. Faldo had cut his finger in a freak accident while putting on a jumper earlier in the week. He caught it on the antlers of a mounted deer's head. After his dreadful opening 83, the cut had reopened, prompting an early-morning hospital visit. Faldo felt he should withdraw. His children took a different view. 'I went back to the hospital and had it glued again and I didn't know what I wanted to do, and then the kids looked at me and said: "Dad, what are we doing?" And when your kids say you're going, you're going.'

Without their intervention, he would have fallen short of his week's objective. The three-time Open Champion wanted to don the famous yellow sweater he had worn when winning the first of his titles at Muirfield in 1987 and stand on the iconic Swilcan Bridge to acknowledge the crowds. He had not looked like a champion on the first day and was ready to throw away the opportunity. However, he followed the advice of his offspring and duly obliged with some magical golf.

The portents were not good for Britain's greatest player of the modern era when he bogeyed the second. He plodded away while playing partners Rose and Rickie Fowler tried to battle their way into contention. Eventually, Faldo made a birdie at the ninth. It had taken 27 holes to collect his first of the championship and another followed at the 28th. Now he was hell bent on matching, or even beating par. He grinded like he used to grind. Measuring his putts, feeling his swings, nothing was going to rush him. It was almost as though he were back in contention for the title.

He collected par after par after par. Then, at the 17th, the celebrated and notorious Road Hole, he came up just short of the green in two. Faldo sized up the putt from down the step at the front, then struck a glorious blow. The ball tracked to the hole and disappeared for one of only half a dozen birdies there in the entire second round. He thrust his arms out wide, looked to the sky and broke into as broad a smile as has ever been seen on the face of Nick Faldo. It was a magical moment. 'Well, 17 made it for me, didn't it,' he said. 'That was special.'

He reached into his bag and pulled out the yellow cashmere he had worn 28 years earlier. He stood with his son Matthew, who was caddying for him, on the Swilcan Bridge to accept the applause of the crowds. Rose and Fowler joined in and it was an appropriately emotional moment for a great champion and all who witnessed it. 'I was just trying to say thank you, St Andrews,' Faldo said. 'That's why I looked at the gods, the St Andrews golfing gods, at 17. I thought, thank you very much for that. That was one of my great moments, making a three there and walking the walk. That won't get any better.'

Faldo, who spends most of his time commentating on television, finished with a par and a remarkable 71 to finish at 10 over. 'I play two tournaments a year,' he explained. 'I can't fall out of a TV tower and really be a golfer. So that's pretty darned good. That might be it. I've just shot 71 and done all that, I think that might be my last walk.'

It was the first of two extraordinary farewells on Friday, with the second proving a more intimate occasion.

As Faldo was finishing, Spieth and Dustin Johnson were setting out, knowing that there would not be sufficient light for them to finish. The three-and-a-quarter hours lost to rain ensured that they would need to return first thing on Saturday.

Spieth made a poor start. There were no early birdies, then a sloppy bogey at the par-5 fifth. It was a wake-up call. He responded with birdies in three of the next four holes and, despite a bogey four at the par-3 eighth, his name was in the mix – provided, of course, that Dustin Johnson didn't build an unassailable lead. That looked to be on the cards when the big-hitting American birdied three of the first seven holes to move to 10 under. He went further clear with a birdie at the 10th. By this time, though, it was heading towards late evening. He bogeyed the next, as did Spieth.

On the 18th, the 22-year-old Irish amateur Paul Dunne made up for a missed short putt two holes earlier with a fine

10-footer for birdie and his second 69. Oosthuizen slotted home a birdie on the seventh to join him on six under while Day also birdied to go one lower. Woods was still toiling, though, with bogeys at the fourth and sixth leaving him six over par.

Darkness was closing in. The R&A gave the players the choice whether or not to play on. With no formal end, it meant that Tom Watson, on the 17th, could continue and would not need to return in the morning to end his Open career in a state of anti-climax.

Day, Oosthuizen and Woods called it quits on the 12th green while Johnson, Spieth and Matsuyama ran out of light two holes further on. Johnson retained the lead at 10 under par. Spieth was five back.

All over the course, groups of players headed for the clubhouse – apart from one. Sportingly, Ernie Els and Brandt Snedeker agreed to continue, to allow Watson to finish. They drove up the last before the horn sounded, allowing them to finish the hole.

This wasn't the scenario Watson would have imagined, heading into his final Open. The five-time champion, who came so close to a sixth title when, aged 59, he was runner-up at Turnberry in 2009, would have envisaged the sort of send-off Jack Nicklaus received in 2005. Then, bright sunshine beamed down on large crowds of spectators who were sent into a state of tumult as the great champion made a farewell birdie. This time it was dark and the grandstands largely deserted.

But there were still plenty of people packed on the road-side adjacent to the 18th fairway. The clubhouse lights shone brightly in the gloaming and the building emptied as R&A members spilled onto the first tee to greet the victor of 1975, 1977, 1980, 1982 and 1983. It was a grand send-off. Watson marched to the Swilcan Bridge, where Faldo had stood earlier. He insisted on his partners joining him for the first photo. Then there was one with his caddie, his son Michael, before finally and briefly, he stood alone, with the flashbulbs illuminating the night sky.

It didn't matter that he finished with a fifth consecutive bogey for an 80 that left him in next-to-last position. It was a fittingly intimate, emotional goodbye to a great champion. 'Well, was that ugly, that finish, I didn't want to go out with a shank. I just didn't want to do that,' Watson smiled. 'On the tee, I told my son: "Michael, there should be no tears, this should be all joy. There have been lots of wonderful memories we've shared here. You and I have shared some and had so many others, so let's go up and go out and enjoy the walk up the last hole."

'I was walking up, about halfway up, just across the road, and I'm looking all the way up the right side, and then to the back, and the road is all jammed with people and I thought of the story about Bobby Jones. When Bobby Jones had won the grand slam, he came back and played a friendly here at the Old Course in St Andrews. I'm not putting myself in the same shoes, but walking up that 18th hole, as the legend goes, Bobby Jones was engulfed by thousands of people who had come out and heard that he was on the golf course, and they watched him finish. And when I was going up there, just across the road, I think I had an inkling of what Bobby Jones probably felt like when he walked up the 18th hole.'

Watson's emotional exit set the seal on a remarkable day, one that had begun with rains of biblical proportions and ended in the worship of one of the most enduring and engaging champions golf has known. Watson's attention turned towards a night of celebration. It was time to party and remember. For the likes of Spieth and Dustin Johnson, though, there was an unfinished second round and an early alarm call to consider.

Saturday, 18 July 2015

Friday's heavy morning rains were replaced on Saturday by bracing winds, gusting at 40 miles per hour. With feelings of trepidation and scepticism, the players set out for the 7 a.m. resumption. These were the same players who had supposedly been favoured by the draw. It didn't seem that way anymore.

Dustin Johnson was faced with a tricky third shot on the par-5 14th. He chose to chip up the steep slope and didn't hit it quite hard enough. He then hesitated before marking his ball. A gust of wind moved the ball a few inches and it then picked up enough momentum to roll off the green, causing playing partner Spieth to jump out of the way. Three putts later and Johnson was entering a bogey on his card.

Another American, Brooks Koepka, refused to play when his ball wouldn't stay still on the 11th green as volleys of wind whistled off the Eden Estuary. The R&A knew the putting surface was going to be on the edge of being playable. Officials said they spent an hour on that green, the most exposed on the course, making sure balls weren't moving, but Koepka's ball simply wouldn't stay still. He took nearly half an hour to hit one putt, marking his ball and protesting with a referee. Finally, he refused to continue when his ball moved a couple of inches on three occasions. A few holes ahead, Oosthuizen putted up to three feet on the 13th. The wind snatched at it and, as the South African laughed at the absurdity, moved it to eight feet away.

At this point, play was suspended, Spieth telling officials that play should never have resumed. With the greens mown to modern championship speeds, there is always the danger that winds will render a venue unplayable. Opens staged on the British coastline are particularly susceptible; this was the third consecutive St Andrews Championship affected in this way. It happened in 2010 and during the Women's British Open in 2013. There are many traditionalists who feel the desire for fast-paced greens is misplaced on such courses.

It was clear this was going to be a long interruption. There was no let-up in the wind speeds forecast, and as it continued to blow the course dried out, firmed up and the greens grew slicker. A restart wasn't possible until 6 p.m., by which time it had been decided that the Championship would have to spill over into a fifth day for the first time since Seve Ballesteros won in 1988.

It took nearly 39 hours to complete a second round that had started at 6.32 a.m. on Friday. Johnson put his drive onto the fringe of the 18th green that Saturday night and two-putted from a vast distance for a birdie that gave him a 69 and meant he was the halfway leader at 10 under par, one ahead of Willett, who had the whole of Saturday to rest and practise. It was the fourth time in his last six rounds at majors that Johnson had at least a share of the lead.

Scotland's Paul Lawrie played bogey-free over the final 14 holes for a 70 and was two shots behind. Oosthuizen (70) and Day (71) joined a large group at seven under, which included Adam Scott and Zach Johnson. Spieth completed a 72 that contained five three-putts and he was five behind. 'I believe I'm still in contention. I still believe I can win this tournament,' Spieth said.

Woods never had a realistic hope of making the cut. He resumed with three straight bogeys and shot 75 to finish at seven over par, his highest 36-hole total in The Open. It came a month after his highest halfway score ever (156) to miss the cut in the US Open. He appeared broken, his golfing year in tatters; another setback in a career that seemed to be rapidly nearing an ignominious end.

−10 Dustin Johnson

−9 Willett

−8 Lawrie

−7 Warren, Zach Johnson, Scott, Streb, Day, Oosthuizen

−6 Dunne (a), Goosen, Donald, Matsuyama

−5 Bowditch, Anirban Lahiri, Geoff Ogilvy, Rose,
   Schwartzel, García, Spieth

Sunday, 19 July 2015

It was a drizzly Sunday morning, there was a bit of breeze
but thankfully the weather was no longer a significant factor.
Indeed, for the later starters the winds were forecast to drop to
negligible levels. Players on level par or better made it to the
final two rounds. Joining Woods in taking an early exit were
1995 champion John Daly, the in-form Shane Lowry, Bubba
Watson, Ian Poulter and Snedeker.

The burly figure of Marc Leishman was glad to make it on
two counts. Firstly, he had scraped through with one stroke to
spare. Secondly, and much more significantly, he had thought
earlier in the year that his days as a touring professional golfer
might be over. Leishman had nearly lost his wife, Audrey, as
she fell seriously ill with toxic shock syndrome, a rare but life-
threatening bacterial infection that led to her being put into
an induced coma. The 31-year-old father-of-two pulled out of
the Masters and feared the worst until she pulled through. 'It
has definitely changed my whole perspective on life,' he said. 'I
feel like I've always had a pretty good outlook, but now it takes
a lot more to worry me. I don't get annoyed about little things
that I can't really help. When you hit a bad shot there's no real
point getting frustrated about it because you tried to hit a good
shot. You didn't. Move on. I feel like even if I do have a bad
day I can still go home and give her a hug and cuddle my boys.

'She's a pretty strong girl. When she woke up from the
coma, she couldn't lift her phone. That's how bad she was. So
you go from lifting weights at the gym to you can't pick up
your phone to send a text message. That hits home, that's how
she went from so strong to basically rock bottom but now she's
recovering really well.'

Leishman admitted that at one stage he had needed to contemplate life without her: 'It was a huge possibility that I wasn't going to be playing golf any more. Travelling with a one-year-old and a three-year-old by yourself wasn't going to happen. I wouldn't do that to the boys. At the time it was just, righto, you're going to have to give it away and stay home with the boys and be a dad, and that was the most important thing.'

Leishman teed off among the back-markers and 11 shots off the lead. He proceeded to compile a remarkable round. He went to the turn in 32 and maintained a blemish-free card. By the 16th he was eight under for his round and he carved out an excellent chance on the hole known as 'Corner O' the Dyke.' Not for the first time during the year, discussion turned towards the prospect of a first major round of 62. Two more birdies were all that he needed, as Leishman's caddie pointed out as they walked down the fairway. But his putt snuck by the edge of the hole by an inch. At the 17th, he carved out another chance and again just missed. Leishman nearly messed up the last, needing to hole from six feet to avoid a dropped shot. It was a slightly subdued ending, but still a superb 64 that lifted him the length of the field, from among the also-rans at one under to nine under par and within a stroke of the leader.

'Yeah, it was disappointing not to go a couple better, but 64 got me right back in it,' Leishman said. He was determined to learn from his closest brush with major glory, which had come at the 2013 Masters when he was paired with eventual champion Adam Scott. 'Playing with him in the last round, having really a front-row seat to see what you actually have to do to win one, that really helped me, I think. I had a chance until a few holes to go, but to be there and see him make some mistakes and recover from them knowing that you don't have to play perfect golf was the big thing I took out of that one.

'You can make mistakes and still win. It's obviously frustrating to make mistakes, but you can't let one mistake ruin your day, which is what has happened to me a few times . . . everything that's gone on in my life in the last six months has helped me with that, too. So I feel like I'm in a pretty good spot with my golf game and my life.'

Out on the course, Englishman Eddie Pepperell moved to eight under par through 14 holes and was within two of the lead. The Oxfordshire professional then added further birdies at the next two holes before spraying his drive on the 17th out of bounds and onto a balcony of the Old Course Hotel. That cost him a double bogey on the most difficult hole on the course.

Dustin Johnson prepared to tee off knowing that the chasing pack were capable of making big moves. Spieth, who had done some extra work on his putting that morning, struck an early blow by stroking home a birdie at the first to get to six under par, the same mark as playing partner Sergio García who sank a monster from the back of the green. At the fifth, the Texan fired in a gorgeous long iron that set up a two-putt birdie to get to within three of the lead. He added another at the seventh but bogeyed the short par-4 ninth to turn in 34.

After all the weather delays, there was a sense that The Open at St Andrews was coming to the boil. It didn't spread to Johnson, though; the metaphorical heat spreading through the championship bypassed the leader's putter, which remained stone-cold. He continued creating early chances but failed to convert. Suddenly the game seemed an awful lot harder than it had in the first two rounds. 'I felt like I was hitting good putts,' Johnson recalled. 'They just weren't going in the hole. There's nothing you can really do about that.'

Amateur Ashley Chesters rolled in a 20-footer across the 18th for a birdie and a round of 67 that took him to six under par and a share of 12th place. He had been planning to turn professional in 2014 but, having defended his European Amateur title and qualified again for this Open, decided to wait. The Shropshire-based player from the Hawkstone Park club that spawned Sandy Lyle was making himself part of a strong amateur narrative at this Open.

Spieth's dropped shot at the ninth proved a turning point for him. A hallmark of his golfing year was his ability to seize the moment and this was the time for him to reassert himself. He grabbed three birdies in a row from the 10th to surge to 10 under par. Bolting from the pack, he catapulted into a share of the lead with Johnson and Louis Oosthuizen.

Johnson was playing with Willett, his closest rival at the halfway stage. The 27-year-old Willett was trying to become the first Yorkshireman to win The Open and began promisingly, a birdie at the par-5 fifth drawing him level at the top of the leaderboard.

Up ahead, Day collected back-to-back birdies by holing out on the sixth to move to nine under par. Suddenly there were 13 players within one stroke of the lead. It was anyone's Open.

Two-time champion Padraig Harrington was among the chasers, rolling back the years with a brilliant 65. But it was another Irishman who stole the limelight. Dunne, the amateur, wedged to four feet on the ninth and knocked in the birdie to join the leaders. It was an astonishing move and he was out in 32, looking calm and in control.

−10 Harrington (16), Spieth (13), Schwartzel (12), Dunne (a) (9), Willett (5), D Johnson (5)

This was a day when you needed eyes everywhere. I was walking with the final pair and Johnson was no longer the force he had been in the first two rounds. He was pressing and straining to make birdies but nothing would happen. The less experienced Willett looked more comfortable but both were being upstaged by Dunne. The youngster, who was one of five Irishmen to play for Great Britain and Ireland in the Walker Cup at Royal Lytham later in the year, grabbed the outright lead with an approach to the 10th to 12 feet. His putt took him to 11 under. He was loving every second of this unlikely charge. 'I felt like I had so much support from the crowd,' he said. 'I kind of felt like I was at home. Every shot I hit was getting cheered, from start to finish.'

Dunne had set out with the objective of shooting a three-under-par 69 but reset his goals. His target became a 66. The chances continued, but the birdies dried up and soon he had company. It came in the shape of the most feared name in the championship. Spieth birdied the 15th to move alongside. Johnson, meanwhile, was fading. A duffed wedge at the par-4 seventh led to him taking four from 70 yards out.

−11 Spieth (15), Dunne (a) (12)
−10 Harrington (F), Oosthuizen (11), Day (11),
    Willett (7)

The rise of the amateur influence continued as 21-year-old American Jordan Niebrugge birdied the last for a magnificent round of 67 and nine under for the tournament. Oosthuizen, meanwhile, dribbled a poor six-foot par putt right of the 12th hole. Behind, Willett plodded on with a par at the short eighth.

At the next, always regarded as a great opportunity to make inroads, Willett created another chance from short range and was equal to the task this time. He went to the turn in 34, two under par, and was back into a share of the lead. Johnson, though, made a limp four. He was one of the very few to be over par for the front nine. Perhaps the trauma of squandering his opportunity at Chambers Bay was catching up with him.

Zach Johnson, meanwhile, was becalmed. He had played 11 holes in 11 pars. Up ahead on the 17th, Spieth found the front of the green in two but overcooked his lag putt and it trundled six feet past. Bravely, he made the return and punched the air. It was only a par, but on that hole a four makes up ground on the field. He shared a friendly fist bump with his Ryder Cup rival García as they headed to the final tee.

The drive on the 18th at St Andrews, like the first, is one of the easiest in championship golf. The target is so broad it is hard to go wrong, but Spieth had struggled with it so far. In the first round he went way left. This time he went right and looked on as his ball flirted with the out-of-bounds road running down the right, in front of a charming parade of shops as the course heads back into town. His ball finished 10 yards on the correct side of the road.

Back at the 10th, Willett was making yet more progress. Another short, wedged approach flew to six feet before he coaxed in the left-to-right downhill putt.

−12 Willett (10)
−11 Spieth (17), Dunne (a) (13), Day (13)
−10 Harrington (F), Goosen (14)

Spieth, coming in from the right, bumped his second shot towards the 18th flag but his ball toppled down into the Valley of Sin. He very nearly drained the uphill putt, judging superbly a big right-to-left break, but settled for a par. He had come back in 32 strokes to sign for a 66. 'When you turn and come into the wind, it's not exactly easy,' he said. 'So to shoot four under with no bogeys on the back was a great comeback.' He was 11 under par and his grand slam hopes were burning bright. That early morning putting session had brought back the feelings that helped him win the first two majors.

'That front nine on the first day was as good as I've played out here, and then for the next 27 holes I was even par. That's poor if you want to win,' Spieth added. He also gave an insight into how he might offset the pressure of history beckoning as he approached the final round. He talked about a 'free-rolling attitude', adding: 'There's really no downside. If we have a chance to win and we don't execute, then we're going to be okay. And with that attitude, it actually frees me up a little bit to say I can take these extra chances. It's always hard to sleep near, or with, the lead in the last round of a major champion-ship. But . . . I think this extra day has given me time to adjust and extra shots to hit, putts to hit out here. I'm going in with plenty of confidence and a higher comfort level.'

The task would be the same as at the US Open – turn a promising 54-hole position into victory – but the kind of golf required was in stark contrast. 'Chambers Bay, you didn't have to manage the conditions. You didn't have to manage the atmosphere, the weather. It was not really going to be windy. It may be a little cool in the morning, but it was links-style golf where you need to play as if you're playing in California. I mean, you can hit it to the moon. You've got to bring it in with high trajectory to carry the false fronts . . . whereas this is more imaginative golf, tee to green. That was a long golf course, wider fairways. Here you've got to split pot bunkers.

'There, if you hit it in the bunkers, you could hit the greens. Off the tee it was, I think, an easier golf course at Chambers, and into the greens you could hit it up in the air. You still need imagination on both green surfaces, given the amount of slope and the crazy slopes that there are. You see some similarities in the leaderboard. I think that, given they're only a month apart, it's just people that are playing good golf. I don't think it's more the golf courses are better for certain people. I think it's just if you're on your game, you're on your game, and you're splitting fairways and you're hitting greens.'

Spieth had guaranteed himself a late tee time and could relax as the remainder of the field came down the closing stretch. Willett missed a good birdie chance at the 11th, pulling his putt after a majestic tee shot to the second of the par 3s. But at the 13th he left short a tricky chip shot, missed the 20-footer and entered a bogey on his card for the first time in the third round. Two holes further on, Dunne rammed home a birdie and suddenly the Irish amateur was out in front on his own.

−12 Dunne (a) (15)
−11 Spieth (F), Oosthuizen (15), Day (14),
    Willett (13)

It was an unsettling setback for Willett because his golf had been immaculate to that point and he had acquired serious momentum around the turn. He wandered back to the 14th tee to take on the inward par 5, a hole that offered a decent chance of a bounce-back birdie. The big danger, though, was out of bounds right. A low stone wall runs down the side of the hole separating it from the neighbouring Eden Course. Willett's drive flew right but he seemed unconcerned. He bent down to pick up his tee and then peered down the fairway. A steward was signalling that the ball had finished the wrong side of the wall. It was a savage blow. 'It must have just kept drifting,' Willett said. 'I don't know, but it was only about six inches over there, so I don't know how it got there. It was riding the breeze a little bit, but must have kept going.' The Yorkshireman made an excellent second-ball birdie, 'a good six in the end,' but it was a second consecutive dropped shot.

Zach Johnson's run of pars ended with a birdie at the 14th and another at the 16th. Although he dropped a shot on the Road Hole, he atoned at the last and signed for an almost unnoticed 70 to move to nine under par. The frustrated Dustin Johnson then came alive with a 60-foot birdie on the 15th that nudged him back to 10 under par.

Dunne, meanwhile, was showing no signs of inexperience. Indeed, he was playing golf worthy of a man at the top of a major leaderboard. He fired a brilliant approach to the 17th that almost yielded a birdie. At the last, with faint strains of a town-centre bagpiper wafting over the 18th green, he holed out for a par and a brilliant round that matched his self-imposed target of 66, the lowest from an amateur in the third round of an Open. He was the leader at 12 under par.

'I just picked conservative targets that gave me room either side and then attacked with my irons and tried to give myself chances,' he explained. 'I went out there thinking that if I could play sensibly and keep the bogeys off my card, you're going to have so many opportunities for birdie that you're bound to make some. I was really pleased to keep the bogeys off the card.

'It's surreal I'm leading The Open,' Dunne added. 'But I can easily believe that I shot the three scores that I shot [69, 69, 66]. If we were playing an amateur event here, I wouldn't be too surprised by the scores I shot. It's just lucky that it happens to be in the biggest event in the world.'

Day and Oosthuizen joined Dunne. Willett made a brave par save on the 15th to stay in touch but Johnson bogeyed the next from a greenside bunker to hand back the shot won on the previous hole. It was the first of three dropped shots in the closing trio of holes, a miserable end to a frustrating round for the halfway leader. His 75 was the second-worst round of the day and he was back to seven under par. Willett also bogeyed the 17th and a round that had promised so much ended in an anti-climactic 72, three strokes off the pace.

−12 Dunne (a), Oosthuizen, Day

−11 Spieth

−10 Harrington

−9 Leishman, Niebrugge (a), García, Rose, Goosen, Streb, Scott, Zach Johnson, Willett

−8 Pepperell, Schwartzel, Bowditch

−7 Fowler, Ryan Palmer, Patrick Reed, Stewart Cink, Anthony Wall, Matsuyama, Warren, Dustin Johnson

---

Severiano Ballesteros (1988), Willie Park Jr (1889) and Bob Martin (1876) were the only men to win Opens on a Monday. Who would join that roll of honour?

Sunday had been extraordinary. Monday would prove magical.

Monday, 20 July 2015

Conditions that morning were benign but with the chance of rain and wind later in the afternoon, making it possible for the early starters to set a challenging target.

Certainly there was scope for low scoring, as Scott Arnold proved. The Australian, who had needed an inward 33 in the second round to make the cut, fired a blemish-free 66 to show what was possible. Ahead of him, New Zealander Ryan Fox, son of the 1987 Rugby World Cup-winning All Black Grant Fox, shot a 67 to cap a fine Open debut. And Bernhard Langer recorded a level-par 72, the 58-year-old making a spirited finish to what was likely to be his final Open appearance at St Andrews.

It was clear that this would be another of those days where players would have to make their scores on the way out, then cling on. Another of the amateur brigade, Ollie Schniederjans of the United States, picked up six birdies in a front-nine 31 en route to a brilliant 67 in his last competitive round before turning professional. Mickelson, Geoff Ogilvy and David Howell all turned in 33, while Branden Grace's outward 31 also set up a 67 that enabled the South African to set the early clubhouse lead at seven under par. Then, shortly before 2 p.m., Brendon Todd came in with a 66 that moved the target to nine under.

By this time, Zach Johnson had begun his final round and was birdieing the second to move to 10 under. He then embarked on a run of five birdies in seven holes. 'I knew the guys in front of me were well accomplished,' Johnson said. 'They're champions. They're not going to back down. I clearly had to be somewhat aggressive early on in the day because those outward holes are the ones where you've got to take advantage.'

Johnson Z emphatically replaced Johnson D on the leaderboard. Despite birdieing the first, Dustin continued in the same inconsistent vein of the previous day. It led to a second successive 75 and a miserable capitulation.

Although Dunne was alongside him in the final pairing, Oosthuizen still felt Spieth was the danger-man. He had quietly worked his way back into contention, keeping alive dreams of a third major in a row. Spieth teed off with Day, who was hoping to land his first major within a month of his dramatic collapse at the US Open. Along with summariser Jay Townsend, I knew there was the potential for something very special as we watched the pair start their rounds. Both hit good tee shots, leaving themselves well-positioned to deal with a first hole that was cut close to the burn running in front of the green.

Ahead, and despite that challenging pin position, Leishman and Harrington had both birdied the first. Harrington, the champion in 2007 and 2008, moved to 11 under and Leishman to nine.

Day fired a percentage approach into the heart of the first green. Then it was Spieth's turn; it transpired that he had hit it further off the tee than it had first appeared and so needed careful consideration before he finessed his second shot.

IC: Wonderful shot from Jordan Spieth! Absolutely dialled in, inch-perfect for distance control and that has come to rest within seven feet to the right of the flag.

JT: Well that's an amazing shot . . . That tells me, number one, that he's not backing off and number two, he's totally comfortable and confident in his game. That shot, right there, tells you a lot about what we can expect to see for the rest of the day.

For the last time Ivor Robson, his voice quivering only slightly, performed his scheduled announcing duties at an Open Championship: 'Ladies and gentlemen, this is the final game of the 144th Open Championship. On the tee from South Africa, Louis Oosthuizen!' And then: 'On the tee from Ireland, Paul Dunne!' Who would have thought a young amateur would be the 18,995th and last name uttered by The Open's most distinctive voice?

The action continued, 350 yards or so further down the course.

IC: Jordan Spieth, then, this for the perfect start to his final round. Seven feet for birdie. Sends it on its waaay . . . and lethally it drops into the cup! It's a birdie start for Jordan Spieth! This man seems unstoppable already, the Masters champion, the US Open champion and now co-leader of The Open after one hole of the final round.

It wasn't just the putt, but the daring approach shot that was so striking. It was a birdie of huge intent and one that would be noted by all his rivals.

JT: This 21-year-old kid, who obviously has won the first two majors of the year, he's won five times this season, he's got nerves of steel. I mean, it's amazing, to take on that shot, downwind as well, we didn't even talk about the margin for error, which was even less because it's downwind. An incredible second shot, followed it up with a great putt. You just wonder, is this real?

Harrington was next to join the pace-setters at 12 under with a birdie at the second; this from a man who had missed 10 cuts in 2015 but was the most decorated of the title contenders. Dunne showed signs of nerves with his approach to the first, which finished short of the burn, very nearly rolling into a watery grave.

There were now 16 players within two shots. Five of them – Dunne, Oosthuizen, Spieth, Day and Harrington – were out in front. But Oosthuizen then broke clear with a birdie at the first for the outright lead, while Dunne failed to get up and down to slip back.

−13 Oosthuizen (1)
−12 Johnson (5) Harrington (2), Spieth (2), Day (1)
−11 Chesters (a) (11), Matsuyama (10), Wall (9),
    García (3), Dunne (a) (1)

At the par-4 second, Dunne sprayed two tee shots wide right and needed to play a second provisional ball – potentially his fifth shot. Fortunately he found the first, on the neighbouring New Course but not out of bounds. It cost him a second successive bogey, though. Showing great spirit, he birdied two of the next three holes to cover the first five in level par. Alas, this was a day when par golf was never going to be enough.

The breeze was playing into the hands of the more experienced players and they formed a peloton at the head of the leaderboard, jockeying for position. Zach Johnson was to the fore, turning in 31. He got to 14 under to overtake Oosthuizen, then doubled his advantage with his birdie at the 10th while Harrington lost his drive in a bush on the sixth, signalling the beginning of the end for the Irishman. Scott then charged into the picture, and the leaderboard shuffled around again.

−15 Johnson (10)
−14 Scott (9)
−13 García (7), Leishman (6), Spieth (5), Day (5),
    Oosthuizen (4)
−12 Niebrugge (a) (7)

The ebb and flow was unrelenting as Spieth and Day collected birdies at the sixth. But Johnson was the pace-setter and, out on the course commentating on 5Live, Chris Jones described him as 'looking every inch an Open champion'. Scott just missed an eagle, but his birdie moved him into a share of the lead with Johnson, who had managed to save par at the 11th. However, the American immediately pulled ahead again at the next, carding a seventh birdie in 12 holes. Now, though, it was time to make the subtle turn left and head for home, into the driving wind and rain.

−16 Johnson (12)
−15 Scott (11)
−14 Spieth (7), Day (7), Oosthuizen (6)
−13 García (9), Leishman (8)
−12 Niebrugge (a) (9), Dunne (a) (6)

The two most prominent Americans on the leaderboard then faltered. 'Aw man!' Spieth cried out as he pushed his tee shot 100 feet right of the hole on the par-3 eighth while Johnson thinned a fairway wood into a pot bunker guarding the front of the 13th green.

IC: Well, news of Jordan Spieth who has putted like a veteran at St Andrews until this moment at the eighth. He had a monstrous birdie putt, I mean it was only a birdie putt in the sense that it was his second shot on this par 3. And it was uphill, but beyond the hole was a severe downslope. He overcooked his putt, gave it too much, it caught the downslope and he has putted off the green.

JT: Well, it was always on if you weren't very careful. I think you were better off coming up six or eight feet short. He was very aggressive and paid the price.

It was a hefty price, too, because from that position Spieth three-putted — four in total — to record a double bogey, one that seemed to spell the end of his chances as he tumbled back to 12 under par and a share of seventh place. The remarkable odyssey that began at Augusta in April seemed to have come to an abrupt and inglorious end on the shortest hole on the Old Course.

'If you make bogey, you're still in it. If you make double bogey, it's a very difficult climb,' Spieth conceded. 'And there was absolutely no reason to hit that putt off the green. I can leave it short, I can leave it eight feet short and have a dead straight eight-footer up the hill where I'll make that, the majority of the time.'

Fortunes continued to swing erratically. Johnson couldn't get up and down despite a fine bunker shot on the 13th while on the 10th García coaxed home a birdie chance that took the Spaniard to 14 under. His supreme ball striking, heading into the heavy homeward winds, would surely be a huge asset. Scott and Day were also prominent and similarly blessed.

Spieth, in contrast, seemed spent. After all the hype and expectation, proverbial betting slips were being crumpled up, ready to be discarded. The young Texan, however, had other ideas. That ability to bounce back from apparently costly errors resurfaced. The ninth? Birdie. The 10th? Birdie. He was back to 14 under.

Scott made a composed par at the 13th to remain in the lead with Johnson. Leishman joined the pair, two-putting from 15 feet for birdie at the 10th. Oosthuizen's birdie at the ninth took him to within a stroke. We were watching spell-binding golf. It was anyone's guess who would emerge as the champion.

García stalled, however, when driving into a bunker on the 12th to drop a shot. The Spaniard had threatened to repeat the Monday success of his celebrated compatriot Ballesteros in 1988, but lost his composure down the closing stretch. The same applied to Scott, who made a mess of the inviting 14th where he missed the tiniest of par putts immediately after the heaviest of the day's rain.

Leishman, meanwhile, was seizing the moment. Birdies at the ninth and 10th were followed by another chance at the 12th, where he was being watched by 5Live's Eilidh Barbour.

EB: Marc Leishman with this birdie putt here on the 12th. He stood up to the ball but he pulled back, something in the crowd made him stop but he's back over the ball now. It goes towards the hole and disappears! Listen to the crowd, that is a roar and I tell you Marc Leishman has the outright lead in The Open Championship at 16 under par!

−16 Leishman (12)
−15 Z Johnson (15)
−14 Scott (14), Day (11), Spieth (11), Oosthuizen (9)
−13 García (12)

Spieth was fortunate to bisect the dangerous bunkers short of the 12th green and then flicked his wedge to 18 feet. His ball clung on to the upper level and Spieth sprinted to the green to mark it before it could tumble down the slope. These were the sort of breaks that suggested destiny was on his side. His birdie attempt, though, somewhat discredited that notion, as he remained two behind.

Zach Johnson parred the 16th and then deliberately sent his drive down the adjacent second fairway at the Road Hole. He lost his footing as he struck his second shot with a rescue club and was well short of the green. The response, though, was brilliant — a wedge to 15 feet. Back on the 12th, Oosthuizen knocked his second to four feet and rolled in the birdie; 15 under. Johnson stepped up to his par save on the 17th and his ball died left at the last moment. The bogey left him two strokes adrift of the unheralded Australian leader.

But Johnson wasn't done. At the last he gave himself a reasonable birdie chance. He faced arguably the biggest putt of his life, and certainly the most important since his 2007 Masters victory.

> Chris Jones: It's a putt that might win The Open Championship, 10, maybe 12 feet. His playing partner Danny Willett just gave him a sighter of this one. Zach Johnson sends it on its way to set the target at 15 under par. Will it disappear? Yes! It's in! And Zach Johnson has finished with a birdie and his caddie does a dance and Johnson punches the air, once, twice, three times. A birdie on 18, a high-five with his caddie and a club-house target of 15 under par. Is that the moment Zach Johnson wins The Open Championship?

Johnson made his way to the recorders' area and took a moment to catch his breath, hands on knees, as the scale of his performance hit home. He then looked to the skies and was hugged by his wife Kim. He declined an invitation to talk to reporters, preferring to ready himself for the prospect of a four-hole playoff. 'I was just trying to stay in the moment,' he said. 'And at that point get to the range, and just warm up and see where things go. I didn't have any expectations.'

Back on the 15th, Leishman was struggling. An indifferent birdie attempt meant he faced a 12-footer for par. It was the first time he had been in trouble all day. He had gone 33 holes without dropping a shot. It should have been a crisis. It wasn't. He kept things in perspective and stroked the ball home.

At the next he drove conservatively with a long iron and his lengthy approach found the greenside bunker. It was a devilishly difficult shot but Leishman maintained his rhythm and sent the ball to four feet. Nevertheless, his golf had become a little ragged. The pressure was mounting. He missed the par save.

−15 Johnson (F), Leishman (16)
−14 Spieth (14), Day (14), Oosthuizen (14)

Spieth, still believing in his hat-trick of majors, hit a fine approach to the 15th. He had ridden his luck throughout the back nine, his ball repeatedly flirting with bunkers. He had kept accumulating pars. Now he had a chance. He was 20 feet away, downwind, but uphill. It was the sort of putt he had made with regularity while landing the Masters and the US Open. He studied his notes intently, trying to work out the subtle borrows that might influence his ball. This was a putt for a share of the lead, with three holes to play.

The ball remained above ground.

Day made a fine par save to stay in the mix. Leishman found the 17th green in two but was a long way from the hole. So was Spieth's approach to the 16th. One hole further back, Oosthuizen fired a brilliant second to eight feet. Leishman's 60-foot birdie attempt on the Road Hole was wonderful but halted an inch short. He tapped in and went to the last tied with Johnson. Attention switched to Spieth.

IC: He has seized the golfing moment all season long. This is your time, Jordan, if you're going to do it. Birdie chance from 50 feet. Sends it on its way, Spieth watches. It looks good. It's moving from right to left. It's moving towards the hole. Will it disappear? Yes! Oh yes! The history boy moves to 15 under par, he holes a monster on 16 and he's in a share of the lead! Jordan Spieth, can you believe it?

JT: Well, that's an amazing putt! I mean, that's certainly seizing the moment. I mean, I've just got chills and it's not because it's cold out here. That was amazing, the guy just does it when he has to. After doubling eight he birdies nine and 10. He had to. The lead is slipping away from him, he's running out of holes, he had to make a putt. That was not a putt you are going to make, but he did.

IC: Wow, wow! Utterly jaw dropping.

Johnson, out on the range, heard the tumultuous roar. 'Was that a birdie?' he asked his caddie Damon Green. 'Birdie,' the bagman said. 'Awesome,' Johnson replied, before getting back to work.

How would the rest respond? Day almost holed his birdie chance from a slightly shorter distance on that 16th green, and Oosthuizen came up short with his opportunity on the 15th.

−15 Z Johnson (F), Leishman (17), Spieth (16)
−14 Day (16), Oosthuizen (15)

Leishman, who had played 35 holes in 14 under par after making the cut with one stroke to spare, came up the last desperate to land a closing birdie and take Zach Johnson out of the equation. He flew his approach over the flag. The ball grabbed and spun back to leave a downhill 15 footer, a putt, it seemed, to win The Open. It was always too far left. He tapped in for a 66 and a share of the clubhouse lead. He signed his card and texted his wife Audrey, who was back home in America. Now it was down to Spieth, Day or Oosthuizen.

Spieth drove conservatively down the second fairway on the penultimate hole and knocked his approach around 40 yards short of the putting surface. He found a delightful lie in the semi-rough and pitched to 10 feet. Day, meanwhile, tugged his second left and then had to putt around the Road Hole bunker, having briefly considered a high-risk flop shot. Both players faced testing par saves.

Only Day succeeded. Spieth's uncharacteristically limp effort died across the hole. 'I just didn't hit a great putt there,' he said. He needed a birdie at the last. So did Day.

−15 Z Johnson (F), Leishman (F)
−14 Spieth (17), Day (17), Oosthuizen (16)

Again, Spieth struggled with his drive up that vast home fairway. He hit way left, leaving him with a pitch from an awkward angle that needed to negotiate the Valley of Sin. Close to the fans, something put him off during his backswing. He aborted and recomposed himself. But he undercooked the shot, the ball sucking back into the Valley.

Day pitched behind the flag and gave himself a much better chance.

Spieth would now have to emulate the Italian Costantino Rocca in 1995, who holed out through the Valley of Sin to force a playoff against John Daly. This was the moment when his great grand-slam dream could die. The flame that had burned so bright after the birdie on the 16th was now barely flickering. Still, this was Jordan Spieth, a player who had spent all of 2015 producing moments that defied expectation.

JT: The one piece of good news is that he only has to think about making the putt. He doesn't have to worry about any shot after it. All he's thinking about is holing it.

IC: Well, that's what he said last night. 'I'm here for the win, not for the place.' And to have any chance of the win he has to hole this putt. It's 13, 14 paces.

JT: Maybe the longest 14 yards of his life. He's going to have to hit it much harder than you would normally for a putt of this distance, because of the severity of the slope. Actually, the vertical climb is probably almost four feet from the very bottom to the top ledge, where it flattens out and leads to the hole.

IC: He has stared at his yardage book where all of the notes have been made as he crammed ahead of this Open, having won in Illinois a week last Sunday. Here we are, eight days on, a Monday evening in St Andrews and Jordan Spieth is now putting for the birdie, for the playoff. It's on its way . . . Oooh it's shaved the left edge and his head just drops and the moment of history has just gone for Jordan Spieth! But what a run at it we have witnessed from the Masters and the US Open champion! And it's only a par 4 and that means that bogey at the 17th has cost the chance of history for Jordan Spieth, because he has come up one shot short of the likely playoff.

Simultaneously, Oosthuizen holed from 15 feet for par on the Road Hole to keep him in the game. Day, meanwhile, had his 20-foot chance of birdie to force his way into the shoot-out.

JT: Well, this is an iconic putt, the type we've seen many times this week in the media centre when they've shown the historic putts that have been made on this green, going back decades and decades. It comes downhill, a little bit left to right.

IC: Louis Oosthuizen is perfectly safe off the 18th tee, he has come up about 30 yards short of this green. And on that green is the solitary figure, all in black, of Jason

Day as he seeks the birdie that would take him into a playoff, surely, for The Open. Twenty feet, sends it on its way looking for it to borrow from left to right. It needs to hurry . . . it needs to hurry and it's short! He's left it short! He can't believe it and his eyes just scrunch into the palm of his hand and he pushes the cap back on his head and he's disconsolate. He left the putt short, the putt that he needed to force his way into the playoff, and poor old Jason Day. It is yet another, yet another, near miss in a major for this very popular 27-year-old from Queensland.

Day shot a two-under-par 70, Spieth a 69 and both exited to huge applause. Spieth was rueful: 'The putt on 18 was a little left the whole way. I know that that putt won't break back to the right. I've watched Opens at St Andrews. It was a very, very straight putt, and when you're swinging that hard it's hard to get it exactly on line. But it was a good putt with the right speed, and that's all I could ask for after the second shot. Just a very poorly placed drive, to not be able to hit my lob wedge in there, where I have great control. Who would have thought a drive on 18 was going to be what really hurt me at the end there? It's kind of hard to not hit a good one on that hole. I just wish I had given myself a little better opportunity.'

Oosthuizen, meanwhile, had a pitch to win The Open from 30 yards. 5Live's Conor McNamara was watching:

CM: A couple of practice swings, thousands and thousands of eyes staring, heads peering out of the windows along the road on the right hand side and now he is ready. He is taking the aerial route, there is no wind, the flag is limp. Here it comes, he's attacking the pin, it bounces short and sticks and rolls. What a shot! Louis

Oosthuizen has given himself the chance of the playoff,
a three-way playoff.

His ball came to rest six feet from the cup and, moments later,
the South African calmly stroked home the birdie putt. 'I felt
I was on the back foot the whole time,' Oosthuizen admitted.
'I was, I think, two behind starting the 12th hole. It was tough
to find birdies out there. I'll take a lot out of the putts I made
to be able to get in the playoff, the shots I pulled off, the little
second on 18.'

So Oosthuizen, Leishman and Johnson faced off. Going
into the four-hole shoot-out, the momentum was undoubtedly
with Oosthuizen. Johnson had been waiting for an hour and
Leishman almost as long, wondering if their day would involve
more golf. Neither had won an Open before. The playoff holes
were the first, second, 17th and 18th. It had been a riveting
day with so many players dreaming of glory: Paul Dunne,
Padraig Harrington, Sergio García, Adam Scott, Jordan Spieth
and Jason Day had all seen their chances disappear. Now we
were down to three.

−15 Johnson (66), Leishman (66), Oosthuizen (69)
−14 Spieth (69), Day (70)
−11 Willett (70), Rose (70), García (70), Niebrugge
       (a) (70)
−10 Koepka (68), Scott (71)

At just gone seven o'clock in the evening, with steady rain
falling, starter Ivor Robson was pressed back into action one
final time. One by one he announced the trio of protagonists
onto the tee and they each dispatched safe drives. Leishman's,
though, finished in a divot. 'To that pin, with the burn right
in front, I had no chance of getting near it,' he said. He hit his
approach to around 40 feet; 'That's about as good as I could

have done.' With all three on the green, Oosthuizen slotted his 18-footer and Johnson followed him in from 12 feet to pile the pressure on the Australian. Leishman buckled, missing from four feet for par and instantly falling two strokes behind.

−1 Oosthuizen, Johnson

+1 Leishman

Johnson was the shortest off the tee at the next, so first to play his second, and he responded with a fizzing approach to inside 20 feet. Oosthuizen replied in kind but Leishman's radar was out and left himself a distant 40 feet away. From there it was a good two-putt, which he executed to remain one over. Oosthuizen shaved the left edge before Johnson stepped up and ruthlessly popped in a second successive birdie. 'I felt like one and two were the ones that certainly you had to get after,' Johnson said. 'I hit four good shots on one and two.'

−2 Johnson

−1 Oosthuizen

+1 Leishman

All week the 17th had served up box-office entertainment for the vast grandstand that horseshoed around the right side of the green. The new seats were navy blue, designed to give The Open a state-of-the-art, corporate look, but no one knew it that Monday evening, because every single place was taken.

All three players hit fine tee shots. Leishman's approach found the front of the green. Johnson pulled his 4-iron left, to yield a desperately difficult pitch. Oosthuizen followed Leishman in.

Pitching over the Road Hole bunker with The Open on the line is as demanding as it gets. Johnson took on the challenge but put too much power into his swing and the ball trundled off the green and into the rough, on the bank leading down to the road. He was in trouble. Leishman, though, already looked a beaten man. His weak putt finished 12 feet short. Oosthuizen was left with six. It was ragged stuff.

Johnson nearly holed his chip but ran it five feet past. Leishman missed his par. He was out of it. Oosthuizen then missed as well, easing the pressure on Johnson. Nevertheless, there are few better players at holing out and that ability didn't desert him when he needed it most. It was for a bogey, but it was a hugely precious putt. One hole to go.

−1 Johnson
 L Oosthuizen
+2 Leishman

There were no tee-shot dramas and Johnson, first to play in, sent his second to within 15 feet. Leishman's attempt to hole out came to a grizzly end in the Valley of Sin while the South African eyed up his attempt to make his second birdie of the day on this famous closing hole. Even that might not prove enough but, undaunted, Oosthuizen bumped and ran his approach to eight feet. He had a chance.

Leishman two-putted for par to end his playoff at two over. 'I'm happy, don't worry about that,' he said a few moments later. 'I've just finished second in The Open. Yeah, I could have won it, but look, my perspective is quite good at the moment. I can go home tomorrow and hug Audrey and the boys and celebrate a little bit. It would have been nice to have a Claret Jug to drink out of to celebrate, but I'll find something else.'

Johnson had secured birdies on all four of his visits to the final hole. One more would give him the title. He sought out a rules official who, after some deliberation, granted his request to repair a blemish on the putting surface, but his birdie attempt slipped wide. Now it was down to Oosthuizen to try to take The Open into sudden-death.

> IC: If he misses then Zach Johnson is the winner, if it goes in, we are back down the 18th. Louis Oosthuizen glances at the hole, looks at the ball, looks at the hole, looks at the ball and then sets the ball in motion. Will it disappear? No, no! It misses on the left, and that means that Zach Johnson from the United States of America, on the final green at St Andrews, is able to hug his cad-die Damon Green and start the celebrations! Because Zach Johnson, after that closing round of 66, is The Open Champion. And who would have predicted this at the start of what has been a truly remarkable day of golf?

Johnson was hugged by his wife after sporting handshakes with his opponents.

> IC: And guess who is walking out to be the next to con-gratulate Zach Johnson? It is none other than Jordan Spieth. We thought so much that this might be the day for Jordan Spieth but it is not. And he is a classy, classy guy. And he's out there to shake hands with the champion who is in floods and floods of tears.

Johnson and Spieth shared a private jet home the following day. They had much to talk about and the Claret Jug was with them, though not in the possession of the man who had been expected to win it. Indeed, if a Johnson was going to win this Open, it would surely have been the big-hitting Dustin. But Zach had proved that shorter hitters could still prosper on the Old Course. His triumph capped a vintage championship.

'I feel like God gave me the ability to play a game,' Johnson explained. 'I try to take it very seriously. I realise it's just a game. I'm just a guy from Iowa that has been blessed with a talent, and this game provides great opportunity. I think if you mentally look at it that way, it kind of takes the pressure off. I don't want to make it any bigger than what it should be. This isn't going to define me or my career, at least I hope it doesn't. It's not my legacy. Granted, as a professional athlete and as a golfer, I'm going to relish this. I'm going to savour this. I'm humbled by this. But my legacy should be my kids, my family, that kind of thing.'

This was a third successive major that had gone the way of the United States, two to Spieth and the next now to the unlikely champion from Iowa. Could there be an American clean sweep of the majors for the first time since 1982? We didn't have long before finding out.

CHAPTER 10

Preparing for the PGA

O f the four majors, the PGA Championship has the least allure. It doesn't have the glamour of the Masters, nor the historical resonance of The Open Championship or the US Open. The PGA, staged in August, is the only one of the big four that feels the need for a marketing slogan. For years, it was billed as 'Glory's Last Shot', but the tag line was dropped after a deal struck with the PGA Tour, who felt it detracted from their September FedEx Cup finale to the season. As a result, 'This is Major' took over as the motto.

Despite the apparent need to remind the sporting public of its status, there is no doubting the championship's place among the big quartet. Indeed, it boasts arguably the strongest field of all. It is run by the PGA of America, a body that represents club and teaching professionals across the United States. This is why there are 20 places in the 156-man field reserved for players whose prime role is to work with the golfing public, rather than play in front of them.

Many argue that this dilutes the field's quality but this is counter-balanced by mechanisms aimed at ensuring that all of the world's top 100 players take part. There is no such guarantee at the other majors and, unlike the two Opens, there are no qualifying competitions or alternative avenues for amateurs, other than gaining an exemption through success in the other majors. The PGA also boasts a vast prize fund. In the last two years, the winner has taken home $1.8 million.

The first PGA Championship was held in October 1916, at Siwanoy Country Club in Bronxville, New York. The winner, Jim Barnes, received $500 and a diamond-studded gold medal donated by a wealthy department store owner called Rodman Wanamaker. To this day, the players compete for the huge silver cup known as the Wanamaker Trophy. It was originally a matchplay event, staged at different times of the year. However, it struggled to make money and in 1958 was switched to traditional 72-hole strokeplay. The tournament was run around the same time of year as The Open Championship, making it difficult for players to compete in both. It switched to August in 1965.

Even so, there are only three weeks between the last two majors of the year and it is often difficult for the PGA to establish its own narrative. There isn't the accompanying drama over who will qualify for the event, and there isn't the sense of anticipation generated by the Masters. The eight months separating August and April is a long time to wait for major golf to return, which is one reason why players and fans so look forward to springtime at Augusta. There isn't such a thirst in the build-up to the PGA because of the quenching effect of The Open. The planet's best players are also drawn together by the World Golf Championships Bridgestone Invitational in Akron in the week prior to the PGA.

If golf had one governing body it would surely structure the calendar differently, creating more spacing between the four biggest tournaments and possibly providing a greater geographical spread. History dictates that three of the four majors are staged in the US, which means the great heartlands of Australia and South Africa are starved of the very best tournaments. The same applies to the emerging markets in Asia.

Golf, though, has a myriad of governing bodies, each taking

responsibility for different facets of the game. They coordinate well but there are inevitably competing interests between such bodies as the Royal and Ancient, the USGA, Augusta National, PGA of America, as well as the PGA and European Tours. This fragmentation is perhaps most apparent during the summer months, when the calendar is concertinaed in both time and place.

The PGA of America have acknowledged this and their former president Ted Bishop even raised the idea of taking the championship abroad. Somewhat mischievously, as it would encroach on Open territory, he mentioned staging it at Royal Portrush in Northern Ireland – a course that staged The Open in 1951 and has subsequently been given a green light to return to The Open rota. The magnificent Royal Melbourne was another potential venue. Bishop, though, was a controversial president, prone to public pronouncements that lacked the gravitas demanded by his position in the game. When he became involved in a social media spat with Ian Poulter in the wake of the 2014 Ryder Cup – Bishop called Poulter a 'lil girl' for critical comments the English player had aimed at Sir Nick Faldo and Tom Watson – he was stripped of his position at the head of the PGA. The notion of taking the tournament outside the US has not been mentioned since.

Wherever it had been played in 2015, it would have been the most eagerly anticipated event in the PGA's history had Jordan Spieth managed to play the final two holes at St Andrews in one under par. That's how close the young American came to keeping alive his challenge for an unprecedented calendar-year grand slam.

Spieth had missed out on the playoff at the Old Course by a single stroke but he still had plenty of history to accomplish at Whistling Straits. The Texan could still become only the third man, behind Ben Hogan and Woods, to win three majors in a year.

This was the third time the championship was to visit the Wisconsin course. Whistling Straits is located north of Sheboygan, an otherwise unremarkable town sitting in rural countryside on the shores of Lake Michigan. There's not much other than vast areas of farmland surrounding it. Over an hour's drive north of the city of Milwaukee, it is, in short, in the middle of nowhere. Whistling Straits is the pet project of billionaire businessman Herb Kohler, who made his fortune in bathroom fittings. The owner of the Old Course Hotel in St Andrews, Kohler enjoys huge influence within the game. He also has the ear of the PGA of America. This helped bring the year's final major to his course in 2004, 2010 and now 2015. It will also stage the Ryder Cup in 2020.

Before the course was built, the property was home to an abandoned airfield called Camp Haven. Having acquired the land, Kohler contracted the famed designer Pete Dye to turn it into a championship layout. During construction, the original landscape was covered with about 800,000 cubic yards of soil and sand.

Fiji's Vijay Singh won the first PGA to be staged there, and Martin Kaymer was the champion in 2010. Both tournaments were settled by three-hole playoffs, Kaymer's victory coming after an infamous rules breach on the 72nd hole by Dustin Johnson. The American grounded his club in one of the hundreds of sandy wastes that pepper the course. These are deemed to be bunkers, where it is illegal to touch the ground when addressing the ball. Although there were notices all over the locker room informing players of the rule, Johnson failed to realise he was in a bunker as he prepared to play his second shot to the final green. He was leading by a shot and the resulting two-stroke penalty cost him a place in the playoff. It was another of those calamitous near-misses that will define Johnson's career unless – or until – he finally wins a major.

Johnson was again a strong part of the narrative heading into the 2015 championship, given his heartbreak at Chambers Bay and his failure to defend his halfway lead at St Andrews.

Whistling Straits was being erroneously billed as the third successive major to be played on a 'links-style' course. Chambers Bay, overlooking Puget Sound, was 'linksy' in character but required much more through-the-air golf. The Old Course is an archetypal seaside course, but had been softened by rain so wasn't fast and running. And Whistling Straits was only reminiscent of a links layout in an aesthetic sense. Yes, there are dunes and fescue grasses in the rough, and it sits on the side of a vast expanse of water – Lake Michigan, after all, is one of the Great Lakes, effectively an inland, freshwater sea. However, the course could only be described as 'links-looking'; its design makes no allowance for playing the ball low and along the ground. To access the greens, players have to fly their balls all the way to their targets.

Open winner Zach Johnson was among those to take exception to the links label. 'I think this golf course is the furthest thing from links,' he said. 'Links golf is using the land, using trajectory control, running things on the green, using the bounces and the rolls. This course is all aerial.

'You have to hit it here to hit it there. It may look like links, standing from the clubhouse looking down, but it does not play like a true links course. The fairways are bent (grass). There's no fescue on the fairway, there's no fescue on the greens, so it's pretty soft. In my opinion, outside of maybe the sand traps and the way they look, it's not a links golf course.'

Rory McIlroy was the reigning champion but it looked as though he would have to miss his title defence for the second consecutive major. When the Northern Irishman injured his ankle, the prognosis was for a six to eight-week absence, although many observers suggested it might be closer to three months. The fact that he had ruptured the ligament in his left ankle was also problematic. That is the area that bears a right-handed golfer's weight when they power through the ball. McIlroy's action is among the most explosive in the game, so the left ankle is one of the most important parts of his anatomy. The good news, though, is that he has a slightly unusual foot action. Many players, Spieth in particular, roll their left ankle through the impact zone. As a result, the outside of their foot bears their entire weight, supported by that ligament. McIlroy, however, flicks the direction of his foot through impact to retain his balance during the follow-through, causing less stress there.

This undoubtedly hastened his recovery. So did the intense rehabilitation programme he undertook with his fitness manager, Steve McGregor. Within a couple of weeks he was embarking on two-hour walks. 'I still had the ankle brace on, but whenever I was rehabbing it, in the gym, I would take the ankle brace off and try to strengthen it up as much as I could,' McIlroy explained. 'That ligament that I ruptured, I don't have that anymore. So I've only got two ligaments on the outside of my ankle instead of three. That ligament is basically just scar tissue now. So it's just about trying to strengthen the ankle and maintain as much integrity in it as possible. For the rest of my career, it's going to be a matter of maybe doing a few extra bits of single-leg stuff in the gym, but it's really not anything to be concerned about in the long-term.'

Even when his foot was stuck in a protective boot, McIlroy wasted no time in re-acquainting himself with his clubs, although he was limited to improvised work on his short game. 'It was more just to try and keep some sort of feel in my hands, hitting some putts,' he said. 'With the boot, my left foot was a little more elevated than my right. So a lot of my weight was on my right side. But more just to get a feeling in my hands and just keep that same feeling of gripping a golf club, of feeling what it was like. So I got some practice in, but whether it was beneficial or not, that's probably another story.'

McIlroy's father, Gerry, was telling all who would listen that his son had always been a quick healer, but the idea that he could return for Whistling Straits seemed fanciful. A week before the PGA, he had withdrawn from the Bridgestone event, which he had also won the year before.

No one outside his tight-knit camp had any idea that he was close to returning. Few people watch McIlroy's career more closely than Greg Allen, golf correspondent for the Irish broad-caster RTÉ. 'I thought there was no chance of him playing the PGA,' Allen told me, 'given the amount of speculation that was going around that he would not return until he was 100 per cent fit. That was more likely to be in or around November, not August. The European Tour's final series, or even their Dubai World Championship, looked a more likely prospect, so that he could perhaps get a victory there to make sure it wasn't a totally lost campaign.'

McIlroy had other ideas. The PGA started on Thursday, 13 August. Eight days earlier, just as the rest of the world's best were readying themselves for the WGC in Akron, McIlroy was in Portugal. He posted a video on Instagram and tweeted a link with the message: 'Working hard every day to come back stronger #dontmindthegrind.' The video showed him balanc-ing on his injured left leg and swinging a medicine ball. It was clear he had made rapid progress. Next day he posted two pic-tures taken four-and-a-half and three-and-a-half weeks earlier. They showed the huge swelling and bruising that came with the injury sustained on 4 July. McIlroy also posted a video of him on the range. 'Feels good to hit driver again,' he said on Twitter and Instagram.

'Once he started tweeting, and knowing the degree to which he makes decisions for himself, it was clear that he felt it was time to let his fans know that he was recovering ahead of schedule,' Allen said. 'I didn't think the tweets were some kind of slow-burn press release, he just didn't want it to be a big shock for his supporters. Clearly, though, he was being counselled by Steve McGregor to be careful not to play the Bridgestone the week before – that's how close a call it was.

'Sensing how strong-minded he is, this must have been in his thoughts . . . having had to sit out the defence of The Open, he must have sat down with his medical team and asked them if there was any chance of making his comeback at Whistling Straits. And if they said, "If you do the work, it's possible", that's all the cue he needed to try.'

With the Portuguese sunshine on his back, McIlroy felt ready to give it a go. At the same time as the players gathered in Ohio in the run-up to the PGA Championship, McIlroy was taking part in his own dress rehearsal. 'I played 72 holes, walking, in Portugal,' he explained. 'And that was basically my fitness test. Four days in a row, 72 holes, playing with no pain, no swelling, no anything like that. Then we knew that, okay, you're ready to go. And if I hadn't passed that test, I wouldn't have gone to the PGA.

'We did contemplate maybe trying to do that at the Bridgestone, but doing that in front of guys in the media, the eyes of the world, it probably wasn't a great idea. So to do it behind closed doors and to see how it reacted, we thought that was a better idea. Once I was able to complete that, then I knew it was the right decision to get on the plane.'

Before take-off he tweeted a picture from the inside of his private jet. The accompanying message came with emoticon symbols, the language of social media. There was a plane, an American flag, a thumbs-up, victory sign and a golf symbol. The message was clear: Rory was coming back. 'It was still a surprise, although not the shock it would have been had he not been tweeting his progress,' Allen said.

McIlroy was still concerned about how his foot might react to a transatlantic flight, but his fears were unfounded. 'It was a nine-hour flight and we had to stop in Vermont just to clear immigration and customs,' he said. 'It was nice to get off the plane and move around a little bit. I was using a couple of machines to compress it and ice it. So I was able to take advantage of that on the plane as well. That kept the inflammation down to a minimum. When I got off the flight I was good to go.'

He told reporters at Whistling Straits, two days before the championship began: 'I did a lot of rehab and a lot of hard work to get back as quickly as I could. I was always going to do that. I wasn't trying to focus on any one event, I just wanted to try and get back as quickly as possible and it just so happened that this is the event that I felt 100 per cent ready to come back and play.'

Someone else had also spent the summer completing an extraordinary recovery. Jason Day's bout of vertigo at Chambers Bay was one of the most distressing images of the golfing year. To have recovered sufficiently from that June episode to challenge as strongly as he did in July at St Andrews had seemed miraculous. After the US Open, he had been placed on anti-viral drugs to counter the problem, which was affecting his inner ear. 'They prescribed two drugs, Zofran and Meclizine,' Day revealed. 'Zofran is given to cancer patients for sickness after chemotherapy. I was pretty sick for the next two days, I didn't feel great. I was shaky but the vertigo symptoms were not as severe.

'I went and saw a doctor in Columbus, Dr Oas. We sat there and talked for at least an hour-and-a-half about the history of it; when I first got it, all that sort of stuff. We de-briefed the last five years. He did tests and prescribed these medicines. I am on them until October and then I go back for more tests. If I need to stay on the medicine, I will stay on the medicine, otherwise I will jump off them. I asked him if this was something I would have to stay on for the rest of my life; he said possibly.'

Life has rarely been straightforward for the Australian who, aged 12, lost his father Alvin to stomach cancer. It was a humble upbringing for the son of two meat-packers in the Queensland town of Beaudesert. He recalled his mother Dening 'cutting the lawn with a knife because we couldn't afford to fix the lawn mower,' adding: 'I remember not having a hot water tank, so we had to use a kettle for hot showers.' Day struggled after his father's death: 'I wasn't in a great spot when he died and then it got worse.' He drank and began to depend on alcohol. He was getting into fights. This young lad of Filipino extraction was fast heading off the rails.

His mother responded by sending him to boarding school. It was a seven-hour drive away, and 'my mom took a second mortgage, borrowed money from my aunt and uncle, just to get me away from where I was'. The decision, though, brought Day into contact with someone who would become one of the most important figures in his life – golf coach Colin Swatton.

This was the same man who, as Day's caddie, helped lift him off the ground after that dizzying collapse at Chambers Bay. That incident could serve as the perfect metaphor for Swatton's overall influence on Day's life.

He has been the ultimate 'father figure'. As a coach, he developed Day's talents, which were first shown at the age of three when his dad returned from the local rubbish tip with a cut-down 3-wood. Then, inspired by the book *How I Play Golf*, written by his hero and now close friend Tiger Woods, Day followed Swatton to Hills International College, a Queensland sporting institution that produced the likes of Adam Scott and Cathy Freeman, the 400-metre gold medallist at the 2000 Sydney Olympics.

Under Swatton's keen and demanding eye, Day worked hard and rapidly earned his place on the PGA Tour. He met his wife Ellie in an Ohio bar and they married at the age of 17. 'We were both so young, figuring everything out,' Ellie said. 'People always thought he was so mature but he was throwing golf clubs and cussing on the course. He had phases where he would almost give up.'

Day also had to contend with a degenerative spinal condition that could only be treated by the strictest of fitness regimes. Nevertheless, he matured as a person and player, winning for the first time at the 2010 Byron Nelson. By the time he arrived at Whistling Straits in 2015 he was in the form of his life.

The despair of leaving short his birdie putt on the Old Course to try to make the playoff with Zach Johnson had been somewhat salved the following week. He birdied the last three holes to claim the RBC Canadian Open, beating Bubba Watson by a single stroke. He faced a very similar putt to the one at St Andrews to claim victory in Ontario. 'The same things were going through my mind – "make sure you get it to the hole" – and fortunately enough for me it was quick enough. I just needed to get it on the line. About six feet out, I knew it was going to come back and go in the hole. This is why we practise. This is why we work so hard and put the hours in, not only on the golf course but off the golf course, with the body and mind. Just to have this one little moment, where you can somehow just freeze it. There is no better feeling. It's just amazing.

'My life-long goal is to get to number one in the world. I know that I can't do that without wins, and big wins in major championships. All of those little hiccups along the way with major championships, just falling short or not doing enough or all of those things, are just setting me up for hopefully later on down the road.'

That road led to the sleepy shores of Lake Michigan. Day arrived with the reigning world number one, McIlroy, back on the scene and the man of the moment, Spieth, desperate for a third major win of the year.

It was no longer 'Glory's Last Shot' but we didn't need the posters to tell us that 'This is Major.'

CHAPTER 11

The PGA's Fitting Finale

Heading into the final major of 2015, the golfing landscape had changed. Yes, a 39-year-old had just won The Open, but professional golf was now a game headlined by the younger generation, with Jordan Spieth, just turned 22 in the vanguard accompanied by the returning Rory McIlroy. Most significantly, the 39-year-old who won The Open was not Tiger Woods.

The seeds of this shift had been sown at a PGA Championship years before. Back in 2009, Woods was going for his 15th major title at a Hazeltine course that seemed to have been built specifically to showcase his daunting strengths. Yet Woods was beaten by an unheralded Korean, Y. E. Yang. It was the first time the then-undisputed world number one had lost a major after leading into the final round. As former *Daily Telegraph* Golf Correspondent Mark Reason wrote, it was 'the end of an aura'.

Later that year, Woods' personal life collapsed, and he has never been the same formidable figure since, especially when major titles have been on the line. He remains stuck on 14 majors, seven years on from his last victory in the 2008 US Open and still four wins short of tying Jack Nicklaus's record. Furthermore, Woods went to Whistling Straits seeking to avoid a third successive missed cut in his last major appearance before turning 40.

'I don't know my exact ranking right now,' Woods admitted on the eve of the tournament (he was 278th in the world). 'I know I'm in the 200s somewhere. But as far as paying attention to it, no; I'm just trying to get better. I'm just trying to get up there where I can win tournaments, get my game organised so I can be consistent, where I'm going to give myself a chance to win each and every event I play in. That's what I have done over most of my career. And I'd like to get to that point again.'

Thursday, 13 August 2015

Woods was out early on the first day, teeing off at the 10th at 8.15 a.m. alongside two other former PGA champions, Martin Kaymer and Keegan Bradley. They were in the group behind Jason Day, Dustin Johnson and Rickie Fowler. McIlroy had to wait until the afternoon to begin his comeback from injury to defend his title, in the company of Spieth and Open winner Zach Johnson.

Woods is prone to nervous starts but he looked secure as he opened up with regulation figures on the short par 4. Johnson, Fowler and Louis Oosthuizen all picked up early birdies to move swiftly into the red but Justin Rose, who had come close in Akron the week before, started poorly. The Englishman was one of the most consistent forces in the majors of 2015, and was keen to make up for the disappointment of losing to Spieth at Augusta despite his hugely impressive 14-under-par total that would have been good enough to win most editions of the Masters. 'I certainly didn't panic earlier in the year when I wasn't playing well,' Rose said. 'I tried to tell myself that my year was going to be built around April through to September, when a lot of the big tournaments rolled around. That's when I wanted to be fresh and at my best.

'I would say throughout my career I've had a bit of trouble with Pete Dye golf courses. He's the master of illusion. His golf courses take some getting used to. At the Zurich Classic this year (at TPC Louisiana), I won on a Pete Dye golf course, and last year I had my best Players' Championship, which is a Pete Dye golf course. I think I'm getting my head around the challenges that he presents. Definitely nothing is done by accident out there. It's very strategic. This Whistling Straits golf course is incredibly tough, but it's a great golf course.'

It perhaps didn't feel that way to the Englishman, who had turned 35 two weeks earlier, when he collected bogeys on the 11th and 13th, leaving him two over par after four holes. By contrast, Dustin Johnson was making another of his characteristic fast starts. He took advantage of the short 10th and par-5 11th to card birdies. Before the tournament, the 31-year-old had addressed the issue of his growing maturity and spoke of the significance of becoming a parent with fiancée Paulina Gretzky to their son Tatum, who was born in January 2015. 'Having a son makes everything so much more easy,' he said. 'You don't worry about golf as much. You don't worry about anything as much. The focus is more on him. So that's been the biggest transformation, the best thing that's happened to me.'

Inevitably, Johnson was also asked to talk about the grounding of his club in the bunker at the last when he was in prime position to win the 2010 PGA at Whistling Straits. We wondered how often he thought back to that fateful moment, which occurred in a hazard that, this time, was covered by a hospitality tent. 'About as many times as I've been asked the question,' he smiled. 'I don't know how many times that is. But I don't really think about it unless someone asks me the question. But this year I don't have to worry about it, there's a grandstand there. Thank you, PGA. I appreciate that.'

Japan's highly promising Hideki Matsuyama was the early pace-setter, going to the turn in four under par. He soon had company. At the par-5 16th, Johnson drained a 30-footer for eagle. Denmark's Thomas Bjørn then accelerated to five under as players took advantage of the relatively soft conditions. 'It was a beautiful morning,' the 44-year-old said. 'Not too warm and the golf course seemed pretty receptive. You never really know when you step out on a golf course in a major championship what to expect, but you felt in the first few holes that it was going to be do-able.'

Playing the inward half first, Jason Day made a quiet start with four pars but then picked up birdies at the 14th and 16th. Once again, his name was on a major championship leaderboard. The winds freshened as the day went on, and Day felt he was in the better half of the draw, playing early on Thursday and late Friday: 'We got out there and got to attack the golf course.' Rose also found his groove and went to the turn in a one-under 35.

Johnson was in one of his first-day moods. Relentless. He swiftly moved to six under par. Day needed an eagle at the par-5 second (his 11th) to keep pace.

−6 D Johnson (11*)

−5 Bjørn (15)

−4 Matsuyama (15*), Harris English (11), Day (11*), Matt Jones (8)

*started on tenth

After back-to-back birdies, Johnson missed the green at the par-3 third, a dramatic downhill short hole with the lake sitting serenely to the left. The American was oblivious to the glorious surroundings as he sought to save par. He failed, but it was only a temporary setback. A birdie followed at the next and Johnson remained on six under for the rest of the round as birdie putts lipped out on the seventh and eighth holes and, at the ninth and last, he bravely avoided three-putting to sign for a fine 66. 'I would prefer to be in the lead,' Johnson said. 'There's less shots you've got to make up. But you've still just got to play your game, especially in majors. When you try to push and try to make things happen, that's when you can make some big numbers.

'All I'm looking for is a chance to get it done on the back nine on Sunday, I was swinging well and I was hitting the shots where I was looking. Any time you're doing that, it makes things a lot easier on you. I really felt like I was just super patient. The ball was going where I was looking, I was controlling it. In this wind it's tough to do.'

Day moved to five under par with four to play but bogeyed the sixth before parring in for a 68. It felt as though the momentum had been maintained from his Canadian Open win. Day was pleased. 'I felt good out there. I was thinking, if I can get 68 or better that would be a good start. If I made a mistake early, I knew that there were opportunities coming in. I just hung in there and then, once I got my first birdie, my game got going and I started driving the ball a lot better. I hit a lot of good greens and felt like I putted pretty solid.'

It was a different yet familiar story for the man playing in the group behind. Woods went to the turn in one over after a bogey at the 18th. It seemed to knock the stuffing out of him and, with no authority on the greens, he laboured to four more bogeys in the next six holes. The only success was a birdie on the 603-yard par-5 fifth. It was a scruffy round, compiled for the most part in the best of the weather and he signed for a disappointing three-over-par 75. 'I hit it great, but I made nothing. Probably one of the worst putting rounds I've had in a very long time,' Woods said. He claimed that tee to green he 'had complete control of his golf ball'. But that was putting a very positive spin on the state of his long game.

Rarely has McIlroy looked forward more to a tee shot than the one he dispatched from the first tee that Thursday afternoon. It was his first competitive stroke since holing out in the final round at Chambers Bay, 53 long days before. He had told me that, in his heart of hearts, he was surprised to have made it back in time. It had been a remarkable recovery, and much of the television build-up to the PGA was devoted to showing images of a sprightly-looking McIlroy sprinting up and down the vast dunes of Whistling Straits. It was as though he was deliberately sending a message that he had returned to full fitness, showing almost superhuman powers of recuperation in the process.

Now, though, it was time for the acid test of competition. He belted a huge drive that caught the left rough. He received a rapturous reception but it was eclipsed by the roar generated by playing partner Spieth, who fired his drive into similar territory.

Zach Johnson was next up and he split the fairway. He was excited to be playing with McIlroy, 'a good friend and a great ambassador', and Spieth, who he holds in the highest esteem. 'He's gritty,' Johnson said. 'He likes to grind. Seems to me he likes it when his back is against the wall. And he doesn't succumb to the pressure of being a favourite, either. I think when there's a little bit of tension and pressure, and I would say even restriction that guys have when you're supposed to rise to the top, for whatever reason that doesn't bother him a bit. It's impressive.'

As they set out, Rose was coming in with a 69. His compatriot James Morrison ended on the same score, while another Englishman, Paul Casey, finished with a 70. 'You've got to be resilient to win these tournaments,' Rose said. 'So whatever happens at the beginning or middle of the week, you have to suck it up and forget that and realise that you're not the only one making that mistake.'

It was a message worth noting for McIlroy on that opening hole. He hacked his approach to the back of the green before showing signs of rustiness as he trundled his long first putt to four feet, then missed the next. Spieth opted to chip from the fringe and bumped to a similar distance before holing out. Johnson carded a regulation par.

At the par-5 second McIlroy looked a lot more composed, smashing an imperious drive and beautifully judged approach into the heart of the green. Two putts later he had returned to level. 'Obviously I was pretty nervous on the first tee,' McIlroy admitted. 'It wasn't the best of starts, but to hit those two shots on the second hole and make birdie, that settled me down and I could get into the round.' Johnson, though, was in trouble from the moment he hit his drive into a fairway bunker and bogeyed. Spieth remained at level par.

On the back nine, David Lingmerth – who had made such an explosive start at St Andrews – began in similar vein. He picked up birdies at the 10th and 11th. The wind was picking up but didn't prevent the elite group of Spieth, McIlroy and Johnson from hitting excellent tee shots into the third green. Only Johnson was able to capitalise, though. McIlroy and Spieth missed good birdie chances at the next as well, but an indication of the worsening conditions came when the Northern Irishman's cap blew from his head shortly before he lined up his 15-foot opportunity. Cranking up the pressure still further, the course scoreboards reminded the trio how many players had taken full advantage of the calmer morning conditions.

–6 D Johnson (F)

–4 Russell Henley (F), Matt Kuchar (F), English (F), J. B. Holmes (F), Day (F), Danny Lee (F), Jones (F)

–3 Brendan Steele (F), Bjørn (F), Morrison (F), Rose (F), Lingmerth (5*)

The fifth at Whistling Straits is a curious hole and provided the first genuine drama for this major-winning group. The long par 5 swings inland from the lakeshore and, like the eighth at

Chambers Bay, there is little scope for spectators to follow the action. This creates an uncharacteristically eerie atmosphere compared with the rest of the course, which offers excellent viewing.

The water down the right gobbled up Johnson's errant drive. Another lake eats into the left side approaching the green and this claimed McIlroy's ball after he chunked a 7-iron approach. It was his third shot after driving into a bunker and playing out sideways. McIlroy's ball was barely submerged and he rolled up his right trouser leg to splash out. His big concern was making sure the protective strapping on his left ankle was not affected. 'If the water gets through this (left) shoe then the tape gets wet and that would be a little more than annoying or uncomfortable for the rest of the day,' he said. 'But it was fine. I just had to remember to hit it hard.' It proved an excellent shot, finishing 10 feet from the hole.

Spieth played in text-book fashion to create an eight-foot birdie chance. He watched as McIlroy holed out for his unlikely par, then squandered his chance to move under par. It was extraordinary that they should record the same scores, given their divergent routes to the hole. Johnson bogeyed and, at two over, didn't look in a mood to challenge.

Lingmerth, meanwhile, hammered his second at the par-5 16th onto the front of the green. The American-based Swede lagged his eagle putt up to a couple of feet and moved into second place. It was a magnificent performance, in increasingly difficult conditions that would prove the worst of the week. 'It's a super-tough course here and they were really windy conditions in the afternoon,' he confirmed. 'But I got off to a flying start, was able to make some putts and give myself a lot of looks. The front nine was really good.'

−6 D Johnson (F)

−5 Lingmerth (7*)

−4 Henley (F), Kuchar (F), English (F), Holmes (F),
  Day (F), Lee (F), Jones (F)
−3 Steele (F), Bjørn (F), Morrison (F), Rose (F)

McIlroy's golf was pretty ragged by contrast, but it was gutsy too. The 26-year-old succumbed to a bogey at the eighth while Spieth continued to collect routine pars. McIlroy birdied the next and moved to one under after hitting a massive drive down the par-5 11th, some 60 yards further than his playing partners, leaving only an 8-iron to the green. Two putts later he was marking down his second birdie in three holes. Spieth, meanwhile, three-putted for a costly, ugly bogey and a score of one over.

Ahead of the tournament, I had shared a bus ride with leading coach Pete Cowen. The man who looks after the swings of many of the best players in the game, including Henrik Stenson, Oosthuizen and Graeme McDowell, is always a good source of information. I sought out his views on who might succeed this week. The name he offered was Brooks Koepka, a big-hitting American whose ball-striking attracts the admiration of his rivals. Koepka cut his teeth on the European Challenge Tour before gaining full playing rights on the continent's main circuit. From there, he progressed to the PGA Tour. He had the game, Cowen said, and was due to start contending in the majors.

Koepka, though, made an unconvincing start and went to the turn in a four-over-par 40. From the 10th, though, he started to show why he is so highly regarded, with five birdies in a row. But it was Lingmerth who continued to steal the show. He had played controlled, par golf after that blistering start and then, at the fifth (his 14th), he took advantage of the par 5 by pitching boldly to five feet for a birdie that took him into a share of the lead with Dustin Johnson. At the next he had a chance for the outright lead, but hit a poor effort, then missed the five-footer back. Koepka also found trouble and slipped back to level.

Spieth did little to inspire in his opening round and, as he struggled to save par from a fairway bunker on the 15th, his group attracted the attention of the timekeeper. The Masters and US Open champion is a very deliberate player and Zach Johnson isn't the quickest either. There are no such problems with McIlroy but, 11 minutes behind schedule, the group was put on the clock. 'There wasn't much you could do about why it was slow,' Spieth said. 'It was because of the conditions. I didn't think much of it. You just kind of go with it. They just said, try and pick up the pace, and nothing happened from there.'

At the next, Spieth drove into trouble but sensibly laid up to 100 yards on the last of Whistling Straits' par 5s. From there he wedged to eight feet and slotted home a welcome birdie putt that took him one under par. He then parred in. Despite Lingmerth's heroics, this represented fine scoring and Spieth was happy with his position, given the weather. 'When we were starting and we saw six-under on the board, we talked about it,' he revealed. 'And we knew that that was probably not feasible for us. It was a different golf course, and we needed to adjust our expectations because of that.' McIlroy also birdied the 16th to go two under par but dropped a shot at the last.

Both superstars signed for 71s, while Lingmerth bucked the afternoon trend with his brilliant 66. 'Under par was a good round, I think one of the better rounds in the afternoon,' Spieth said. 'Whatever David ate this morning, I'd like to eat it tomorrow, because that's a heck of a round of golf in those conditions. I definitely had chances to shoot a lower score, but the par saves on 15 and 17 were huge.'

McIlroy was equally satisfied. 'It was a solid round of golf and I was happy with the way I struck the ball,' he said. 'It was an unfortunate bogey on the last. I just hit a 3-iron and held it up a little bit too much into the wind and leaked it right. But as I said, anything under par is a good score.' As for his injured ankle, there was no issue. 'I have full confidence in it,' he said.

Zach Johnson never looked comfortable in a ragged 75. 'There was a lot of struggling with my ball-striking off the tee,' he said. Koepka, meanwhile, couldn't sustain his birdie rush and stumbled to a disappointing 73.

Aside from Lingmerth's brilliant performance, there was little movement at the top of the leaderboard that windswept afternoon, on the shoreline of Lake Michigan.

−6 D Johnson

−5 Lingmerth

−4 Henley, Kuchar, English, Holmes, Day, Lee, Jones,
   Scott Piercy

−3 Steele, Bjørn, Morrison, Rose

Friday, 14 August 2015

Spieth had been uncharacteristically quiet on the opening day of the PGA but, with perfect conditions on the second morning, he made his move. It would have been out of keeping with the rest of the year, indeed, had he not forced his name up onto the leaderboard. His route around Whistling Straits began on the 10th. There wasn't much to suggest he would be generating headlines early on. He took advantage of both par 5s but after eight holes was only one under par for his round and two under for the championship. McIlroy moved alongside with a birdie at the long 16th, but two holes later fortunes swung wildly for both players.

The 18th is a dramatic downhill par 4 named 'Dye-abolical', in honour of course designer, Pete Dye. It points due west, with the lake immediately behind the tee box. Evening rounds finish directly into blinding sunshine but this was mid-morning and not an issue. The second shot requires a long carry over thick rough and a water hazard, and the green is well protected by bunkers. It was into one of these hazards that Spieth deposited a 230-yard approach with a hybrid. McIlroy, who had bogeyed the hole at the end of his first round the previous evening, blamed that memory for pulling a long iron into thick rough to the left of the green. 'The second shot on 18 was definitely a reaction to the second shot in the first round,' he explained. 'I did not want to miss it right, especially with that right pin. I just double-crossed it. I was in between clubs there, as well. I was trying to cut a 3-iron. Maybe I should have hit a committed 4-iron.'

His ball was sitting up, nestling in the top of the grass, and his wedge travelled right under the ball, barely moving it. His second attempt was rather clumsy, and he missed a 10-footer for bogey. An ugly six was entered onto his scorecard.

Spieth pounced on those errors. He was facing a very tricky escape from the hazard and, potentially, a dropped shot. He was on a downslope in the bunker to the front-right of the green. The backswing was awkward and there was little room with which to work. It required a stroke of the utmost delicacy. Spieth splashed out carefully, his ball dropped onto the fringe before hopping forward and curling into the cup. It was an astonishing birdie, on the hardest hole on the course. He turned in two under par, three under for the championship and three strokes better than the man he was trying to usurp as world number one.

The success of that shot was another example of Spieth's scrupulous attention to detail. 'I talked to local caddies ahead of time,' he revealed. 'That bunker, and I think there is one other, always has much more sand than the rest of the bunkers on the golf course. When I was hitting my approach shot I knew that, because it was a hybrid, it wasn't going to plug. If it went into that bunker and it was on the flat or the upslope, it wasn't a bad place to be. You didn't want to be long left to that pin today (like McIlroy). So I hit it over there and I thought it was going to be okay, just be in the flat part. And it ended up being kind of against the back lip. We were thinking about playing 10 feet out to the right, given my (hampered) back swing.

'It had to be almost straight up and straight down. The chances of hitting that the right way are so slim you could easily catch that thin, and then you're left with a very likely double bogey. So I lined up a little to the right and, as I took it back, just tried to kind of cut across it a bit. I just struck it absolutely perfectly. It was sitting nicely on top of the sand, but, no, I was not looking to make that. I would have taken four and walked off a very, very happy guy.

'I was staring at being one over on the round and instead made the turn in two under. That was a nice kind of two-shot swing in one shot.' Suddenly the year's most dangerous name was back on a major leaderboard.

Lingmerth, meanwhile, had made a fast start that took the Swede into a two-stroke advantage at eight under par. He quickly fell back into the pack, though, while American Scott Piercy picked up a couple of early birdies to join the later-starting Dustin Johnson in a share of the lead.

−6 Piercy (5 holes), D Johnson

−5 Justin Thomas (13*), Y. E Yang (12),
    Lingmerth (8)

−4 Henley, Kuchar, English, Holmes, Day, Lee, Jones

−3 George Coetzee (13), Spieth (9*) Billy
    Horschel (7), Marcel Siem (7*), Steele, Bjørn,
    Morrison, Rose

Spieth was ready to hit the accelerator and he embarked on the second half of his round with a wedged approach to 10 feet. In familiar style, he addressed the putt, gripping left hand below right, then came the small forward press with the hands and that metronomic rock of the shoulders to generate the most certain of putting strokes. His ball disappeared into the hole. He was now within two strokes.

There is much excitement over the prospect of an enduring rivalry between Spieth and McIlroy; they look set to vie for the world number one position for years to come. The very next hole illustrated why this is such an enticing prospect. Having watched Spieth's fireworks, McIlroy was inspired into some box-office golf of his own. He struck a fine drive and lengthy approach into the par 5 to set up a certain looking birdie chance. He was just off the front right of the green, 25 feet away. His chip never deviated from its intended path, taking a gentle right-to-left curl. The eagle wiped out the double bogey at the 18th. McIlroy returned to two under par.

Spieth had sent his tee shot into sand and could only manage a par but, at the next, he rammed home a birdie chance and moved to five under. George Coetzee, however, had got to six under, following an eagle-birdie blast on the 16th and 17th holes. Even that standard of play was being eclipsed by Hiroshi Iwata. The unheralded Japanese player, competing in his first American major, was making up for a disappointing first-round 77. He reached the turn in a two-under-par 34 before eagling the 11th and following up with birdies at the next two holes. Yet again, the prospect of a record-breaking 62 was raised. The conditions, calm and hot, seemed ideal.

Lingmerth was also bouncing back and three consecutive birdies, seven in all, took the Swede into the outright lead. At the short par-4 sixth (their 15th), Spieth and McIlroy collected birdies, taking the American to one shot off the pace and the Northern Irishman to within four. Lingmerth's extraordinary round then took a turn for the worse with a bogey at the 15th. Spieth was now sharing the lead.

−6 Lingmerth (15), Spieth (15*), D Johnson
−5 Coetzee (F), Horschel (15*)

McIlroy dropped a shot at the seventh despite a fine chip from an awkward lie that fully tested his injured ankle. Attention swung back towards Iwata. The 34-year-old added three more birdies. One more at the last – no easy task – would yield the first ever 62 in a major championship. The record seemed safe when his second shot finished 30 yards from the hole. But Iwata's exquisite pitch threatened the cup, only to finish inches away. Had it gone in, a 42-year-old record would have been smashed by a player little known outside his own shores. He tapped in to come home in a magical 29 strokes and complete a round that, extraordinarily, took him from five *over* to four *under*. He became the 25th player to shoot a 63 in a major (Greg Norman and Vijay Singh having managed it twice).

Speaking through an interpreter, Iwata thought his inward half might have been even lower. 'On the back nine, after 13, I was thinking that I'm going to shoot 27,' he smiled.

While Iwata was unable to birdie the last, Lingmerth concluded his remarkably inconsistent round by picking up a shot on that most difficult of closing holes. He had recorded eight birdies, four bogeys, a double bogey and only five pars. It added up to a two-under 70, to go with an opening 67, and he took the lead. 'I saw nine under as a possibility, I wish I could have done that, but there were too many bad shots,' he said. 'I got a good start at The Open, too, at St Andrews, but was very disappointed with how I continued my play in that tournament. To get two solid rounds in is a good feeling.'

Spieth, McIlroy and Zach Johnson were just behind. McIlroy would finish with a second successive 71 while Spieth stole the show with his 67. Johnson had battled to make the cut but came up short, bowing out after a level-par 72 left him three over for the tournament.

It was clear McIlroy was frustrated. He felt he had played better than he had scored. He also saw first-hand how adept Spieth had become at contending for the biggest prizes. 'He's the prime example of someone whose game is very efficient, when he gives himself chances,' McIlroy noted.

As with all of Spieth's rounds in the 2015 majors, his next port of call was the media centre. Only the leading scorers are dragged away from the recorders' area for such duties. For the young Texan, it had become routine at Augusta, Chambers Bay, St Andrews and now Whistling Straits.

He was asked whether he enjoyed playing in the company of McIlroy. 'No, we hate each other, it's very challenging to talk to him,' Spieth laughed, before returning to his complimentary self. 'I've been friends with Rory since maybe the middle-to-end of the first year that I was out here, when we first played together. His game is extremely exciting. Watching him drive the golf ball is just inspirational. It's unbelievable when he is hitting his driver good. I would argue there's nobody like it.'

Spieth felt he still had plenty left in the tank. 'I feel good,' he insisted. 'I've got a chance to win a major championship. Just thinking about that gets you enough adrenaline, so there won't be any issues. This year, I've done a better job of when I take time off, when I limit the practice coming back, and how to prepare. But as far as mentally in this position, the way the year's gone, I approach each event as if it's the only event of the year when I stand on the first tee. That gets me through it. Just looking at the board, grinding it out – I don't feel any fatigue.'

Spieth seemed in total control. Perhaps the biggest question of the day, however, surrounded Dustin Johnson's ability to cope mentally with holding yet another early lead in a major. He started his second round in solid, unspectacular style, collecting pars until he recorded his first birdie at the seventh. He moved to two under, and eight under for the championship, with a birdie at the 10th. Thereafter, though, his game became ragged. There were three bogeys in his next four holes. He began to look uncertain and unconvincing, just as he had done when closing with two 75s at St Andrews.

Day, on the other hand, was going in the other direction, with three birdies in his first six holes. He went to the turn in 34 and was bubbling with the confidence of a man in form. A hat-trick of birdies from the 11th took him to nine under. Up ahead, Rose was also making good progress despite a double bogey at the fourth. The Englishman matched the Australian's outward half and was seven under for the tournament when he birdied the 14th. Then came a bogey at the next, and a birdie at the 16th.

All this time, storm clouds were brewing. Dirty, thick, black masses were gathering over the lake. Rose added another birdie at the 17th. He was firmly in the mix of the championship and thought he was going to catch a helpful break from the weather. He commented to his playing partners that it looked as though they would finish just before the inevitable storm broke, thereby avoiding an early wake-up call on Saturday. Behind, Day was surveying a birdie putt that would take him to 10 under.

As Rose arrived on the 18th tee, his hopes were dashed. 'I opened my big mouth to the boys playing with us, I said, the end is in sight, and 30 seconds later they blew the horn,' he said. Tournament director Kerry Haigh knew what was coming. Claps of thunder could be heard as the players rushed from the course. The wind picked up and suddenly Whistling Straits was in the eye of the storm.

The media tent covering us began to billow violently. The metal supports creaked loudly and the banners advertising future PGA venues started to sway erratically. Rain pounded on the canvas. Within minutes, portable toilets on the course were overturned and Haigh wasted no time in informing the players that there would be no further play. They would be coming back at 7 a.m. the next day to complete their second rounds. 'At the time I didn't think that we would finish for the day,' Rose said. 'I thought that the storm would blow through for maybe an hour and then go. Calling it for the day is a bit of a drag.'

It was also the only sensible decision. Locals said the violence of the storm was a rarity, but for the best part of an hour the Sheboygan area took a hammering. The evacuation had been timely; throughout the locality, trees and branches came crashing down. 'There was trouble lurking there for a second,' Day said as he left. 'Right around the 15th the horn blew and I was glad that we were taken in. It's a mess out there.'

The players departed with an enticing leaderboard swaying precariously in the wind.

−9 Day (14), Jones (12*)

−8 Rose (17)

−7 Lingmerth (F), English (15*), Tony Finau (13*)

−6 Spieth (F), Piercy (F), Steele (F), Henley (17*), Holmes (14*)

−5 Coetzee (F), Johnson (14), Lee (13*)

−4 Iwata (F), Horschel (F), Marcel Siem (F), Hideki Matsuyama (F), Charles Howell III (F), Kuchar (F), Brandt Snedeker (17), Paul Casey (16), Anirban Lahiri (13*)

Saturday, 15 August 2015

Saturday opened with glorious, clear skies and turned into another stunning day of golf. The humidity that had triggered the violent weather had been swept away. Rose returned to face the toughest hole on the course and was equal to it, getting up and down from 90 feet for a round of 67. Day couldn't make his birdie at the 15th. He signed for the same score and remained one shot clear of Rose. 'I feel pretty good,' he said. 'I've been here before, so I know that it's not the right time to get panicked. Because once you get anxious, things start to multiply and that's when you start making mental errors. So I just know that if I make a mistake, it's okay. I've just got to keep plodding along and be patient, and hopefully it falls.'

Day's Aussie compatriot, Matt Jones, completed a 65 that propelled him into the lead at 11-under-par. 'It's hard to say if you ever feel a week like this coming,' said the 35-year-old, whose only PGA Tour win had come at the 2014 Shell Houston Open. 'You're a golfer, so you expect weeks like this. I had some good weeks this year, and I've had bad weeks and that's the nature of the game. I'm a streaky player, I know that. I'm trying to get better at that part of my game. But I'm just managing my golf ball better this week than I probably have in previous years and I'm putting well.'

As for Woods, he resumed knowing that he needed something special to avoid another missed cut. It didn't materialise. His miserable season ended with a second-round 73 that left him six over, missing out by three strokes. It was only the bad weather first at St Andrews and now Whistling Straits that had allowed him to compete on a major weekend for the first time since the Masters.

Never before had he experienced such a run. His remodelled swing had a long way to go. Woods effectively spent the year being left behind by the very generation he had inspired to take up the game. If it was the end of an aura at the 2009 PGA, it felt like the end of an era in 2015.

'I came back at Augusta and had my short game back,' Woods said. 'Then I started getting my ball striking in order, but I lost my putting. I hit too many balls and neglected my chipping, because I thought that was sound again. I just need to do both at the same time. I haven't done that. I haven't put together ball striking and putting. It's been one or the other.'

Despite this result almost certainly ending his PGA Tour season, well ahead of the FedEx Cup playoffs, Woods remained optimistic. But his message rang hollow, his words contradicted by his scores. 'The confidence is growing quickly,' he claimed. 'That's the fun part. I'm hitting shots and able to hit shots that I haven't been able to hit in years, and that's nice again. And to have the control that I need to have going forward, it's starting to come back. I just need to get more consistent in tournament golf. The only way you can do that is by playing, I have a lot of golf to be played around the world.'

−11 Jones

−9 Day

−8 Rose

−7 Lingmerth, Finau, Lahiri

−6 Spieth, Piercy, Steele

−5 Coetzee, Henley, English, Johnson, Holmes

−4 Iwata, Horschel, Siem, Matsuyama, Howell III, Kuchar, Casey, Hunter Mahan, Kaymer, Grace

---

Resuming on two under, McIlroy required a fast start to his third round if he was to have any chance of defending his title. Playing with Koepka, he received rapturous applause when he arrived on the first tee and nearly rewarded those fans with an outrageous opening birdie. Having driven into sand, his second shot finished on the front fringe of the green. His attempt from 60 feet came within millimetres of dropping. Encouraged, McIlroy birdied two of the next three holes before arriving at the par-5 fifth. He put his second shot within putting range and then slotted home a 65-footer for an eagle. Suddenly he was six under par and in share of seventh place.

The joy, though, was short-lived. Bogeys at two of the next three holes followed. 'I guess that probably showed just a lack of competitiveness, considering it was the first week back in a few weeks,' he admitted. But McIlroy showed signs of shedding that rust in the rest of his round. There were four birdies on the way home, offset by a couple of bogeys, adding up to a satisfying 68 that took him back to six under. 'I was aggressive with my shots, I was committed to most shots and most swings that I took,' he said. 'I was just getting back into the rhythm of it. I thought it might have taken me a few weeks, but I feel like it's right there and feels like I wasn't away for that long.'

Dustin Johnson's second round ended in disappointment. Hoping to build on his first-round lead, he could only manage a one-over-par 73. Nevertheless, he was still in the mix. Although his putter remained relatively cold in the third round, two birdies and a bogey helped the American to the turn in a one-under-par 35. It proved an ideal platform for a fine inward half. There were birdies at the 11th, 14th and 16th and no dropped shots. His 68 took Johnson to nine under. 'I thought I played really well,' he said. 'I thought I rolled it well, I just didn't make any putts. All in all, I hit it very well and I'm very pleased with it. It could have been a really nice day.'

Going out again, the all-Australian pairing of Day and Jones made big statements of intent on their opening holes. Both fired brilliant approaches and calmly knocked in birdie putts to send a convincing message: they would take some catching. Moments earlier, Rose started in dramatic fashion by draining a 50-footer for birdie on the first. However, at the fourth he ran into trouble and matched his double bogey of the previous day. One of the 2013 US Open champion's most impressive traits is the way he deals with setbacks. There was no change to his body language in the ensuing holes and he clawed his way back into contention by going to the turn in a two-under-par 34. Three more birdies on the way home maintained his momentum, only checked by a bogey at the last. Nevertheless, he put together a fine 68 to move to 12 under par.

'Obviously anything in the 60s on moving day is not going to do you any harm,' Rose observed. 'Before I even started my round, I could see that there were scores to be had out there. A few guys were going low. But when I got on the golf course, it certainly wasn't easy. The breeze was up, it was from a slightly different direction.'

This didn't seem to disturb Jones, who was showing remarkable composure as he glided through the front nine. 'I was totally fine,' he said. 'I wasn't nervous at all, especially after birdieing the first hole.' Jones pulled three strokes clear with a birdie at the sixth taking him to 13 under. Nothing seemed to perturb him until he came to the ninth where he pulled his drive into the hospitality area. He examined the options, which included a free drop, before choosing to play from the decking where his ball lay. This was a brave move, generating a big sense of theatre — and providing a huge bonus for the corporate guests.

'It was crazy. It was exciting to get up close like that,' Jones said. 'I was happy where the ball was. The spot where I had to have gone would have been much harder. And I hit a very good shot. I actually hit it exactly on the line I picked, but I picked the wrong line. I thought the wind was off to the left, but it was straight down.' The mistake led to his only bogey on the outward half.

Playing partner Day waited until the sixth hole for his first par, having scored two untidy bogeys and three birdies in a topsy-turvy start. While the Jones drama was playing out, Day collected a calm birdie that took him to 11 under par. He was alongside a charging Kaymer and Finau, and one stroke behind Jones.

−12 Jones (9)
−11 Kaymer (17), Grace (17), Finau (10), Day (9)
−10 Rose (9)

Not much was happening for Spieth, though. He followed an opening birdie with nine straight pars. Arriving on the 11th tee, the young American knew he needed his round to catch fire. He was only seven under par and his aims of winning a third major and claiming the world-number-one spot were hanging in the balance. There was little to suggest what was going to happen next.

His birdie at the 11th merely felt as though it was a long overdue improvement. But it proved the first of six birdies in the closing eight holes. Remarkably, Spieth had turned a humdrum round into a scintillating 65. I'm always reluctant to use the phrase 'moving day' for third rounds. It's a cliché and erroneous, in the sense that every day is a moving day. Shots count the same on a Thursday, Friday, Saturday or Sunday. However, this was certainly a move from Spieth in the third round, and a big one, which reverberated through the leaderboard.

Spieth credited his caddie for maintaining his focus during the frustrating early part of his round. 'I was impatient on the front nine,' Spieth said. 'I felt like I was playing some solid golf . . . I just wasn't scoring. My score did not reflect the way that I was playing.

'Once the one on 11 went in, even though it was a simple up and down, I at least saw another birdie. The one on 12 was nice, and we were off to the races. The holes started to look bigger. A lot of times it just takes one to go for me to really find that extra confidence, that extra little pop in my stroke.

'I remember telling Michael [Greller], we've got birdie opportunities on this side, let's try to get to 10 under. I thought the lead would be somewhere around 13.'

It wasn't just Spieth who was tearing up a course softened by the previous day's storm. Day was moving as well. He coaxed in a 20-footer at the 10th, then set about the par-5 11th. He hammered a monstrous drive before firing his second to six feet. Jones, meanwhile, up-and-downed from the back of the green to move to 13 under. It was a momentary lead, though; Day stroked home his eagle putt and was out in front.

−14 Day (11)
−13 Jones (11)
−12 Grace (F), Finau (12)
−11 Kaymer (F), Rose (12)
−10 Spieth (13), Lahiri (12)

Adrenaline was coursing through Day's veins as he rode the momentum with two more birdies that took him seven under for his round. He was two shots clear of Jones as they came to the 15th. After an excellent drive, the leader pulled his approach into a greenside bunker and Jones found the same hazard. Day took two shots to escape and ran up an expensive double bogey, while Jones pushed an easy-looking par save to drop one shot. Their woes offered encouragement to the chasing pack.

On the next, Day failed to take advantage of the last par 5 but then made a superb birdie on the difficult short 17th. A par at the last gave him a superb 66, which had included just 24 putts. Jones, by contrast, finished with 73 and Rose 68.

The big movers on this dramatic third day, one that had been thoroughly in keeping with the excitement of the other 2015 majors, had been two familiar figures – Jason Day and Jordan Spieth.

Day was two clear of the field and knew that he had carved out yet another opportunity. He also knew that the man who had won the first two majors of the year would be his biggest challenger on the final day.

'I felt like I tried to stay as patient as I could, even with the few mistakes that I did make,' Day said. 'Overall, I was very happy with how I played. I've been in position where I've been close to the lead going into a Sunday. The US Open, I was tied for the lead this year going into the last day [as he was at The Open]. To have a two-shot lead is pretty sweet.'

There was a determined look in his eye as Day addressed

reporters at the end of what had been an exceptionally long day. He had been among those needing to return first thing in the morning to complete their second rounds, so his performance late in the afternoon was all the more praiseworthy. 'I've played phenomenal golf leading up to this,' he said. There was not a hint of conceit in his voice, just a confidence that suggested he was ready for the next step. 'I need to make sure that I focus and prepare myself, make sure I get enough rest, make sure I get hydrated, because it is going to be warm. And really mentally prepare myself, to know that things may go wrong tomorrow and things maybe go right. But you've got to make sure that you just keep pushing forward. That's the mindset I need to take.'

It was the second major running that Day and Spieth would be paired together for the closing round. This time, though, unlike St Andrews, they would be the final pairing, an appropriate scenario to end the year's majors.

−15 Day

−13 Spieth

−12 Grace, Rose

−11 Kaymer

−10 Finau, Jones

 −9 Johnson, Lahiri

 −8 Kuchar, Horschel, Holmes

 −7 Koepka, Snedeker, Henley, Coetzee

Sunday, 16 August 2015

A year and one week earlier, McIlroy had returned to the top of the world rankings. His victory in the WGC Bridgestone Invitational followed his triumph at The Open Championship at Royal Liverpool. These two wins satisfied the complex, rolling calculations that take into account two years of results in producing the rankings. Everyone knew McIlroy was the best player in the world, and by the time he won in Akron in August 2014 the statistics caught up and confirmed the fact. After a year at the top, though, his reign was under threat.

The fact that McIlroy had not been able to defend his Open and WGC crowns, combined with Spieth's outstanding year, meant that, going into the PGA, there were several scenarios that would enable Spieth to go top of the rankings. If he won the year's final major, McIlroy needed to finish second to stay ahead. If the American was second on his own, then his rival had to finish in the top six. A share of second with one other player would mean McIlroy would have to finish in the top 13. And so the permutations went on.

For the American, though, the all-important first step was to try to land a third major in a remarkable season.

McIlroy's hopes of a successful title defence were almost non-existent as he teed off nine strokes behind Day, and seven behind Spieth. The course was still soft and receptive, the weather was good and, despite a fluctuating breeze, there was scope for low scoring. No one had ever finished a major 20 strokes below par but, with Day resuming at 15 under, that record looked under threat. All that concerned the Australian, though, was winning. He had served his time on major leaderboards. Now was the time to top one.

McIlroy began 90 minutes ahead of the final pair. A year before, he had scrapped his way to victory by beating Phil Mickelson and Rickie Fowler in near-darkness at a rain-soaked Valhalla. The Northern Irishman had been in his element. He loves to be centre of attention and thrives in that environment. Teeing off back in the pack on the final day, though, was relatively unfamiliar territory for him.

On that final day at Whistling Straits, he sought to mount the sort of charge that put him on the fringe of contending in the US Open at Chambers Bay. There were no early fireworks, though, just five straight pars. McIlroy then collected birdies at the sixth and seventh and made the most of the short par-4 10th. It was a steady, but largely unspectacular performance. There was a bogey at the 13th, cancelled out by another birdie at the long 16th. He parred in for a 69 to finish the championship at nine under par.

'I feel I did well to come back and shoot the scores that I did,' McIlroy said. 'I progressed each and every day. If I was to take back anything, it would just be probably that second day, when we teed off in benign conditions in the morning and I didn't take advantage. I'm walking away pretty happy. It isn't a win and I didn't get myself into contention but, considering six weeks ago I wasn't able to walk, it's not a bad effort.'

It was indeed a respectable performance, especially so soon after such a serious injury. However, it capped an ultimately disappointing year. The dominant figure in 2014 had not contended in any of the big four tournaments. His fourth place at Augusta was his best performance, having finished in a share of ninth at Chambers Bay. At Whistling Straits, he came home in 17th place.

McIlroy, though, remains a fine ambassador for the game. Before leaving the course, he accepted that if Spieth were to overhaul him in the rankings it would be thoroughly deserved. He also said that Day was ready to win his first major.

Some might argue the PGA is the least attractive of the majors, but it didn't feel that way on the final afternoon. The atmosphere crackled with anticipation. With McIlroy a mere footnote, it was all about Day and Spieth. Grace and Rose were in striking distance at 12 under, but they never assumed centre stage.

Day and Spieth made confident, routine pars at the first. At the par-5 second, both hit fine tee shots, with Day edging his rival for distance, as he would do all day long. He found a greenside bunker with his approach but his ball was lying well. Spieth came up short, pitched to 10 feet and was unable to convert the birdie. Day, meanwhile, splashed beautifully and moved into a three-stroke lead.

Spieth produced a trademark response, firing his tee shot at the par-3 third into birdie range. Day did well to hold his nerve and make a demanding two-putt par, but the Texan made no mistake with his chance. This was just the sort of cut-and-thrust golf that had been expected. But trouble awaited Spieth on the fourth. He failed to find the green in two after an errant tee shot and recorded his first bogey in 37 holes. With Grace having moved to 13 under, Spieth was now sharing second place. Day was three clear once again.

The fifth, the second of the par 5s, served up plenty of drama. Day didn't like his tee shot as it landed off the fairway to the left of the dogleg. Spieth found the middle of the fairway but his second drifted into the rough short of the green. He didn't look comfortable with his chip and overcooked it, leaving it 20 feet away. Day chipped to closer range. Knowing the Aussie was well placed, Spieth needed something special and responded brilliantly, draining a birdie to pile the pressure onto the leader. Day stood up to it by curling in his eight footer, which had grown in difficulty following his rival's birdie. Up ahead Grace and Rose both birdied the sixth.

−17 Day (5)

−15 Grace (6)

−14 Spieth (5)

−13 Rose (6)

−12 Lahiri (7)

Grace added another birdie at the seventh as roars sprung up all over the course. Day and Spieth took advantage of the sixth to power on at the top of the leaderboard. The Australian was displaying all the credentials of a major champion. He surveyed every shot deliberately, sticking to his lengthy, meticulous routine, which involved a deep breath in and a relaxing exhalation before addressing the ball. He found the green on the short seventh but was some way from the hole. Sometimes it is your moment, though, and this felt like his. Calmly he rolled in yet another birdie to motor to 19 under. He was three strokes clear of Grace and, more significantly, four clear of Spieth.

Day's drive at the eighth found an awkward lie in a fairway bunker and led to his first dropped shot. Spieth parred. There were more worries at the ninth as Day showed signs of nerves with a wedged approach that he chunked short of the green. Spieth was in trouble off the tee this time, however, and had to lay up on the downhill par 4. The American failed to get up and down while the leader recovered his composure to scramble a par that must have felt like a birdie. As importantly, it gave him momentum heading into the back nine.

Up ahead, Grace overshot the 10th green, then failed to find the putting surface from below the bank at the rear. He double-bogeyed, while Rose burst back into the picture with a textbook birdie.

−18 Day (9)
−15 Rose (10)
−14 Spieth (9)
−14 Grace (10)

Four strokes back, Spieth needed to make progress early on the inward half. He hit a superb approach to the 10th and, after Day left his birdie attempt short, the American seized his chance. As he addressed his birdie putt, a gust of wind swept in off the lake and disturbed his concentration. With the maturity of a veteran, he backed off, set himself again and holed. He was within three.

Day, however, showed that he could respond as decisively as his pursuer. No one drove the ball better all summer and, on the par-5 11th, he crunched his tee shot 382 yards right down the middle. Spieth later revealed: 'I actually turned to him and said holy – you know – and I yelled it over to him and I said: "You've got to be kidding me!" And then he gave me a little bicep.'

Spieth, shorter and less accurate, played out a relatively messy hole, recording just a par when he needed better. Day, meanwhile, had a straightforward approach and a comfortable two putts for the birdie that restored his three-stroke advantage.

With Grace reeling from his double bogey, Rose was now looking the biggest threat. But the Englishman, needing faultless golf, caught an awful lie in a bunker on the 13th and struggled to a miserable six that ended his chances. 'The double bogey on 13 took the wind out of my sails,' Rose admitted. 'That's the thing about this golf course, there are birdies to be had, but if you get in the wrong spot you can get up a double real quick.'

Day performed more profitably from the sand on the short 12th and nervelessly made par while Spieth squandered his birdie chance after an excellent tee shot.

−19 Day (12)
−15 Spieth (12)
−15 Grace (13)
−14 Rose (13)

Each time one of the final pair faltered, the other sought to capitalise. At the 13th, Day could not find the correct level with a second shot that came up short, while his playing partner landed his approach within 12 feet. The Australian steadied his nerves to make a difficult two-putt par, only to watch the ever-dangerous Spieth slot home a birdie.

The homeward stretch at Whistling Straits offers boundless permutations. While there are several birdie chances and an eagle opportunity on the 16th, the holes are also riddled with danger. Day had double bogeyed the 15th only 24 hours earlier, and the 18th could also cause big problems.

The route back towards the clubhouse begins on the 14th. Day drove into a fairway bunker. His ball was lying well, though, and there would be no second successive slip-up. The opposite, in fact; he found the green, sank the putt and went to 20 under par. Spieth overshot the green from 134 yards out, then held his nerve to escape with a par. Day now had one hand on the Wanamaker Trophy.

But fortunes reversed again at the next. Day again struggled with the 15th, although this time he limited the damage to a single dropped shot. He hit a poor chip from a difficult lie at the back of the green while Spieth needed to hole a four-and-a-half footer for par. He was back to within three of the lead, but the holes were running out.

−19 Day (15)
−16 Spieth (15)
−15 Rose (16)
−14 Lahiri (17)
−14 Grace (16)

Rose had found the green in two at the 16th and two-putted for a birdie. What the leading pair would have given for the same outcome! Both hit thunderous tee shots, with Day's again the longer, but neither could match Rose with their seconds. Day's approach caught a fortunate bounce, landing on a ridge that propelled the ball close to the putting surface. From 250 yards out, Spieth found sand. He had an awful stance, yet conjured a magical escape that set up a straightforward birdie. Day, putting from the fringe of the green, saw his ball bobble during the first part of its journey only to cosy up next to the hole for a tap-in. He was back on that magical mark of 20-under par and the job was almost done.

As long as Day missed the cavernous drop to the left of the par-3 17th, he would surely end his tortuous wait for a major title. He watched Spieth find the green with his tee shot. Again, Day relied on his well-ingrained pre-shot routine to reply in kind. The last remaining danger was avoided in champion style. Both players two-putted before preparing to hit into the bright evening sunlight on the home hole.

−20 Day (17)
−17 Spieth (17)
−15 Rose (17)
−15 Grace (17)

Peering through those rays, the leading pair might have caught sight of Rose finishing with a bogey that allowed Grace to claim third place outright. 'I thought 14-under par would be great. It's ironic that's what I finished on, I thought that would be a winning score,' Rose said.

Day needed just one more imperious drive. This was the strength of his game, as it had been at St Andrews and Chambers Bay. Those were heart-breaking near-misses but here at Whistling Straits things would be different. Day nailed his tee shot. 'I honestly said, don't double bogey, don't hit it left, don't double bogey,' Day recalled. 'Hit it as hard as you can up the right side. And I mean, I hammered the drive up the right side.'

Spieth was also equal to the task. His chances of victory had all but gone, but he still had the world-number-one ranking to play for. His Titleist golf ball always bears a printed red number one. It's a permanent reminder of his ambition to live at the top of the game.

The Texan played first into a green surrounded by huge grandstands. Applause rang out to greet his ball's safe arrival. Now for the final approach of the major season. From 185 yards, Day struck a beauty that found the heart of the green. 'I'm being honest here, I was over the second shot, and I'm like, don't hit it short in the water,' he said. 'All those things run through your head.'

Suddenly the tears began to well up in his eyes. What a journey he had taken, from his traumatic, alcohol-fuelled youth to the status of a major champion. The injuries, the illness and the missed opportunities helped make it a remarkable story. One man had been by his side throughout and, at this crowning moment, Colin Swatton was still there. 'We were a blubbering mess,' the bagman happily divulged.

There was no grandstand finish, no birdie putt to seal the end of an astonishing year. Both players two-putted for pars that heralded landmark moments for both. Spieth was the new world number one. Day was a major champion, and the first to finish 20 under par, overhauling Tiger Woods' record of 19 under in the 2000 Open at St Andrews.

Inevitably the Australian broke down in tears. His young son Dash ran onto the green to cuddle his dad, so did his wife Ellie, and there was a special hug for Swatton. They had completed an extraordinary story together. 'I learned a lot about myself, being able to finish the way I did,' Day said. 'The experiences that I've had in the past with previous major finishes definitely helped me prepare myself for a moment like this. To be able to walk up the 18th hole and finish the way I did, it was just a lot of emotion that came out of me. I guess you can take me off the list of best players without a major now.'

Day acknowledged that, had he faltered again, the experience might have proved catastrophic: 'It would have been very tough for me to come back from a major championship such as this, if I didn't finish it off. Knowing that I had the 54-hole lead, or tied for the 54-hole lead, for the last three majors and not being able to finish, it would have been tough mentally to come back from that.' Maybe, he said, he would have been scarred by the thought that 'I really can't finish it off'.

And the key to getting the job done? It was that mantra of one shot at a time.

'Really trying to stay in the present. Trying to pull myself back, especially on the back nine, because all I could think about was this,' Day added, pointing to the enormous Wanamaker Trophy. 'And it was hard to not think about it. I had to pull myself back and really grind.'

Moments after receiving the trophy, he added: 'I wouldn't have been here if my father didn't pass away. And that's just because that door closed for me and another opportunity opened up. That was for my mom to sacrifice and my sisters to sacrifice for me, so I could get away to a golf academy and work hard and meet Col. And to be able to have Colin on the bag at my first major championship win, walking up 18 knowing that I've got the trophy, it was just hard.

'I was trying to hold back tears over the first putt. And when I saw the putt go up to half a foot, I just couldn't stop crying. It's just a lot of hard work that I've been putting into this game, to dedicate myself to have a shot at glory; have a shot at greatness. That's what we all work towards.'

Spieth also congratulated the victor. 'It was fantastic,' he said. 'We played a lot of major championship rounds together and that was the best I've ever seen him play. Just given the timing of it and whatever, he's impressive to watch strike the ball.

'I'm really proud of the way that we fought. I'm proud of the way that we finished the round off. A couple of the up-and-downs I had today were among the best ones I ever had in my life. It was Jason's day. I mean, power to him. Congratulations! He played like he had won seven or eight majors before.'

Spieth's comments were made in the knowledge that he was now officially the best player in the world. 'That will never be taken away from me now,' Spieth stated. He had joined golf's most exclusive club. 'I'll always be a number one player in the world. When I look back on this year, the consistency that we have had and especially being able to step it up on the biggest stages, that's a huge confidence-builder and that's what's allowed us as a team to become the best, the number-one ranked.'

His major results told us as much. Masters – win; US Open – win; Open – tied fourth; PGA – runner up. Extraordinary.

The build-up to the PGA had been dominated by McIlroy's missives on social media, detailing his comeback from injury. Appropriately enough, his Twitter feed provided the perfect closing message: '2 inevitable things happened today, @JDayGolf winning a major and @JordanSpieth getting to 1 in the world! Congrats guys!! Inspiring stuff!'

Epilogue

Justin Rose departed Whistling Straits a cumulative 34 under par for the four majors of 2015. It was the fourth-best tally against par in the history of men's golf, yet all the Englishman had to show for his efforts were the hefty cheques that accompanied his finishes of tied-second at Augusta, 27th at Chambers Bay, tied-sixth at St Andrews and fourth at Whistling Straits. These figures help illustrate the high level of golf played in the biggest tournaments of 2015.

Jordan Spieth set a new record by finishing 54-under for those 16 rounds. That was a stroke better than Tiger Woods' astonishing season in 2000 when he romped to victory at the US Open, Open and PGA by an aggregate margin of 23 shots. Woods' campaign that year remains the benchmark in the modern era, but Spieth came very close to eclipsing it.

Having won the first two majors, he was only a stroke shy of making The Open playoff and three shots behind Jason Day at the PGA. So it could be argued that he was a mere four strokes away from a grand slam. Given all the variables that dictate this capricious sport, and the strength in depth at the top of the world game, that amounted to a truly amazing performance.

Spieth is not one for the 'ifs and buts' of golfing life but recognised that his year would have had a very different complexion had Dustin Johnson sunk an eminently makeable eagle putt on the 72nd green at Chambers Bay. To put that 12-footer into context, I holed it at my first attempt the very next day, and I'm a very rusty eight handicapper. Of course, there was no pressure on me and had my attempt missed it would have trundled on – just as Johnson's did to prompt the three-putt that handed Spieth his victory.

'You can look at it as four shots shy of the grand slam or you could look at it from a negative view,' Spieth said. 'Maybe one putt and I would only have one major this year, if Dustin's went in at the US Open. I'm fortunate that we caught a break there. Then we had a chance to win another one. It was amazing. You only get four a year, to have an opportunity to win all of them is so cool. I hope to have a season like this one at the biggest stages again. I hope that we can do this again. It's not easy, it takes a lot out of you. It really does wear you out mentally, trying to grind that much. There's a reason I have a receding hairline and it's because I've got that kind of pressure building up and that kind of stress. And as much of a thrill as it is, it can wear you down.'

It was repeated close calls with no celebratory cigar that had been wearing down the remarkable Jason Day. Never mind the health concerns that had dogged his young career, he is a player of immense talent and he finally came to the fore with his record-breaking 20-under-par victory at the PGA. He heads into the future with ambition undimmed by the fulfilment of his major dream. 'As long as I am healthy, I feel like I'm going to be there a long time,' he stated. 'I still want to accomplish that number-one goal of mine, which is to be the best player in the world. I'm still motivated and still very hungry for that, even after this win. Stuff like this is just the icing on the top of the cake, when you work so hard and being able to achieve something like this.'

Within weeks, Day claimed two more victories in the PGA Tour's season-ending FedEx Cup series and those results allowed him to realise his lifelong ambition: to be ranked number one player in the world. Reflecting the ultra-competitive environment that emerged at golf's pinnacle in 2015, Spieth allowed him to reign for only a single week. Fittingly, the Texan rounded off his year with victory at the Tour Championship at East Lake Golf Club in Atlanta, giving him the playoff title and a $10 million bonus in a season in which he netted $22 million in prize money.

'I think golf is in a very healthy stage now,' Day continued. 'I felt a few years ago it was kind of struggling a little bit with the identity of who was really going to be that number one player in the world; who was going to be the next best thing? Rory came out and was really dominating. But there was no one really challenging him for that role.'

The injured Rory McIlroy was a frustrated spectator as Zach Johnson triumphed on a soft Old Course that was perfectly suited to the Northern Irishman's game. Johnson showed that golf is not just the preserve of this exciting young generation. The 39-year-old was a thoroughly deserving Open champion and provides another indication of just how many players are capable of winning each and every major championship.

Johnson, the 2007 Masters champion, entered exalted company in becoming only the sixth man to win majors at Augusta and St Andrews. He joined Woods, Jack Nicklaus, Sir Nick Faldo, Seve Ballesteros and Sam Snead in triumphing on golf's most evocative stages. 'It's extremely special,' Johnson smiled. 'You're talking where the game was essentially founded, invented. The true pioneers that played the game stepped foot there and played there and obviously won there.

'I've been getting that question a lot about Augusta and St Andrews. I'm not trying to think about it because I can get caught up in it. If anything, I'm pretty proud of the way I handled it because I never really thought about that when I was competing, thank the Lord, because it's a small list, and it's a special thing. You're talking about two places, two venues that, whether you're a player or a spectator, you probably admire and certainly respect. Those two places are venues that just exude golf. It's an honour to play in both of those. It's hard to put into words what it is to win on both of those sites.'

For me, the abiding memory of the majors in 2015 came at St Andrews, but not from the champion. When Spieth sank his long, raking putt for birdie on the 16th green it felt as though a third successive major victory was inevitable. Once again, he had seized the golfing moment. It was the story of the year. The spectators leapt from their seats in celebration, competitors watching from their Old Course Hotel balconies punched the air and the player himself thought he was going to remain on track for a unique grand slam. A par at the 17th, a birdie at the last were all he needed to claim the Claret Jug.

But golf remains an unpredictable game and will for evermore. Spieth could only manage a bogey-par finish and the door opened for Johnson and his playoff companions Marc Leishman and Louis Oosthuizen.

Nevertheless, Spieth had produced a magnificent effort that will live long in the memory. Despite defeats in the last two majors, it was still his year. It served to inspire McIlroy on his return to full fitness, while at the same time Day was also breathing the rarefied air at the very top of the game.

By the time the 2015 season drew to a close, Tiger Woods found himself recovering from another back operation. 'I'm a fighter,' he insisted, but the game had moved on. Woods was once the ultimate driving force but golf has now entered an era of a new 'big three' – Jordan Spieth, Jason Day and Rory McIlroy.

One element remained unchanged, however; the way that golfing status is measured. As Spieth said: 'Major championships are what we're remembered for in this sport. It's what I imagine all of our dreams were as kids, to play professional golf and to compete and try and win major championships.'

The events at Augusta, Chambers Bay, St Andrews and Whistling Straits made it an unforgettable golfing year.

Acknowledgements

This book is dedicated to Iain Thomas, who sadly passed away this year. Iain was my boss at the BBC World Service when I first moved to London in the early 1990s. He was an inspirational figure, a constant source of encouragement and determined that his reporters should go about their work in the correct way. He sought out opportunities for his teams of broadcasters and producers and gave me my first golf reporting assignments. Iain sent me to the World Matchplay at Wentworth in 1990 and three years later, in and around my cricket and rugby duties, found ways for me to cover the Masters, Open and Ryder Cup. Witnessing Bernhard Langer claim his second green jacket at Augusta and Greg Norman triumphing at Royal St George's were my first experiences of life in major media centres. They proved the stepping stones for my career as the BBC's golf correspondent. I will always feel a huge debt of gratitude to Iain Thomas for giving me those opportunities.

More than two decades on I remain grateful to my bosses and thanks go to BBC Radio's head of sport Richard Burgess for his continued support and encouragement. The majors of 2015 were covered with a new 5Live production team headed by editor Simon Clancy and producer James Peacock. They inherited the fine template left by Graham McMillan and are due thanks for all their help and laughs through such an exciting year. Thanks also to Catherine Archer, Steve Jones, George Cottam, John Murray, Alistair Bruce-Ball, Chris Jones, Eilidh Barbour and Conor McNamara for their brilliant production and broadcasting, as well as for their company and sense of fun along the way.

Much of my time on the road is spent in the company of other golf correspondents. Thanks to the *Telegraph*'s James Corrigan, the *Mail*'s Derek Lawrenson, Ewan Murray from the *Guardian* and the *Sun*'s David Facey for the many shared meals, bottles of Sauvignon Blanc and invaluable insights into the game. I'm grateful to the *Augusta Chronicle*'s Scott Michaux for his time and expertise and for pointing me in the direction of David Owen's superb *The Making of the Masters*.

Without the hard work of the fantastic team at Elliott and Thompson this book would never have existed. To Lorne Forsyth and Jennie Condell thank you for the lunch where the idea of chronicling the 2015 Majors was first suggested. As with our previous effort, *Showdown: The Inside Story of the Gleneagles Ryder Cup*, there was a rapid turn-around to have it so swiftly on the shelves. Editor Pippa Crane was constantly supportive, despite my homework arriving a tad late and I'm greatly indebted to the detailed eye of copy-editor Tony Lawrence. Thanks also to publicist Alison Menzies.

Special thanks to a great, great golfing figure, three-time major champion Padraig Harrington, for providing the Foreword. I'm also grateful to Michele Mair and Adrian Mitchell from IMG for their help with this book.

It is impossible to cover the major golf championships without the help of the media support teams from Augusta, the USGA, R&A and PGA of America. All do an excellent job that helps us bring these great events to life on the air or on pages and screens. Thanks also to the media departments of the European and PGA Tours.

There are several occasions in this book where I mention players getting back strokes with birdies following holes where they have dropped shots. Although this is a technique to describe golfers atoning for errors, it will infuriate my long term on-air sidekick Jay Townsend. 'You can never get a shot back,' he insists. Technically he is correct, as he is about so many aspects of the game of golf. So, Jay, apologies if this aspect infuriates you, but thank you for so willingly sharing so much of your knowledge of the game. Now this book is written I can concentrate on implementing your chipping tips as well.

The final mention is the most important one. I have been able to continue enjoying a job that is the most fulfilling one I could do because of the love and support of the two people closest to me. While this book is dedicated to my old boss Iain, it is also for my wife Sarah and son Ollie who put up with my absences with remarkable grace. Not only that, they encourage and embrace projects such as this. For that I'm very grateful.

Index